# The Core of Mysticism

Down through the ages the phenomenon of mysticism has been locally interpreted in terms of a particular culture, creed, or doctrine.

In this fascinating volume, Walter T. Stace observes the characteristics common to all forms of mysticism—religious or non-religious, ancient or modern. He analyzes, interprets, and explains the differences and similarities in mystical experience as described by the great mystical writers of the world . . . and he evaluates the meaning mysticism holds for us today.

"If anyone thinks that mysticism consists in useless dreaming, or in the idle and selfish enjoyment of wonderful experiences without any practical and valuable effects in life, he has . . . his answer. It is the universal testimony of those who know that mystical experience transforms human life and alters character—often from the squalid and mean to the noble and selfless."      —W. T. Stace

———

WALTER T. STACE was born in London and graduated in philosophy from Trinity College, Dublin University. A man of two careers, he has been successful in both. While serving as a British Civil Servant in Ceylon (1910-32), he wrote distinguished books on Greek philosophy, the philosophy of Hegel, and problems of aesthetics. Later, as Stuart Professor of Philosophy at Princeton University, he continued to write technical treatises, as well as popular articles, on nearly every aspect of philosophy. He retired from Princeton in 1955, but has continued to teach and to write. *Mysticism and Philosophy* (Lippincott) is among his most recent books.

# SIGNET and MENTOR Books of Interest

# THE TEACHINGS
## OF
# THE MYSTICS

BEING SELECTIONS FROM THE GREAT MYSTICS
AND MYSTICAL WRITINGS OF THE WORLD,
EDITED, WITH INTRODUCTION, INTERPRETIVE
COMMENTARIES, AND EXPLANATIONS, BY

## WALTER T. STACE

A MENTOR BOOK
Published by THE NEW AMERICAN LIBRARY

---

## ACKNOWLEDGMENTS AND COPYRIGHT NOTICES

(The page following constitutes an extension
of this copyright page)

The author wishes to thank the authors, publishers, and authors' representatives listed below for permission to use the following selections, which may not be reproduced in any form without the consent of the copyright owners:

George Allen & Unwin Ltd., London, for excerpts from *Plotinus,* edited and translated by A. H. Armstrong, and *Rumi: Poet and Mystic,* translated by R. A. Nicholson.

Cambridge University Press, New York, for the excerpt from *Eastern Poetry and Prose,* by R. A. Nicholson.

William Collins Sons & Company Ltd., with Messrs. Hamish Hamilton Ltd., London, for the excerpt from *The Invisible Writing* by Arthur Koestler.

Bruno Cassirer (Publishers) Ltd., Oxford, for the excerpt from *Buddhist Texts Through the Ages,* edited by E. Conze and others.

J. M. Dent & Sons Ltd., London, for excerpts from *The Adornment of the Spiritual Marriage* and *The Book of Supreme Truth* by Jan van Ruysbroeck, translated by C. A. Wynschenck Dom.

E. P. Dutton & Co., Inc., New York for the excerpt from *A Buddhist Bible,* edited by Dwight Goddard, Copyright, 1938, by E. P. Dutton & Co., Inc.

---

Library of Congress Catalog Card No. 60-15528

MENTOR BOOKS are published *in the United States* by The New American Library of World Literature, Inc., 501 Madison Avenue, New York, New York 10022, *in Canada* by The New American Library of Canada Limited 156 Front Street, West, Toronto 1, Ontario

Harper & Brothers, New York, for excerpts from *Meister Eckhart: A Modern Translation*, by Raymond B. Blakney. Copyright 1941 by Harper & Brothers.

Harvard University Press, Cambridge, for the excerpt from *Buddhism in Translations* by H. C. Warren, No. 3 in the Harvard Oriental Series.

The Janus Press, London, for the excerpt from *The Conference of the Birds*, by Farid al-Din Attar, translated by S. C. Nott.

Longmans, Green & Co., Inc., New York, for the excerpt for *The Philosophy of Plotinus*, by W. R. Inge, Third Edition, 1929, Vol. II, New Impression, 1948.

Luzac & Company Ltd., London, for excerpts from *Readings from the Mystics of Islam*, by Margaret Smith.

The Macmillan Company, New York, for the excerpt from *The Invisible Writing* by Arthur Koestler. Copyright 1954 by Arthur Koestler.

The New American Library of World Literature, Inc., New York, for excerpts from *The Way of Life: Tao Té Ching*, by Lao Tzu, translated by R. B. Blakney, Copyright 1955 by Raymond B. Blakney; and *The Teachings of the Compassionate Buddha*, edited by E. A. Burtt.

A. D. Peters, London, for the excerpt from *The Invisible Writing*, by Arthur Koestler.

Pantheon Books, Inc., New York, for the excerpt from *The Method of Zen*, by Eugen Herrigel, edited by Hermann Tausend, translated by R. F. C. Hull. Copyright 1960 by Pantheon Books, Inc.

Philosophical Library, Inc., New York for the excerpt from *Buddhist Texts Through the Ages*, edited by E. Conze and others.

Rider & Co., London, for the excerpt from *Essays in Zen Buddhism*, by D. T. Suzuki.

Schocken Books, Inc., New York, for the excerpts from *Zohar, the Book of Splendor*, by Gershom G. Scholem. Copyright 1949 by Schocken Books, Inc.

Sheed & Ward, Inc., New York, for the excerpt from *The Complete Works of Saint Teresa*, translated and edited by E. Allison Peers, from the critical edition of P. Silverio de Santa Teresa, C. D., published in three volumes by Sheed & Ward, Inc., New York.

Sheed & Ward Ltd., London, for the excerpt from *The Complete Works of Saint Teresa*, translated and edited by E. Allison Peers.

Society for Promoting Christian Knowledge, London, for the excerpt from *Dionysius the Areopagite on the Divine Names and the Mystical Theology*, translated by C. E. Rolt.

Frederick Ungar Publishing Co., New York, for the excerpt from *The Dark Night of the Soul*, by St. John of the Cross, translated by Kurt F. Reinhardt. Copyright 1957 by the Frederick Ungar Publishing Co., from the series Milestones of Thought.

The Vedanta Society of Southern California, Hollywood, California, for the excerpts from *The Upanishads: Breath of the Eternal*, published in hardbound version by the Vedanta Press and in paperbound version by the New American Library of World Literature.

# Contents

# -1-

# What Is Mysticism?

(1) *Terminological*. In these pages I shall often use the expressions "mysticism," "mystic," "mystical experience," "mystical consciousness," "mystical idea." "Mysticism," of course, is the general name of our entire subject, and its meaning will be gradually developed. By the word "mystic" I shall always mean a person who himself has had mystical experience. Often the word is used in a much wider and looser way. Anyone who is sympathetic to mysticism is apt to be labeled a mystic. But I shall use the word always in a stricter sense. However sympathetic toward mysticism a man may be, however deeply interested, involved, enthusiastic, or learned in the subject, he will not be called a mystic unless he has, or has had, mystical experience. The phrases "mystical experience" and "mystical consciousness" will be used as synonymous with each other. But "mystical consciousness" is the better term, the word "experience" being misleading in certain respects. It will be seen that both "mysticism" and "mystic" are defined in terms of mystical experience or consciousness. This is therefore the basic thing on which we have to fasten attention and in terms of which we have to understand the whole subject. Our question "What is mysticism?" really means "What is mystical experience?"

The phrase "mystical idea" has also to be defined in terms of mystical experience. It means an idea, belief, opinion, or proposition which was originally based on mystical experience, although the connection between the experience and the opinion may have been quite forgotten. The point is that a mystical idea is a product of the conceptual intellect, whereas a mystical experience is a nonintellectual mode of consciousness. The proposition that "time is unreal" is an example of a mystical idea. It must have arisen because mystics usually feel (a) that their experience is timeless and (b) it is more "real" (in some sense) than any other experience. But many philosophers who have never had any mystical experience, nor any knowledge of how the idea originated, yet come to adopt it in their philosophies and treat it as if it were a product of a process of reasoning. A mystical idea may be either true or false, though it must have originated in a genuine mystical experience.

(2) *Experience and Interpretation.* On a dark night out of doors one may see something glimmering white. One person may think it is a ghost. A second person may take it for a sheet hung out on a clothesline. A third person may suppose that it is a white-painted rock. Here we have a single experience with three different interpretations. The experience is genuine, but the interpretations may be either true or false. If we are to understand anything at all about mysticism, it is essential that we should make a similar distinction between a mystical experience and the interpretations which may be put upon it either by mystics themselves or by nonmystics. For instance, the same mystical experience may be interpreted by a Christian in terms of Christian beliefs and by a Buddhist in terms of Buddhistic beliefs.

(3) *Some Things Which Mysticism Is Not.* The word "mysticism" is popularly used in a variety of loose and inaccurate ways. Sometimes anything is called "mystical" which is misty, foggy, vague, or sloppy. It is absurd that "mysticism" should be associated with what is "misty" because of the similar sound of the words. And there is nothing misty, foggy, vague, or sloppy about mysticism.

A second absurd association is to suppose that mysticism is sort of mystery-mongering. There is, of course, an etymological connection between "mysticism" and "mystery." But mysticism is not any sort of hocus-pocus such as we commonly associate with claims to the elucidation of sensational mysteries. Mysticism is not the same as what is commonly called the "occult"—whatever that may mean. Nor has it anything to do with spiritualism, or ghosts, or table-turning. Nor does it include what are commonly called parapsychological phenomena such as telepathy, telekinesis, clairvoyance, precognition. These are not mystical phenomena. It is perhaps true that mystics may sometimes claim to possess such special powers, but even when they do so they are well aware that such powers are not part of, and are to be clearly distinguished from, their mystical experience. Such powers, if they exist—as to which I express no opinion—may be possessed by persons who are not mystics. And conversely, even the greatest mystics may be devoid of them and know nothing about them. The closest connection one can admit will be to say that it may be the case that the sort of persons who are mystics also tend to be the sort of persons who have parapsychological powers.

Finally, it is most important to realize that visions and voices are not mystical phenomena, though here again it seems to be the case that the sort of persons who are mystics may often be the sort of persons who see visions and hear voices. A few years ago it was reported that certain persons in Italy saw a vision of the Virgin Mary in the clouds. Even if we suppose that these persons really did have this vision, it must be emphatically asserted that this was not a mystical experience and had nothing to do with mysticism. Nor are the voices which certain persons in history, such as Socrates, Mohammed, and Joan of Arc, are supposed to have heard to be classed as mystical experiences. Socrates, Mohammed, and Joan of Arc may have been mystics for all I know, but they are not to be classed as such because of these voices. Returning for a moment to the subject of visions, it is well known that certain mystics saw visions but that they did not themselves regard these visions as mystical experiences. A case in point is St. Teresa of Avila. She had frequent visions, but she knew that they were not the experiences she desired. Some of them, she thought, may have been sent to her by God to comfort and encourage her in trying to attain the mystical consciousness. Others, she supposed, might have been sent by the devil in order to confuse her and distract her from the true mystic quest.

The reader may perhaps suppose that the exclusion of visions and voices from the class of mystical phenomena is a matter of arbitrary choice on the part of the present writer. Of course, one is logically entitled to define his terms as he pleases. Therefore if anyone says that he intends to use the phrase "mystical experience" so as to include visions and voices, spiritualism, telepathy, and the like, we do not say that he is wrong. But we say that his usage does not conform to that which has been usual with those who have been recognized as the great mystics of the world. The case of St. Teresa has just been mentioned. St. John of the Cross specifically warns his readers not to seek visions, not to be misled by them, and not to mistake them for the true mystical union. And there are, one must add, good reasons for this. What mystics say is that a genuine mystical experience is nonsensuous. It is formless, shapeless, colorless, odorless, soundless. But a vision is a piece of visual imagery having color and shape. A voice is an auditory image. Visions and voices are sensuous experiences.

(4) *A New Kind of Consciousness*. In his book *The Varieties of Religious Experience* William James suggests, as a result of his psychological researches, that "our normal consciousness, rational consciousness as we call it, is but one special type of consciousness, whilst all about it, parted from it by the filmiest of screens, there lie potential forms of consciousness entirely different." This statement exactly fits mystical consciousness. It is entirely unlike our everyday consciousness and is wholly incommensurable with it. What are the fundamental characteristics or elements of our ordinary consciousness? We may think of it as being like a building with three floors. The ground floor consists of physical sensations—sights, sounds, smells, tastes, touch sensations, and organic sensations. The second floor consists of images, which we tend to think of as mental copies of sensations. The third floor is the level of the intellect, which is the faculty of concepts. On this floor we find abstract thinking and reasoning processes. This account of the mind may be open to cavil. Some philosophers think that colors, sounds, and so on, are not properly called "sensations"; others that images are not "copies" of sensations. These fine points, however, need not seriously concern us. Our account is sufficiently clear to indicate what we are referring to when we speak of sensations, images, and concepts as being the fundamental elements of the cognitive aspects of our ordinary consciousness. Arising out of these basic cognitive elements and dependent upon them are emotions, desires, and volitions. In order to have a name for it we may call this whole structure—including sensations, images, concepts, and their attendant desires, emotions, and volitions—our *sensory-intellectual consciousness*.

Now the mystical consciousness is quite different from this. It is not merely that it involves different kinds of sensation, thought, or feeling. We are told that some insects or animals can perceive ultraviolet color and infrared color; and that some animals can hear sounds which are inaudible to us; even that some creatures may have a sixth sense quite different from any of our five senses. These are all, no doubt, kinds of sensations different from any we have. But they are still sensations. And the mystical consciousness is destitute of any sensations at all. Nor does it contain any concepts or thoughts. It is not a sensory-intellectual consciousness at all. Accordingly, it cannot be described or analyzed in terms of any of the elements of the sensory-intellectual consciousness, with which it is wholly incommensurable.

This is the reason why mystics always say that their experiences are "ineffable." All words in all languages are the products of our sensory-intellectual consciousness and express or describe its elements or some combination of them. But as these elements (with the doubtful exception of emotions) are not found in the mystical consciousness, it is felt to be impossible to describe it in any words whatever. In spite of this the mystics do describe their experiences in roundabout ways, at the same time telling us that the words they use are inadequate. This raises a serious problem for the philosophy of mysticism, but it is not possible for us to dwell on it here.

The incommensurability of the mystical with the sensory-intellectual consciousness is also the ultimate reason why we have to exclude visions and voices, telepathy, precognition, and clairvoyance from the category of the mystical. Suppose someone sees a vision of the Virgin Mary. What he sees has shape, the shape of a woman, and color—white skin, blue raiment, a golden halo, and so on. But these are all images or sensations. They are therefore composed of elements of our sensory-intellectual consciousness. The same is true of voices. Or suppose one has a precognition of a neighbor's death. The components one is aware of—a dead man, a coffin, etc.—are composed of elements of our sensory-intellectual consciousness. The only difference is that these ordinary elements are arranged in unfamiliar patterns which we have come to think cannot occur, so that if they do occur they seem supernormal. Or the fact that such elements are combined in an unusual way so as to constitute the figure of a woman up in the clouds, perhaps surrounded by other humanlike figures with wings added to them—all this does not constitute a different *kind* of consciousness at all. And just as sensory elements of any sort are excluded from the mystical consciousness, so are conceptual elements. It is not that the thoughts in the mystical consciousness are different from those we are accustomed to. It does not include any thoughts at all. The mystic, of course, expresses thoughts about his experience after that experience is over, and he remembers it when he is back again in his sensory-intellectual consciousness. But there are no thoughts *in* the experience itself.

If anyone thinks that a kind of consciousness without either sensations, images, or thoughts, because it is totally unimaginable and inconceivable to most of us, cannot exist, he is surely being very stupid. He supposes that the possibilities of this vast universe are confined to what can be imagined and understood by the brains of average human insects who crawl on a minute speck of dust floating in illimitable space.

On the other hand, there is not the least reason to suppose that the mystical consciousness is miraculous or supernatural. No doubt it has, like our ordinary consciousness, been produced by the natural processes of evolution. Its existence in a few rare men is a psychological fact of which there is abundant evidence. To deny or doubt that it exists as a psychological fact is not a reputable opinion. It is ignorance. Whether it has any value or significance beyond itself, and if so what—these, of course, are matters regarding which there can be legitimate differences of opinion. Owing to the comparative rarity of this kind of consciousness, it should no doubt be assigned to the sphere of abnormal psychology.

(5) *The Core of Mysticism*. I shall, for the present, treat it as an hypothesis that although mystical experiences may in certain respects have different characteristics in different parts of the world, in different ages, and in different cultures, there are nevertheless a number of fundamental common characteristics. I shall also assume that the agreements are more basic and important, the differences more superficial and relatively less important. This hypothesis can only be fully justified by an elaborate empirical survey of the descriptions of their experiences given by mystics and collected from all over the world. But I believe that enough of the evidence for it will appear in the following pages to convince any reasonable person.

The most important, the central characteristic in which all *fully developed* mystical experiences agree, and which in the last analysis is definitive of them and serves to mark them off from other kinds of experiences, is that they involve the apprehension of *an ultimate nonsensuous unity in all things,* a oneness or a One to which neither the senses nor the reason can penetrate. In other words, it entirely transcends our sensory-intellectual consciousness.

It should be carefully noted that only fully developed mystical experiences are necessarily apprehensive of the One. Many experiences have been recorded which lack this central feature but yet possess other mystical characteristics. These are borderline cases, which may be said to shade off from the central core of cases. They have to the central core the relation which some philosophers like to call "family resemblance."

We should also note that although at this stage of our exposition we speak of mystical experience as an apprehension *of* the Unity, the mystics of the Hindu and Buddhist cultures, as well as Plotinus and many others, generally insist that this is incorrect since it supposes a division between subject and object. We should rather say that the experience *is* the One. Thus Plotinus writes: "We should not speak of seeing, but instead of seen and seer, speak boldly of a simple Unity for in this seeing we neither distinguish nor are there two." But we will leave the development of this point till later. And often for convenience' sake we shall speak of the experience *of* the unity.

(6) *Extrovertive Mysticism*. There appear to be two main distinguishable types of mystical experience, both of which may be found in all the higher cultures. One may be called extrovertive mystical experience, the other introvertive mystical experience. Both are apprehensions of the One, but they reach it in different ways. The extrovertive way looks outward and through the physical senses into the external world and finds the One there. The introvertive way turns inward, introspectively, and finds the One at the bottom of the self, at the bottom of the human personality. The latter far outweighs the former in importance both in the history of mysticism and in the history of human thought generally. The introvertive way is the major strand in the history of mysticism, the extrovertive way a minor strand. I shall only briefly refer to extrovertive mysticism and then pass on, and shall take introvertive mysticism as the main subject of this book.

The extrovertive mystic with his physical senses continues to perceive the same world of trees and hills and tables and chairs as the rest of us. But he sees these objects transfigured in such manner that the Unity shines through them. Because it includes ordinary sense perceptions, it only partially realizes the description given in section (4). For the full realization of this we have to wait for the introvertive experience. I will give two brief historical instances of extrovertive experience. The great Catholic mystic Meister Eckhart (circa 1260–1329) wrote as follows: "Here [i.e., in this experience] all blades of grass, wood, and stone, all things are One. . . . When is a man in mere understanding? When he sees one thing separated from another. And when is he above mere understanding? When he sees all in all, then a man stands above mere understanding."

In this quotation we note that according to Eckhart seeing a number of things as separate and distinct, seeing the grass and the wood and the stone as three different things, is the mark of the sensory-intellectual consciousness. For Eckhart's word "understanding" means the conceptual intellect. But if one passes beyond the sensory-intellectual consciousness into the mystical consciousness, then one sees these three things as being "all one." However, it is evident that in this extrovertive experience the distinctions between things have not wholly disappeared. There is no doubt that what Eckhart means is that he sees the three things as distinct and separate and yet at the same time as not distinct but identical. The grass is identical with the stone, and the stone with the wood, although they are all different. Rudolph Otto, commenting on this, observes that it is as if one said that black is the same as white, white the same as black, although at the same time white remains white and black remains black. Of course this is a complete paradox. It is in fact contradictory. But we shall find that paradoxicality is one of the common characteristics of all mysticism. And it is no use saying that this is all logically impossible, and that no consciousness of this kind can exist, unless we wish, on these a priori grounds, to refuse to study the evidence—which is overwhelming.

What some mystics simply call the One other mystics often identify with God. Hence we find Jakob Böhme (1575-1624) saying much the same thing about the grass and the trees and the stones as Eckhart does, but saying that they are all God instead of just all One. The following is a statement of one of his experiences: "In this light my spirit saw through all things and into all creatures and I recognized God in grass and plants."

It is suggested that the extrovertive type of experience is a kind of halfway house to the introvertive. For the introvertive experience is wholly nonsensuous and nonintellectual.

But the extrovertive experience is sensory-intellectual in so far as it still perceives physical objects but is nonsensuous and nonintellectual in so far as it perceives them as "all one."

We may sum up this short account of the extrovertive consciousness by saying that it is a perception of the world as transfigured and unified in one ultimate being. In some cultures the one being is identified with God; and since God is then perceived as the inner essence of all objects, this type of experience tends toward pantheism. But in some cultures—for example, Buddhism—the unity is not interpreted as God at all.

(7) *Introvertive Mysticism.* Suppose that one could shut all physical sensations out of one's consciousness. It may be thought that this would be easy as regards some of the senses, namely sight, hearing, taste, and smell. One can shut one's eyes, stop up one's ears, and hold one's nose. One can avoid taste sensations by keeping one's mouth empty. But one cannot shut off tactual sensations in any simple way of this kind. And it would be even more difficult to get rid of organic sensations. However, one can perhaps suppose it possible somehow to thrust tactual and organic sensations out of conscious awareness—perhaps into the unconscious. Mystics do not, as far as I know, descend to the ignominious level of holding their noses and stopping their ears. My only point is that it is possible to conceive of getting rid of all sensations, and in one way or other mystics claim that they do this.

Suppose now, after this has been done, we next try to get rid of all sensuous *images* from our minds. This is very difficult. Most people, try as they will not to picture anything at all, will find vague images floating about in consciousness. Suppose, however, that it is possible to suppress all images. And suppose finally that we manage to stop all thinking and reasoning. Having got rid of the whole empirical content of sensations, images, and thoughts, presumably all emotions and desires and volitions would also disappear, since they normally exist only as attachments to the cognitive content. What, then, would be left of consciousness? What would happen? It is natural to suppose that with all the elements of consciousness gone consciousness itself would lapse and the subject would fall asleep or become *un*conscious.

Now it happens to be the case that this total suppression of the whole empirical content of consciousness is precisely what the introvertive mystic claims to achieve. And he claims that what happens is not that all consciousness disappears but that only the ordinary sensory-intellectual consciousness disappears and is replaced by an entirely new kind of consciousness, the mystical consciousness. Naturally we now ask whether any description of this new consciousness can be given. But before trying to answer that difficult question, I propose to turn aside for a brief space to speak about the methods which mystics use to suppress sensuous images, and thinking, so as to get rid of their sensory-intellectual consciousness. There are the Yoga techniques of India; and Christian mystics in Catholic monasteries also evolved their own methods. The latter usually call their techniques "prayers," but they are not prayers in the vulgar sense of asking God for things; they are much more like the "meditation" and "concentration" of Yogis than may be commonly supposed. This is too vast a subject to be discussed in detail here. But I will give two elementary illustrations.

Everyone has heard of the breathing exercises undertaken by the yogins of India seeking samadhi—samadhi being the Indian name for mystical consciousness. What is this special method of breathing, and what is it supposed to accomplish? The theory of the matter is, I understand, something like this: It is practically impossible, or at least very difficult, to stop all sensing, imaging, and thinking by a forcible act of the will. What comes very near to it, however, is to concentrate one's attention on some single point or object so that all other mental content falls away and there is left nothing but the single point of consciousness. If this can be done, then ultimately that single point will itself disappear because contrast is necessary for our ordinary consciousness, and if there is only one point of consciousness left, there is nothing to form a contrast to it.

The question then is: On what single thing should one concentrate? A simple way is to concentrate on the stream of one's own breath. Simple instructions which I have heard given are these. One first adopts a suitable physical position with spine and neck perfectly erect. Then breathe in and out slowly, evenly, and smoothly. Concentrate your attention on this and nothing else. Some aspirants, I believe, count their breaths, 1, 2, 3, . . . up to 10, and then begin the count again. Continue this procedure till you attain the desired results.

A second method is to keep repeating in one's mind some

short formula of words over and over again till the words lose all meaning. So long as they carry meaning, of course, the mind is still occupied with the thought of this meaning. But when the words become meaningless there is nothing left of consciousness except the monotonous sound-image, and that too, like the consciousness of one's breath, will in the end disappear. There is an interesting connection between this method and a remark made by the poet Tennyson. From childhood up Tennyson had frequent mystical experiences. They came to him spontaneously, without effort, and unsought. But he mentions the curious fact that he could induce them at will by the odd procedure of repeating his own name over and over again to himself. I know of no evidence that he studied mysticism enough to understand the theory of his own procedure, which would presumably be that the constantly repeated sound image served as the focus of the required one-pointed attention.

This leads to another curious reflection. Mystics who follow the procedure of constantly repeating a verbal formula often, I believe, tend to choose some religious set of words, for instance a part of the Lord's Prayer or a psalm. They probably imagine that these uplifting and inspirational words will carry them upwards toward the divine. But Tennyson's procedure suggests that any nonsense words would probably do as well. And this seems to agree with the general theory of concentration. It doesn't seem to matter what is chosen as the single point of concentration, whether it be one's breathing, or the sound of one's own name, or one's navel, or anything else, provided only it serves to shut off all other mental content.

Another point on which mystics usually insist in regard to spiritual training is what they call "detachment." Emphasis on this is found just as much in Hinduism and Buddhism as in Christianity. What is sought is detachment from desire, the uprooting of desire, or at any rate of all self-centered desires. The exact psychology of the matter presents great difficulties. In Christian mysticism the idea of detachment is usually given a religious and moral twist by insisting that it means the destruction of self-will or any kind of self-assertiveness, especially the rooting out of pride and the attainment of absolute humility. In non-Christian mysticism detachment does not usually get this special slant. But in the mysticism of all cultures detachment from desires for sensations and sensory images is emphasized.

We will now return to the main question. Supposing that the sensory-intellectual consciousness has been successfully supplanted by the mystical consciousness, can we find in the literatures of the subject any descriptions of this consciousness that will give us any idea of what it is like? The answer is that although mystics frequently say that their experiences are ineffable and indescribable, they nevertheless do often in fact describe them, and one can find plenty of such descriptive statements in the literature. They are usually extremely short—perhaps only three or four lines. And frequently they are indirect and not in the first person singular. Mystics more often than not avoid direct references to themselves.

I will give here a famous description which occurs in the Mandukya Upanishad. The Upanishads are supposed to have been the work of anonymous forest seers in India who lived between three thousand and twenty-five hundred years ago. They are among the oldest records of mysticism in the world. But they are of an unsurpassable depth of spirituality. For long ages and for countless millions of men in the East they have been, and they remain, the supreme source of the spiritual life. Of the introvertive mystical consciousness the Mandukya says that it is "beyond the senses, beyond the understanding, beyond all expression. . . . It is the pure unitary consciousness, wherein awareness of the world and of multiplicity is completely obliterated. It is ineffable peace. It is the Supreme Good. It is One without a second. It is the Self."

It will repay us, not to just slur over this passage, but to examine it carefully clause by clause. The first sentence is negative, telling us only what the experience is *not*. It is "beyond the senses, beyond the understanding." That is to say, it is beyond the sensory-intellectual consciousness; and there are in it no elements of sensation or sensuous imagery and no elements of conceptual thought. After these negatives there comes the statement that "it is the unitary consciousness, wherein all awareness of multiplicity has been obliterated." The core of the experience is thus described as an undifferentiated unity—a oneness or unity in which there is no internal division, no multiplicity.

I happen to have quoted a Hindu source. But one can find exactly the same thing in Christian mysticism. For instance the great Flemish mystic Jan van Ruysbroeck (1293-1381) says of what he calls "the God-seeing man" that "his spirit is undifferentiated and without distinction, and therefore it feels nothing but the unity." We see that the very words of the faithful Catholic are almost identical with those of the ancient Hindu, and I do not see how it can be doubted that they are describing the same experience. Not only in Christianity and Hinduism but everywhere else we find that the essence of the experience is that it is an *undifferentiated unity*, though each culture and each religion interprets this undifferentiated unity in terms of its own creeds or dogmas.

It may be objected that "undifferentiated unity" is a conceptual thought, and this is inconsistent with our statement that the experience is wholly nonintellectual. The answer is that concepts such as "one," "unity," "undifferentiated," "God," "Nirvana," etc., are only applied to the experience *after* it has passed and when it is being *remembered*. None can be applied during the experience itself.

The passage of the Upanishad goes on to say that the undifferentiated unity "is the Self." Why is this? Why is the unity now identified with the Self? The answer is plain. We started with the full self or mind of our ordinary everyday consciousness. What was it full of? It was full of the multiplicity of sensations, thoughts, desires, and the rest. But the mind was not merely this multiplicity. These disparate elements were held together in a unity, the unity of the single mind or self. A multiplicity without a unity in which the multiple elements are together is inconceivable—e.g., many objects in one space. Now when we emptied all the multiple contents out of this unity of the self what is left, according to the Upanishad, is the unity of the self, the original unity minus its contents. And this is the self. The Upanishads go further than this. They always identify this individual self with the Universal Self, the soul of the world. We will consider this in Chapter 2. For the moment we may continue to think in terms of the individual self, the pure ego of you or me. The undifferentiated unity is thought to be the pure ego.

I must draw the reader's attention to several facts about this situation. In the first place it flatly contradicts what David Hume said in a famous passage about the self. He said that when he looked introspectively into himself and searched for the I, the self, the ego, all he could ever introspect was the multiplicity of the sensations, images, thoughts, and feelings. He could never observe any I, any pure self apart from its contents, and he inferred that the I is a fiction and does not really exist. But now a vast body of empirical evidence, that of the mystics from all over the world, affirms that Hume was simply mistaken on a question of psychological fact, and that it is possible to get rid of all the mental contents and find the pure self left over and to experience this. This evidence need not mean that the self is a thing or a "substance," but can be taken as implying that it is a pure unity, the sort of being which Kant called the "transcendental unity" of the self.

The next thing to note is that the assertion of this new kind of consciousness is completely paradoxical. One way of bringing out the paradox is to point out that what we are left with here, when the contents of consciousness are gone, is a kind of consciousness which has no objects. It is not a consciousness *of* anything, but yet it is still consciousness. For the contents of our ordinary daily consciousness, the colors, sounds, wishes, thoughts are the same as the objects of consciousness, so that when the contents are gone the objects are gone. This consciousness of the mystics is not even a consciousness of consciousness, for then there would be a duality which is incompatible with the idea of an undifferentiated unity. In India it is called *pure* consciousness. The word "pure" is used in somewhat the same sense as Kant used it—meaning "without any empirical contents."

Another aspect of the paradox is that this pure consciousness is simultaneously both positive and negative, something and nothing, a fullness and an emptiness. The positive side is that it is an actual and positive consciousness. Moreover, all mystics affirm that it is pure peace, beatitude, joy, bliss, so that it has a positive affective tone. The Christians call it "the peace of God which passeth all understanding." The Buddhists call it Nirvana. But although it has this positive character, it is quite correct to say also that when we empty out all objects and contents of the mind *there is nothing whatever left*. That is the negative side of the paradox. What is left is sheer Emptiness. This is fully recognized in all mystical literature. In Mahayana Buddhism this total emptiness of the mystical consciousness is called the Void. In Christian mysticism the experience is identified with God. And this causes Eckhart and others to say that God, or the Godhead, is pure Nothingness, is a "desert," or "wilderness," and so on. Usually the two sides of the paradox are expressed in metaphors. The commonest metaphor for the positive side is light and for the negative side darkness. This is the darkness of God. It is called darkness because all distinctions disappear in it just as all distinctions disappear in a physical darkness.

We must not say that what we have here is a light *in* the darkness. For that would be no paradox. The paradox is that the light *is* the darkness, and the darkness *is* the light. This statement can be well documented from the literature of different cultures. I will give two examples, one from Christianity, one from Buddhism—and from the Buddhism of Tibet of all places in the world. Dionysius the Areopagite, a Christian, speaks of God as "the dazzling obscurity which outshines all brilliance with the intensity of its darkness." And the Tibetan book of the Dead puts the same paradox in the words, "the clear light of the Void." In Dionysius we see that the obscurity, or the darkness, *is* the brilliance, and in the Tibetan book we see that the Void itself *is* a clear light.

(8) *Mysticism and Religion.* Most writers on mysticism seem to take it for granted that mystical experience is a religious experience, and that mysticism is necessarily a religious phenomenon. They seem to think that mysticism and religious mysticism are one and the same thing. But this is far from being correct. It is true that there is an important connection between mysticism and religion, but it is not nearly so direct and immediate as most writers have seemed to think, nor can it be simply taken for granted as an obvious fact.

There are several grounds for insisting that intrinsically and in itself mystical experience is not a religious phenomenon at all and that its connection with religions is subsequent and even adventitious. In the first place, it seems to be clear that if we strip the mystical experience of all intellectual interpretation such as that which identifies it with God, or with the Absolute, or with the soul of the world, what is left is simply the undifferentiated unity. Now what is there that is religious about an undifferentiated unity? The answer seems to be, in the first instance, "Nothing at all." There seems to be nothing religious about an undifferentiated unity as such.

In the theistic religions of the West, in Christianity, Judaism, and Islam, the experience of the undifferentiated unity is interpreted as "union with God." But this is an interpretation and is not the experience itself. It is true that some Christian mystics, such as St. Teresa of Avila, invariably speak simply of having experienced "union with God," and do not talk about an undifferentiated unity. St. Teresa did not have a sufficiently analytical mind to distinguish between the experience and its interpretation. But other Christian mystics who are more analytically minded, such as Eckhart and Ruysbroeck, do speak of the undifferentiated unity.

These considerations are further underlined by the fact that quite different interpretations of the same experience are given in different cultures. The undifferentiated unity is interpreted by Eckhart and Ruysbroeck in terms of the Trinitarian conception of God, but by Islamic mystics as the unitarian God of Islam, and by the leading school of the Vedantists as a more impersonal Absolute. And when we come to Buddhism we find that the experience is not interpreted as any kind of God at all. For the Buddhist it becomes the Void or Nirvana. Buddha denied the existence of a Supreme Being altogether. It is often said that Buddhism is atheistic. And whether this description of Buddhism is true or not, it is certainly the case that there can exist an atheistic mysticism, a mystical experience naked and not clothed in any religious garb.

In view of these facts, we have a problem on our hands. Why is it that, in spite of exceptions, mysticism *usually* takes on some religious form and is usually found in connection with a definitely religious culture and as being a part of some definite religion? The following are, I think, the main reasons.

First, there is a very important feature of the introvertive mystical experience which I have not mentioned yet. I refer to the experience of the "melting away" into the Infinite of one's own individuality. Such phrases as "melting away," "fading away," "passing away" are found in the mystical literature of Christianity, Islam, Hindusim, and Buddhism. Among the Sufis of Islam there is a special technical term for it. It is called fanā. It must be insisted that this is not an inference or an interpretation or a theory or a speculation. It is an actual experience. The individual, as it were, directly experiences the disappearance of his own individuality, its fading away into the Infinite. To document this, one could quote from Eckhart, or from the Upanishads or the Sufis. But I believe I can bring home the point to a modern reader better by quoting a modern author. I referred earlier to the fact that Tennyson had frequent mystical experiences. His account of them is quoted by William James in his *The Varieties of Religious Experience*. Tennyson wrote, "All at once, as it were out of the intensity of the consciousness of individuality, individuality itself seemed to dissolve and fade away into boundless being. . . . the loss of personality, if such it were, seeming no extinction but the only true life." "Boundless being" seems to have the same meaning as "the Infinite." The Infinite is in most minds identified with the idea of God. We are finite beings, God is the only Infinite Being. One can see at once, therefore, how this experience of the dissolution of one's own individuality, its being merged into the Infinite, takes on a religious meaning. In theistic cultures the experience of melting away into boundless being is interpreted as union with God.

A second reason for the connection between mysticism and religion is that the undifferentiated unity is necessarily thought of by the mystics as being *beyond space and beyond time*. For it is without any internal division or mulitplicity of parts, whereas the essence of time is its division into an endless multitude of successive parts, and the essence of space is its division into a multitude of parts lying side by side. Therefore the undifferentiated unity, being without any multiplicity of parts, is necessarily spaceless and timeless. Being timeless is the same as being eternal. Hence Eckhart is constantly telling us that the mystical experience transcends time and is an experience of "the Eternal Now." But in religious minds the Eternal, like the Infinite, is another name for God. Hence the mystical experience is thought of as an experience of God.

A third reason for this identification of the undifferentiated unity with God lies in the emotional side of the experience. It is the universal testimony of the mystics that their kind of consciousness brings feelings of an exalted peace, blessedness, and joy. It becomes identified with the peace of God, the gateway of the Divine, the gateway of salvation. This is also why in Buddhism, though the experience is not personified or called God, it nevertheless becomes Nirvana which is the supreme goal of the Buddhist religious life.

Thus we see that mysticism naturally, though not necessarily, becomes intimately associated with whatever is the religion of the culture in which it appears. It is, however, important to realize that it does not favor any particular religion. Mystical experience in itself does not have any tendency to make a man a Christian or a Buddhist. Into the framework of what creed he will fit his experience will tend to depend mostly on the culture in which he lives. In a

Buddhist country the mystic interprets his experience as a glimpse of Nirvana, in a Christian country he may interpret it as union with God or even (as in Eckhart) as penetrating into the Godhead which is beyond God. Or if he is a highly sophisticated modern individual, who has been turned by his education into a religious skeptic, he may remain a skeptic as regards the dogmas of the different religions; he may allow his mystical experience to remain naked without any clothing of creeds or dogmas; but he is likely at the same time to feel that in that experience he has found something *sacred*. And this feeling of the sacred may quite properly be called "religious" feeling though it does not clothe itself in any dogmas. And this alone may be enough to uplift his ideals and to revolutionize his life and to give it meaning and purpose.

(9) *The Ethical Aspects of Mysticism.* It is sometimes asserted that mysticism is merely an escape from life and from its duties and responsibilities. The mystic, it is said, retreats into a private ecstasy of bliss, turns his back on the world, and forgets not only his own sorrows but the needs and sorrows of his fellow-men. In short, his life is essentially selfish.

It is possible that there have been mystics who deserved this kind of condemnation. To treat the bliss of the mystical consciousness as an end in itself is certainly a psychological possibility. And no doubt there have been men who have succumbed to this temptation. But this attitude is not the mystic ideal, and it is severely condemned by those who are most representative of the mystics themselves. For instance, St. John of the Cross condemns it as "spiritual gluttony." Eckhart tells us that if a man were in mystical ecstasy and knew of a poor man who needed his help, he should leave his ecstasy in order to go and serve the poor man. The Christian mystics especially have always emphasized that mystical union with God brings with it an intense and burning love of God which must needs overflow into the world in the form of love for our fellow-men; and that this must show itself in deeds of charity, mercy, and self-sacrifice, and not merely in words.

Some mystics have gone beyond this and have insisted that the mystical consciousness is the secret fountain of all love, human as well as divine; and that since love in the end is the only source of true moral activity, therefore mysticism is the source from which ethical values ultimately flow. For all selfishness and cruelty and evil result from the separateness of one human being from another. This separateness of individuals breeds egoism and the war of all against all. But in the mystical consciousness all distinctions disappear and therefore the distinction between "I" and "you" and "he" and "she." This is the mystical and metaphysical basis of love, namely the realization that my brother and I are one, and that therefore his sufferings are my sufferings and his happiness is my happiness. This reveals itself dimly in the psychological phenomena of sympathy and more positively in actual love. For one who had no touch of the mystical vision all men would be islands. And in the end it is because of mysticism that it is possible to say that "no man is an island" and that on the contrary every man is "a part of the main."

(10) *Alternative Interpretations of Mysticism.* We have seen that the same experience may be interpreted in terms of different religious creeds. There is also another set of alternative interpretations which we ought to mention. We may believe that the mystic really is in touch, as he usually claims, with some being greater than himself, some spiritual Infinite which transcends the temporal flux of things. Or we may, on the other hand, adopt the alternative solution of the skeptic who will think that the mystical consciousness is entirely subjective and imports nothing outside itself. My own vote would be cast for the former solution. I would agree with the words of Arthur Koestler which are quoted in the final selection printed in this book. He speaks of a higher order of reality which for us is like a text written in invisible ink. "I also liked to think," he says, "that the founders of religions, prophets, saints and seers had at moments been able to read a fragment of the invisible text; after which they had so much padded, dramatised and ornamented it, that they themselves could no longer tell what parts of it were authentic." [1]

But I wish to point out that even if one should choose the skeptical alternative and suppose that the mystical consciousness reveals no reality outside its owner's brain, one is far from having disposed of mysticism as some worthless delusion which ought to be got rid of. Even if it is wholly subjective, it still reveals something which is supremely great in human life. It is still the peace which passeth all

[1] See p. 235.

understanding. It is still the gateway to salvation—not, I mean, in a future life, but as the highest beatitude that a man can reach in this life, and out of which the greatest deeds of love can flow. But it must be added, of course, that it belongs among those things of which Spinoza wrote in those famous words: "If the road which I have shown is very difficult, it yet can be discovered. And clearly it must be very hard if it is so rarely found. For how could it be that it is neglected by practically all, if salvation . . . could be found without difficulty. But all excellent things are as difficult as they are rare."

(11) *The Method of These Selections.* Some explanation is due to the reader as to the method which has been followed in making these selections. I have been guided by a general principle, although I do not claim that it has been consistently carried through. It has seemed to me important to emphasize the value of mystical experiences themselves rather than the interpretative theories and philosophies which have been built upon them, whether by the mystics or by others. In my view, as will have been made plain in this introduction, the supreme gift of the mystic is his experience. Directly he begins to interpret it intellectually, he has become a thinker and a philosopher who is as liable to error and confusion as the next man. He may be a good philosopher or he may be a poor one. His theories are not sacrosanct, but his experience is.

Therefore my guiding principle has been to choose, wherever possible, those selections in which the mystical experience of the writer is directly described and emphasized. But there are severe limitations on the possibilities here. There are, of course, a few mystics, such as St. Teresa and Henry Suso, who have written autobiographies and have given in them uninhibited and detailed accounts of their experiences. But more often the mystic does not wish to draw attention to himself at all. He tends to write down his reflections on life in general, his beliefs and opinions, his philosophical or theological ideas, his aspirations and ideals, the advice he feels himself competent to give to others. He will only refer to his own intimate inner life in a most roundabout and indirect way, or not at all. We often get mere scraps and hints and glimpses which occupy two or three lines in a chapter about something else. Brief remarks appear from time to time which we feel could not have been written except on the basis of the writer's own experience, although he does not say it is his own. And we have to be sensitive enough to spot these passages.

But worse is to come—worse from the point of view of carrying through our principle. In some areas of our subject it is practically impossible to find any writings which are representative of that area and of which one can feel sure that their authors were mystics at all in the strict sense of having had their own mystical experiences. This is especially true of Buddhism. Mr. Alan Watts very aptly refers to "the tediously repetitious and scholastic style of most of the Buddhist scriptures" and adds "there can be little doubt that the greater part of both Buddhist Canons [he means the Hinayana and the Mahayana] is the work of pandits of the . . . Buddhist monastic order, for it shows every sign of being the reverential elaboration of an original doctrine." [2] In other words, one does not find in the Buddhist scriptures the living breath of the mystic, but only dry bones left behind. My own estimate is a little more favorable as regards some of the Mahayana texts, which seem to be more inspired and less arid than the texts of the Pali canon. But even with the most famous of the Mahayana sutras one cannot be sure whether their authors were mere Buddhist philosophers or whether they themselves had attained that "Supreme Enlightenment" whereof they speak. For instance, I have chosen a selection from *The Awakening of Faith*. The reading of it gives me the impression that the author probably had the enlightenment experience or some measure of it. But one cannot be sure.

It is for this reason that in the subtitle of this book I speak of it not solely as "selections from the great mystics" but as "selections from the great mystics and mystical writings of the world." I think it reasonable to claim that *The Awakening of Faith* and the rest of my Buddhist selections are "great mystical writings" even if they were not in all cases the authentic work of the mystics themselves.

Wherever possible I have chosen the work of those who were plainly mystics themselves. But although this has not always been possible, I think I can claim that in no case have I selected writings of poor quality. I believe they are all "great" in one way or another, and that every one of them deserves its place in this book.

---

[2] Alan W. Watts, *The Way of Zen*. New York: Pantheon Books, Inc., 1957; New York: New American Library (Mentor Books), 1959, p. 42.

# -2-

# Hindu Mysticism

The philosophy known as Vedantism has from ancient times been the leading philosophy of India, although there have been a great variety of rival philosophies, several of which were also very influential. Vedantism, although it regards itself as a philosophy, and therefore as a product of the intellect, is in reality rooted in mysticism. It is an intellectual interpretation of the kind of mystical experience described in the quotation from the Mandukya Upanishad on page 20. The main operative clause of that description reads: "The unitary consciousness, wherein awareness . . . of multiplicity is completely obliterated . . . is the Self." Vedantism itself divided into several divergent streams of thought, but we shall here speak only of what must be regarded as the main stream, the so-called "nondualistic" version of it.

Nondualistic Vedantism, if reduced to its simplest possible expression, is seen to be the result of two great interpretative steps based upon the mystical experience described above. These two steps had already been fully developed in the Upanishads and were merely elaborated by the later Vedantists. The first step of the interpretation consisted in taking the undifferentiated unity in which all multiplicity has been obliterated to be the pure self of the individual. The explanation of this was given in the previous chapter. The undifferentiated unity was reached by emptying the individual self of its manifold contents of sensations, images, thoughts, desires, etc. What is left is naturally taken to be the pure unity of the individual self itself.

We have now to examine the second step. This consisted in identifying the individual self, the pure unity of the finite

ego, with the Universal Self, the Infinite Self, Brahman, the
Absolute. This transition of thought was believed by the composers of the Upanishads to be the secret of salvation. It
was their supreme discovery—that in the mystical consciousness the soul realizes its own identity with the divine and
thereafter passes beyond all sorrow.

We find that by the time of the Upanishads—say a mil-
lennium before Christ—the Indian mind had come to accept
belief in reincarnation. And the further belief that all life
is essentially sorrowful had taken deep root. Hence the Indian sages sought release from reincarnation. The seers of
the Upanishads believed that whoever can attain and hold
fast to the mystical identification with Brahman will never
again be reborn, but will pass into the life of the Infinite. But
the question that we have here to ask is how and why this
second interpretative step was made; how the individual self
becomes identified with the Universal Self.

The matter is obscured by the fact that in the wording of
the passage in the Mandukya Upanishad the two steps are
telescoped into one. "The unitary consciousness . . . is the
Self." In this sentence the word "Self" means both the individual self and the Universal Self. They are simply taken to
be identical without any question. We have separated the
two steps in order to understand them. The first step has
been explained. We have now to explain the second.

Why, then, is the pure self of the individual which is
reached in the mystical consciousness declared to be the
Universal Self of the world? In principle the reasons for
this transition have been given in our first chapter, where we
inquired why the undifferentiated unity, which is not itself
a religious phenomenon, becomes religious. We have only
to apply the principle to the present case. The experience of
the pure self in the Upanishads is identified with the experience of the Universal Self for the same reasons as it is identified with the experience of the primal being in other
cultures and in general takes on the character of the divine.

First, there is the experience of the "melting away" of the
individual soul into the Infinite, or into "boundless being," as
Tennyson phrased it. This is found in the mysticisms of all
cultures. It was also part of the experience of the seers of
the Upanishads. In the selection from the Brihadaranyaka
Upanishad which is given below, the reader will find it stated:
"The individual self, dissolved, is the Eternal. . . . With the
disappearance of consciousness of the many in divine il-

lumination it disappears. Where there is consciousness of the Self, individuality is no more." It is not, according to the Upanishads, that the individual self *becomes* the Universal Self. It always was that Self. What happens in the moment of illumination is only that it realizes that truth.

The second reason for this identification is that the undifferentiated unity is necessarily spaceless and timeless—since space and time are both differentiated existences. Hence the experience is transcendental and eternal, and therefore identical with the Divine Being.

The third reason is the felt peace, the bliss, the beatitude of the experience. Herein all sorrow ends. The goal of the soul's aspiration is reached. And the goal of aspiration is naturally conceived in a religious culture as the Divine Being.

It will be understood that this identification of the finite self with the Infinite Self, which is realized in the mystical consciousness, is the Hindu equivalent of what the Christian mystics call "union with God." We shall see later that the Christian theory of the nature of union with God is vastly different from the Vedantic theory of the nature of identity with Brahman. But for the moment it is the equivalence that is to be noted.

The realization that the individual self is the same as the Supreme Self is the sole point of our selection from the Chandogya Upanishad. It is not found only there, however. There is scarcely a page in the Upanishads in which it is not either explicit or implicit. But here in the Chandogya the point is made in a very dramatic form. The father Uddalaka teaches it to his son Svetaketu. In his school days with the Brahman priests Svetaketu had learned to repeat the Vedas by heart—the kind of formalistic religious education one expects from a priesthood. The question his father asks is whether Svetaketu has learned "that knowledge by which we hear the unhearable, by which we perceive the unperceivable, by which we know the unknowable." The knowledge that his father wishes Svetaketu to learn is not any kind of intellectual knowledge, but mystical illumination. That which is learned in that illumination is nonsensuous—"unhearable" and "unperceivable"—and also nonintellectual, "unknowable" by the intellect. Then comes the great revelation. "He, the One" is "the subtle essence" of all things. He manifests himself in all beings. "He is the Self. And that, Svetaketu, THAT ART THOU." And Uddalaka forces home that supreme discovery of the seers of the Upanishads, by the dramatic repetition, again and again, of those tremendous words.

The period of the composition of the Upanishads is generally believed to have extended from about 1000 B.C. to 400 B.C.—although Indian chronology may be called the despair of scholars. The authors of the Upanishads are unknown. But they are commonly believed to have been the work of "forest seers"—men who, having renounced the common desires of men, retired into the forest to live the life of contemplation.

## FROM *the Chandogya Upanishad*[1]

When Svetaketu was twelve years old, his father Uddalaka said to him, "Svetaketu, you must now go to school and study. None of our family, my child, is ignorant of Brahman."

Thereupon Svetaketu went to a teacher and studied for twelve years. After committing to memory all the Vedas, he returned home full of pride in his learning.

His father, noticing the young man's conceit, said to him: "Svetaketu, have you asked for that knowledge by which we hear the unhearable, by which we perceive the unperceivable, by which we know the unknowable?"

"What is that knowledge, sir?" asked Svetaketu.

"My child, as by knowing one lump of clay, all things made of clay are known, the difference being only in name and arising from speech, and the truth being that all are clay; as by knowing a nugget of gold, all things made of gold are known, the difference being only in name and arising from speech, and the truth that all are gold—exactly so is that knowledge, knowing which we know all."

"But surely those venerable teachers of mine are ignorant of this knowledge; for if they had possessed it, they would have taught it to me. Do you therefore, sir, give me that knowledge."

"Be it so," said Uddalaka, and continued thus:

"In the beginning there was Existence, One only, without a second. Some say that in the beginning there was non-existence only, and that out of that the universe was born. But how could such a thing be? How could existence be born of non-existence? No, my son, in the beginning there

[1] *The Upanishads: Breath of the Eternal*, translated by Swami Prabhavananda and Frederick Manchester. Hollywood, Calif.: The Vedanta Society of Southern California, 1957; New York: New American Library (Mentor Books), 1957, pp. 68-69.

was Existence alone—One only, without a second. He, the One, thought to himself: Let me be many, let me grow forth. Thus out of himself he projected the universe; and having projected out of himself the universe, he entered into every being. All that is has its self in him alone. Of all things he is the subtle essence. He is the truth. He is the Self. And that, Svetaketu, THAT ART THOU."

"Please, sir, tell me more about this Self."

"Be it so, my child:

"As the bees make honey by gathering juices from many flowering plants and trees, and as these juices reduced to one honey do not know from what flowers they severally come, similarly, my son, all creatures, when they are merged in that one Existence, whether in dreamless sleep or in death, know nothing of their past or present state, because of the ignorance enveloping them—know not that they are merged in him and that from him they came.

"Whatever these creatures are, whether a lion, or a tiger, or a boar, or a worm, or a gnat, or a mosquito, that they remain after they come back from dreamless sleep.

"All these have their self in him alone. He is the truth. He is the subtle essence of all. He is the Self. And that, Svetaketu, THAT ART THOU."

"Please, sir, tell me more about this Self."

"Be it so, my son:

"The rivers in the east flow eastward, the rivers in the west flow westward, and all enter into the sea. From sea to sea they pass, the clouds lifting them to the sky as vapor and sending them down as rain. And as these rivers, when they are united with the sea, do not know whether they are this or that river, likewise all those creatures that I have named, when they have come back from Brahman, know not whence they came.

"All those beings have their self in him alone. He is the truth. He is the subtle essence of all. He is the Self. And that, Svetaketu, THAT ART THOU."


The selection from the Brihadaranyaka Upanishad which next follows repeats and reinforces the lesson of the previous selection—the realized identity of the individual self with the Universal Self. The Self is all creatures—that is, the essence of everything in the world. This is the pantheistic doctrine of the identity of God and the world. Hence the text says: "Let us ignore him who thinks that anything whatever is different from the Self."

We have next the assertion, already explained, that individuality disappears "in divine illumination."

Finally there is the famous saying: "The Self is described as *not this, not that*. It is incomprehensible, for it cannot be comprehended." From one point of view this is a statement of the negative side of the mystical paradox. Is God mind? No. Is he matter? No. Is he this? No. Is he that? No. There is no positive predicate whatever which can be applied to him. To say that he is "incomprehensible" is a way of saying this. To comprehend, to understand, is the function of the intellect. It operates by applying concepts to its object or, what is the same thing, asserting attributes or relations of it. But the sensory-intellectual consciousness cannot reach the Self. The Self can only be "known" in the direct experience of the mystical consciousness. It is difficult not to use such phrases as "the direct experience *of* the mystical consciousness." But always one must correct this by reminding ourselves that the mystical consciousness does not experience the Self in the sense of having it as an object. The correct statement is that true mystical experience *is* the Self.

### FROM *the Brihadaranyaka Upanishad*[2]

#### *Yagnavalkya (to his wife)*

Maitreyi, I am resolved to give up the world and begin the life of renunciation. I wish therefore to divide my property between you and my other wife, Katyayani.

#### *Maitreyi*

My lord, if this whole earth belonged to me, with all its wealth, should I through its possession attain immortality?

#### *Yagnavalkya*

No. Your life would be like that of the rich. None can possibly hope to attain immortality through wealth.

#### *Maitreyi*

Then what need have I of wealth? Please, my lord, tell me what you know about the way to immortality.

2 *Ibid.*, pp. 86-89.

## Yagnavalkya

Dear to me have you always been, Maitreyi, and now you ask to learn of that truth which is nearest my heart. Come, sit by me. I will explain it to you. Meditate on what I say. . . .

It is not for the sake of itself, my beloved, that anything whatever is esteemed, but for the sake of the Self.

The Self, Maitreyi, is to be known. Hear about it, reflect upon it, meditate upon it. By knowing the Self, my beloved, through hearing, reflection, and meditation, one comes to know all things.

Let the Brahmin ignore him who thinks that the Brahmin is different from the Self.

Let the Kshatriya ignore him who thinks that the Kshatriya is different from the Self.

Let the higher worlds ignore him who thinks that the higher worlds are different from the Self.

Let the gods ignore him who thinks that the gods are different from the Self.

Let all creatures ignore him who thinks that the creatures are different from the Self.

Let all ignore him who thinks that anything whatever is different from the Self.

The priest, the warrior, the higher worlds, the gods, the creatures, whatsoever things there be—these are the Self.

As, when the drum is beaten, its various particular notes are not heard apart from the whole, but in the total sound all its notes are heard; as, when the conch-shell is blown, its various particular notes are not heard apart from the whole, but in the total sound all its notes are heard; as, when the vina is played, its various particular notes are not heard apart from the whole, but in the total sound all its notes are heard—so, through the knowledge of the Self, Pure Intelligence, all things and beings are known. There is no existence apart from the Self.

As smoke and sparks arise from a lighted fire kindled with damp fuel, even so, Maitreyi, have been breathed forth from the Eternal all knowledge and all wisdom—what we know as the Rig Veda, the Yajur Veda, and the rest. They are the breath of the Eternal.

As for water the one center is the ocean, as for touch the one center is the skin, as for smell the one center is the nose, as for taste the one center is the tongue, as for form the one center is the eyes, as for sound the one center is the ears, as for thought the one center is the mind, as for divine wisdom the one center is the heart—so for all beings the one center is the Self.

As a lump of salt when thrown into water melts away and the lump cannot be taken out, but wherever we taste the water it is salty, even so, O Maitreyi, the individual self, dissolved, is the Eternal—pure consciousness, infinite and transcendent. Individuality arises by identification of the Self, through ignorance, with the elements; and with the disappearance of consciousness of the many, in divine illumination, it disappears. Where there is consciousness of the Self, individuality is no more.

This it is, O my beloved, that I wanted to tell you.

### Maitreyi

"Where there is consciousness of the Self, individuality is no more": this that you say, my lord, confuses me.

### Yagnavalkya

My beloved, let nothing I have said confuse you. But meditate well the truth that I have spoken.

As long as there is duality, one sees *the other*, one hears *the other*, one smells *the other*, one speaks to *the other*, one thinks of *the other*, one knows *the other*; but when for the illumined soul the all is dissolved in the Self, who is there to be seen by whom, who is there to be smelt by whom, who is there to be heard by whom, who is there to be spoken to by whom, who is there to be thought of by whom, who is there to be known by whom? Ah, Maitreyi, my beloved, the Intelligence which reveals all—by what shall it be revealed? By whom shall the Knower be known? The Self is described as *not this, not that*. It is incomprehensible, for it cannot be comprehended; undecaying, for it never decays; unattached, for it never attaches itself; unbound, for it is never bound. By whom, O my beloved, shall the Knower be known?

This it is that I teach you, O Maitreyi. This is the truth of immortality.

So saying, Yagnavalkya entered upon the path of renunciation.

Only brief extracts were given from the Chandogya and Brihadaranyaka Upanishads. But the whole Svetasvatara Upanishad as it appears in the translation of Swami Prab-

havananda and Frederick Manchester in this series is given
below.

The Svetasvatara shows many signs of being the work of a
time much later than the Chandogya and Brihadaranyaka.
Yet though the form and style are different, the essence of
the spiritual message is the same. He who has carefully read
the brief extracts from the two earlier Upanishads given
above should have little difficulty in perceiving, under the
guise of a new style, the insights which he has already received. The fundamental pantheism is the same. Brahman,
though stated in the opening section to be the first cause of
the universe, is yet identical with the universe. "He alone
is *all this*—what has been and what shall be. He has become the universe." The omnipresence of Brahman is expressed in a striking passage. "This great Being has a thousand heads, a thousand eyes, and a thousand feet. . . . His
hands and feet are everywhere; his eyes and mouths are
everywhere. His ears are everywhere." Many Westerners must
often have wondered at what may seem to them the
grotesque appearance of Hindu temple architecture and
sculpture—the twisted figures with the many arms and legs
and faces. The words just quoted show us how these figures
symbolize Hindu pantheism. In the second stanza of the
poem which forms the last part of the Svetasvatara Upanishad, in the nineteen lines beginning "Thou art the fire,"
this pantheism expresses itself in a burst of magnificent
poetry.

We find here also, as in the earlier selections, the supreme
message of the identity of the human spirit with God as
realized in the mystical consciousness; also the salvation and
the liberation from rebirth which this realization brings.

There are, however, at least two new ideas, not found in
the previous selections, to which it may be useful to draw
the reader's attention. The section beginning at the fifteenth
paragraph gives some information and instructions as to the
techniques to be employed in achieving the mystical consciousness. One should "sit upright, holding the chest,
throat, and head erect." With the aid of "spiritual disciplines" one is to control the senses and the mind, and detach
oneself from "objects of pleasure." "Controlling the breath,"
one is to "turn . . . the mind inward to the lotus of the heart"
—i.e., practice introversion. One should then "meditate upon
pure consciousness as distinct from the ordinary consciousness of the intellect." This last is an explicit reference to
the difference between the sensory-intellectual consciousness

and the pure or mystical consciousness which is explained in our first chapter.

The other new subject matter is the concept of Maya which appears in the last part of the Upanishad. Quite definitely this concept belongs to Indian philosophy rather than to mysticism proper. It is an intellectual interpretation or "mystical idea" as that term was explained in Section (1) of the first chapter. Moreover, it is peculiar to Indian philosophy—although it has its counterparts elsewhere—and is not found, for example, in Christian mysticism. It is therefore no part of the heritage of mysticism as such. Hence a very brief statement about Maya—sufficient only to make the text intelligible—will suffice here.

Westerners usually think of Maya as meaning "illusion." Although the thought that the world is illusion was not fully developed till a time later than the Upanishads, the translation of "Maya" as "illusion" is not incorrect, but is oversimple. The word originally means a work of art, an artifice, and hence a deceit, fraud, conjuring trick, magical performance, etc. But it is also used as the name of the power which Brahman puts forth in producing the magical performance of the world. Hence we get three connected ideas: Brahman, Maya, and the world. Brahman (1) puts forth his Maya (power) (2) and thereby produces the world (3). Maya is then thought of as a link or middle term between Brahman and the world. Finally this intermediary becomes the wife or "divine consort" of Brahman, by uniting with whom he procreates the world. This latter is the image mostly used in this Upanishad.

## The Svetasvatara Upanishad[3]

DISCIPLES INQUIRE within themselves:

What is the cause of this universe?—is it Brahman? Whence do we come? Why do we live? Where shall we at last find rest? Under whose command are we bound by the law of happiness and its opposite?

Time, space, law, chance, matter, primal energy, intelligence—none of these, nor a combination of these, can be the final cause of the universe, for they are effects, and exist to serve the soul. Nor can the individual self be the cause, for, being subject to the law of happiness and misery, it is not free.

The seers, absorbed in contemplation, saw within them-

3 *Ibid.*, pp. 118-28.

selves the ultimate reality, the self-luminous being, the one God, who dwells as the self-conscious power in all creatures. He is One without a second. Deep within all beings he dwells, hidden from sight by the coverings of the gunas— *sattwa, rajas,* and *tamas.* He presides over time, space, and all apparent causes.

This vast universe is a wheel. Upon it are all creatures that are subject to birth, death, and rebirth. Round and round it turns, and never stops. It is the wheel of Brahman. As long as the individual self thinks it is separate from Brahman, it revolves upon the wheel in bondage to the laws of birth, death, and rebirth. But when through the grace of Brahman it realizes its identity with him, it revolves upon the wheel no longer. It achieves immortality.

He who is realized by transcending the world of cause and effect, in deep contemplation, is expressly declared by the scriptures to be the Supreme Brahman. He is the substance, all else the shadow. He is the imperishable. The knowers of Brahman know him as the one reality behind all that seems. For this reason they are devoted to him. Absorbed in him, they attain freedom from the wheel of birth, death, and rebirth.

The Lord supports this universe, which is made up of the perishable and the imperishable, the manifest and the unmanifest. The individual soul, forgetful of the Lord, attaches itself to pleasure and thus is bound. When it comes to the Lord, it is freed from all its fetters.

Mind and matter, master and servant—both have existed from beginningless time. The Maya which unites them has also existed from beginningless time. When all three—mind, matter, and Maya—are known as one with Brahman, then is it realized that the Self is infinite and has no part in action. Then is it revealed that the Self is all.

Matter is perishable. The Lord, the destroyer of ignorance, is imperishable, immortal. He is the one God, the Lord of the perishable and of all souls. By meditating on him, by uniting oneself with him, by identifying oneself with him, one ceases to be ignorant.

Know God, and all fetters will be loosed. Ignorance will vanish. Birth, death, and rebirth will be no more. Meditate upon him and transcend physical consciousness. Thus will you reach union with the lord of the universe. Thus will you become identified with him who is One without a second. In him all your desires will find fulfillment.

The truth is that you are always united with the Lord. But you must *know* this. Nothing further is there to know.

Meditate, and you will realize that mind, matter, and Maya (the power which unites mind and matter) are but three aspects of Brahman, the one reality.

Fire, though present in the firesticks, is not perceived until one stick is rubbed against another. The Self is like that fire: it is realized in the body by meditation on the sacred syllable OM.

Let your body be the stick that is rubbed, the sacred syllable OM the stick that is rubbed against it. Thus shall you realize God, who is hidden within the body as fire is hidden within the wood.

Like oil in sesame seeds, butter in cream, water in the river bed, fire in tinder, the Self dwells within the soul. Realize him through truthfulness and meditation.

Like butter in cream is the Self in everything. Knowledge of the Self is gained through meditation. The Self is Brahman. By Brahman is all ignorance destroyed.

To realize God, first control the outgoing senses and harness the mind. Then meditate upon the light in the heart of the fire—meditate, that is, upon pure consciousness as distinct from the ordinary consciousness of the intellect. Thus the Self, the Inner Reality, may be seen behind physical appearance.

Control your mind so that the Ultimate Reality, the self-luminous Lord, may be revealed. Strive earnestly for eternal bliss.

With the help of the mind and the intellect, keep the senses from attaching themselves to objects of pleasure. They will then be purified by the light of the Inner Reality, and that light will be revealed.

The wise control their minds, and unite their hearts with the infinite, the omniscient, the all-pervading Lord. Only discriminating souls practice spiritual disciplines. Great is the glory of the self-luminous being, the Inner Reality.

Hear, all ye children of immortal bliss, also ye gods who dwell in the high heavens: Follow only in the footsteps of the illumined ones, and by continuous meditation merge both mind and intellect in the eternal Brahman. The glorious Lord will be revealed to you.

Control the vital force. Set fire to the Self within by the practice of meditation. Be drunk with the wine of divine love. Thus shall you reach perfection.

Be devoted to the eternal Brahman. Unite the light within you with the light of Brahman. Thus will the source of ignorance be destroyed, and you will rise above karma.

Sit upright, holding the chest, throat, and head erect. Turn the senses and the mind inward to the lotus of the heart. Meditate on Brahman with the help of the syllable OM. Cross the fearful currents of the ocean of worldliness by means of the raft of Brahman—the sacred syllable OM.

With earnest effort hold the senses in check. Controlling the breath, regulate the vital activities. As a charioteer holds back his restive horses, so does a persevering aspirant hold back his mind.

Retire to a solitary place, such as a mountain cave or a sacred spot. The place must be protected from the wind and rain, and it must have a smooth, clean floor, free from pebbles and dust. It must not be damp and it must be free from disturbing noises. It must be pleasing to the eye and quieting to the mind. Seated there, practice meditation and other spiritual exercises.

As you practice meditation, you may see in vision forms resembling snow, crystals, smoke, fire, lightning, fireflies, the sun, the moon. These are signs that you are on your way to the revelation of Brahman.

As you become absorbed in meditation, you will realize that the Self is separate from the body and for this reason will not be affected by disease, old age, or death.

The first signs of progress on the path of yoga are health, a sense of physical lightness, clearness of complexion, a beautiful voice, an agreeable odor of the person, and freedom from craving.

As a soiled piece of metal, when it has been cleaned, shines brightly, so the dweller in the body, when he has realized the truth of the Self, loses his sorrow and becomes radiant with bliss.

The yogi experiences directly the truth of Brahman by realizing the light of the Self within. He is freed from all impurities—he the pure, the birthless, the bright.

He is the one God, present in the north, the east, the south, and the west. He is the creator. He enters into all wombs. He alone is now born as all beings, and he alone is to be born as all beings in the future. He is within all persons as the Inner Self, facing in all directions.

Let us adore the Lord, the luminous one, who is in fire, who is in water, who is in plants and trees, who pervades the whole universe.

The one absolute, impersonal Existence, together with his inscrutable Maya, appears as the divine Lord, the personal God, endowed with manifold glories. By his divine power he holds dominion over all the worlds. At the periods of creation and dissolution of the universe, he alone exists. Those who realize him become immortal.

The Lord is One without a second. Within man he dwells, and within all other beings. He projects the universe, maintains it, and withdraws it into himself.

His eyes are everywhere; his face, his arms, his feet are in every place. Out of himself he has produced the heavens and the earth, and with his arms and his wings he holds them together.

He is the origin and support of the gods. He is the lord of all. He confers bliss and wisdom upon those who are devoted to him. He destroys their sins and their sorrows.

He punishes those who break his laws. He sees all and knows all. May he endow us with good thoughts!

O Lord, clothed in thy most holy form, which is calm and blissful, and which destroys all evil and ignorance, look upon us and make us glad.

O Lord, thou hast revealed thy sacred syllable OM, which is one with thee. In thy hands it is a weapon with which to destroy ignorance. O protector of thy devotees, do not conceal thy benign person.

Thou art the supreme Brahman. Thou art infinite. Thou hast assumed the forms of all creatures, remaining hidden in them. Thou pervadest all things. Thou art the one God of the universe. Those who realize thee become immortal.

Said the great seer Svetasvatara:

I have known, beyond all darkness, that great Person of golden effulgence. Only by knowing him does one conquer death. There is no other way of escaping the wheel of birth, death, and rebirth.

There is nothing superior to him, nothing different from him, nothing subtler or greater than he. Alone he stands, changeless, self-luminous; he, the Great One, fills this universe.

Though he fills the universe, he transcends it. He is untouched by its sorrow. He has no form. Those who know him become immortal. Others remain in the depths of misery.

The Lord God, all-pervading and omnipresent, dwells in the heart of all beings. Full of grace, he ultimately gives liberation to all creatures by turning their faces toward himself.

He is the innermost Self. He is the great Lord. He it is that reveals the purity within the heart by means of which he, who is pure being, may be reached. He is the ruler. He is the great Light, shining forever.

This great Being, assuming a form of the size of a thumb,

forever dwells in the heart of all creatures as their inner-most Self. He can be known directly by the purified mind through spiritual discrimination. Knowing him, men become immortal.

This great Being has a thousand heads, a thousand eyes, and a thousand feet. He envelops the universe. Though transcendent, he is to be meditated upon as residing in the lotus of the heart, at the center of the body, ten fingers above the navel.

He alone is *all this*—what has been and what shall be. He has become the universe. Yet he remains forever change-less, and is the lord of immortality.

His hands and feet are everywhere; his eyes and mouths are everywhere. His ears are everywhere. He pervades everything in the universe.

Without organs of sense, yet reflecting the activities of the senses, he is the lord and ruler of all.

He is the friend and refuge of all.

He resides in the body, the city of nine gates. He sports in the world without in innumerable forms. He is the master, the ruler, of the whole world, animate and inanimate.

He moves fast, though without feet. He grasps every-thing, though without hands. He sees everything, though without eyes. He hears everything, though without ears. He knows all that is, but no one knows him. He is called the Supreme, the Great One.

Subtler than the subtlest, greater than the greatest, the Self is hidden in the heart of all creatures. Through his grace a man loses his cravings, transcends grief, and realizes him as Brahman Supreme.

> O Brahman Supreme!
> Formless art thou, and yet
> (Though the reason none knows)
> Thou bringest forth many forms;
> Thou bringest them forth, and then
> Withdrawest them to thyself.
> Fill us with thoughts of thee!
>
> Thou art the fire,
> Thou art the sun,
> Thou art the air,
> Thou art the moon,
> Thou art the starry firmament,
> Thou art Brahman Supreme:
> Thou art the waters—thou,
> The creator of all!

Thou art woman, thou art man,
Thou art the youth, thou art the maiden,
Thou art the old man tottering with his staff;
Thou facest everywhere.

Thou art the dark butterfly,
Thou art the green parrot with red eyes,
Thou art the thunder cloud, the seasons, the seas.
Without beginning art thou,
Beyond time, beyond space.
Thou art he from whom sprang
The three worlds.

Maya is thy divine consort—
Wedded to thee.
Thou art her master, her ruler.
Red, white, and black is she,
Each color a guna.
Many are her children—
The rivers, the mountains,
Flower, stone, and tree,
Beast, bird, and man—
In every way like herself.
Thou, spirit in flesh,
Forgetting what thou art,
Unitest with Maya—
But only for a season.
Parting from her at last,
Thou regainest thyself.

Thou, Brahman Immortal,
And thou, woven of clay
(Two beings, yet one)—
Like two beautiful birds,
Golden of plumage,
Companions inseparable,
Perched high up on the branches
Of the selfsame tree—
As man thou tastest
The sweet fruits of the tree,
The sweet and bitter fruits;
But as Brahman, master of Maya,
Thou remainest unseen,
Immobile,
Calmly observing.

Forgetting his oneness with thee,
Bewildered by his weakness,
Full of sorrow is man;
But let him look close on thee,
Know thee as himself,
O Lord, most worshipful,
And behold thy glory—
Lo, all his heavy sorrow
Is turned to joy.

Changeless thou art,
Supreme, pure!
In thee dwell the gods.
The source of all scriptures thou art;
Yet what shall scriptures avail
If they be smooth on the lip
But absent from the heart?
To him who knows thee comes fullness—
To him alone!

Thou art lord and master of Maya,
Man is her slave.
With Maya uniting, thou hast brought forth the
    universe.
The source of all scriptures thou art,
And the source of all creeds.
The universe is thy Maya;
And thou, great God, her lord,
Wherever the eye falls,
There, within every form,
Thou dwellest.

One thou art, one only.
Born from many wombs,
Thou hast become many:
Unto thee all return.
Thou, Lord God, bestowest all blessings,
Thou the Light, thou the Adorable One.
Whoever finds thee
Finds infinite peace.

Thou art Lord God of all gods,
All the worlds rest in thee;
Thou art ruler of the beasts,
Two-footed, four-footed:
Our heart's worship be thine!

Thou art the blissful Lord,
Subtler than the subtlest.
In thee alone is there peace.

Thou, sole guardian of the universe,
Thou, lord of all,
In the hearts of thy creatures
Thou hidest thyself.
Gods and seers become one with thee.
Those who know thee die not.

Of all religions thou art the source.
The light of thy knowledge shining,
There is nor day nor night,
Nor being nor non-being—
Thou alone art.

Thou alone art—thou the Light
Imperishable, adorable;
Great Glory is thy name.
No one is there beside thee,
No one equal to thee.

Invisible is thy form,
Invisible to mortal eyes;
The seers alone,
In their purified hearts—
They alone see thee.
They alone are immortal.

Neither male nor female art thou,
Nor neuter;
Whatsoever form thou assumest,
That thou art.

Thou dost pervade the universe,
Thou art consciousness itself,
Thou art creator of time.
All-knowing art thou.

At thy bidding Maya,
Thy power divine,
Projects this visible universe,
Projects name and form.

Thou art the Primal Being.

Thou appearest as this universe
Of illusion and dream.
Thou art beyond time.
Indivisible, infinite, the Adorable One—
Let a man meditate on thee
Within his heart,
Let him consecrate himself to thee,
And thou, infinite Lord,
Wilt make thyself known to him.

Thou, womb and tomb of the universe,
And its abode;
Thou, source of all virtue,
Destroyer of all sins—
Thou art seated in the heart.
When thou art seen,
Time and form disappear.
Let a man feel thy presence,
Let him behold thee within,
And to him shall come peace,
Eternal peace—
To none else, to none else!

Thou art the eternal among non-eternals,
The consciousness of the conscious;
Though one, thou fulfillest
The desires of many.

Let a man devote himself
To knowledge of thee,
Let him follow thy path,
And he shall know thee:
All his fetters shall be loosed.

Can a man roll up the sky
Like a piece of skin?
Can he end his misery
And know not thee?

If the truths of these scriptures are meditated upon by
a man in the highest degree devoted to God, and to his
Guru as to his God, they will shine forth. They will shine
forth indeed!

OM ... Peace—peace—peace.

# Sri Aurobindo

When we turn from the earliest Hindu mysticism as represented in the Upanishads to the latest contemporary mysticism of Sri Aurobindo we find—considering that nearly three thousand years separate the two—astonishingly little change of thought. In one sense, of course, this is not surprising, because the mystical consciousness is the same in all ages. But it usually clothes itself in the cultural ideas and philosophies of the age or country in which it appears. And this causes it to seem very different—to the eye which cannot penetrate below surfaces—at different times and places. And yet even in this sense the change from the composers of the Upanishads to Sri Aurobindo is surprisingly small. That he is a direct spiritual descendant of those seers makes itself evident on almost every page of his writings. He bases his chapters directly on the Upanishads, and references to them in his writings appear more often than references to any other book in the world—with the possible exception of the Bhagavad-Gita. This is but one more instance of the fact that the Upanishads have always been the supreme source of Indian spirituality.

We must not, of course, think of Sri Aurobindo's work as a mere wooden reproduction of the ancient wisdom. This is a charge which can with some justice be brought against some contemporary Indian philosophers. But it cannot be brought against the Indian mystics. For they are by nature inspired men, not copyists. Along with the identity of spirit as between the Upanishads and Aurobindo there has, of course, been change of form. Perhaps one might characterize this change as a conscious attempt by Aurobindo to adapt the timeless message of Indian mysticism to the thought of the modern and Western world, especially as it has been molded by the spirit of science.

Aurobindo was born in India in 1872. He was educated at Cambridge, England, where he obtained a senior scholarship in classics. He won numerous prizes and honors in Latin and Greek. He was fluent in French, German, and English. He spent, all told, fourteen years in England. Returning to India, he worked for a time in the service of the government of Baroda. He became the professor of English literature in Baroda College. At a later date he was drawn into the nationalistic politics of India, then in the midst of its struggle for independence. He was arrested for sedition by the British and accused of taking part in terrorist activities. He affirmed that though he was working for Indian independence he had never taken any part in a policy of violence, and had never approved it. He was put on trial and acquitted. Soon after this he abandoned politics and "retired from the world," as the Indian phrase is, in order to spend the remainder of his life in the practice of yoga and the pursuit of the goal of the mystic.

He published a large number of books in English. His most elaborate and complete expression of his thought and experience is found in *The Life Divine*, from which the following selections are taken. This enormous book covers a thousand closely packed pages and contains over 400,000 words. His English style is in many respects exceedingly beautiful and powerful. Yet it is enormously prolix, and for this reason tends to become wearisome. Moreover, although his own mystical experience—which was unquestionably of a high order of development—shines out occasionally in brilliant flashes, yet his writing is mostly concerned with the philosophical ideas in terms of which he interpreted the experiences. Readers of these selections will have to become accustomed to this fact—that mystics, with some notable exceptions, tend to write of their opinions rather than their mystical experience. They are shy of wearing their hearts on their sleeves. Yet their experience is their priceless gift, while their opinions may or may not be valuable. There is perhaps only one sudden beacon light of his own mystical illumination in the present selection, but this is of very great importance. I will reproduce it in full here in order to comment on it.

He writes (page 64): "At the gates of the Transcendent stands that mere and perfect spirit described in the Upanishads, luminous, pure, sustaining the world . . . , without flaw of duality, without scar of division, unique, identical, free from all appearance of relation and multiplicity,—the pure Self of the Adwaitins, the inactive Brahman, the transcendent Silence. *And the mind when it passes those gates suddenly . . . receives a sense of the unreality of the world and the sole reality of the Silence which is one of the most powerful and convincing experiences of which the human mind is capable.*" (Italics mine.) It is obvious that this is a transcript of his own experience. It is to be noted that "silence" is a metaphor for the pure consciousness having the same meaning as the word "darkness." Both stand for the emptiness of the negative, darkness being the absence of light, silence the absence of sound.

The point to make here is that the idea of the unreality or illusoriness of the world is plainly based on this kind of experience. It is an interpretation of the mystical experience which for the most part the mystics of other cultures do not universally support. The philosophy which goes with mysticism in the Western religions, Christianity, Islam, and Judaism, is usually realism as regards the external world. Being interpretations, realism and illusionism might either be true or false. I shall not discuss that question. But it should be clear that the idea that the world is appearance, not reality, is rooted in mystical experience and not in logical argument. Afterwards it floats off in the atmosphere of thought free from the experience. What happens then is that philosophers who have never had the experience seize hold of it, repeat it, and because they are ignorant of its mystical origin begin to invent arguments for it or against it and finally come to believe that it is based on reasoned arguments. Those who accept it think the arguments good, those who reject it think them bad.

In the present selections Aurobindo is mostly concerned to do justice to what he regards as two poles of human thought, Western scientific materialism and Eastern idealistic mysticism. Each tends to run to unacceptable extremes. He blames Indian mysticism for its extreme otherworldliness. To this he thinks Western materialism, which is the other extreme, is a valuable counterweight. Moreover, he thinks that the mystical mind which is not restrained and kept straight by a clear, austere, and trained intellect—such as scientific education produces—is apt to lose itself in a world of fantasies and perverting superstitions. The function of Western materialistic science in the evolution of the human spirit has therefore been to clarify and discipline the mind so that it can advance on a more solid basis to the heights of spirituality. He even writes that "we should observe with respect and wonder the work which atheism has done in the service of the Divine."

Aurobindo's metaphysics, which he believes to be based on his total experience, both sensory-intellectual and mystical, is a kind of emergent evolutionism, the terms of which from lower to higher are: matter, life, mind, and supermind —i.e., the mystical mind. This is an eternal or timeless development. Nevertheless the goal of man in time is the final term, the embodiment of the divine mind in the flesh. But the emergence of any higher term is only possible because the higher is already present in the lower. Even matter, as the Upanishads already insisted, is Brahman. Crass matter could not produce life, much less mind and supermind, were not these later terms potential in it from the beginning.

FROM *The Life Divine*

## FROM *Chapter* 1. *The Human Aspiration* [4]

The earliest preoccupation of man in his awakened thoughts and, as it seems, his inevitable and ultimate preoccupation,—for it survives the longest periods of scepticism and returns after every banishment,—is also the highest which his thought can envisage. It manifests itself in the divination of Godhead, the impulse towards perfection, the search after pure Truth and unmixed Bliss, the sense of a secret immortality. The ancient dawns of human knowledge have left us their witness to this constant aspiration; today we see a humanity satiated but not satisfied by victorious analysis of the externalities of Nature preparing to return to its primeval longings. The earliest formula of Wisdom promises to be its last,—God, Light, Freedom, Immortality.

These persistent ideals of the race are at once the contradiction of its normal experience and the affirmation of higher and deeper experiences which are abnormal to humanity and only to be attained, in their organised entirety, by a revolutionary individual effort or an evolutionary general progression. To know, possess and be the divine being in an animal and egoistic consciousness, to convert our twilit or obscure physical mentality into the plenary supramental illumination, to build peace and a self-existent bliss where there is only a stress of transitory satisfactions besieged by physical pain and emotional suffering, to establish an infinite freedom in a world which presents itself as a group of mechanical necessities, to discover and realise the immortal life in a body subjected to death and constant mutation,— this is offered to us as the manifestation of God in Matter and the goal of Nature in her terrestrial evolution. To the ordinary material intellect which takes its present organisa-

4 Sri Aurobindo, *The Life Divine*. Calcutta: Arya Publishing House, 139, Vol. I, pp. 1-6; Madras: Sri Aurobindo Library, Inc., 1949. Copyright, 1949, by Sri Aurobindo Library, Inc.

tion of consciousness for the limit of its possibilities, the direct contradiction of the unrealised ideals with the realised fact is a final argument against their validity. But if we take a more deliberate view of the world's workings, that direct opposition appears rather as part of Nature's profoundest method and the seal of her completest sanction. . . .

We speak of the evolution of Life in Matter, the evolution of Mind in Matter; but evolution is a word which merely states the phenomenon without explaining it. For there seems to be no reason why Life should evolve out of material elements or Mind out of living form, unless we accept the Vedantic solution that Life is already involved in Matter and Mind in Life because in essence Matter is a form of veiled Life, Life a form of veiled Consciousness. And then there seems to be little objection to a farther step in the series and the admission that mental consciousness may itself be only a form and a veil of higher states which are beyond Mind. In that case, the unconquerable impulse of man towards God, Light, Bliss, Freedom, Immortality presents itself in its right place in the chain as simply the imperative impulse by which Nature is seeking to evolve beyond Mind. . . . For if evolution is the progressive manifestation by Nature of that which slept or worked in her, involved, it is also the overt realisation of that which she secretly is. . . . If it be true that Spirit is involved in Matter and apparent Nature is secret God, then the manifestation of the divine in himself and the realisation of God within and without are the highest and most legitimate aim possible to man upon earth.

Thus the eternal paradox and eternal truth of a divine life in an animal body, an immortal aspiration or reality inhabiting a mortal tenement, a single and universal consciousness representing itself in limited minds and divided egos, a transcendent, indefinable, timeless and spaceless Being who alone renders time and space and cosmos possible, and in all these the higher truth realisable by the lower term, justify themselves to the deliberate reason as well as to the persistent instinct or intuition of mankind.

FROM *Chapter 2. The Two Negations*[5]

## 1. *The Materialist Denial*

He energised conscious-force (in the austerity of thought) and came to the knowledge that Matter is the Brahman. For

5 *Ibid.*, pp. 8-23.

from Matter all existences are born; born, by Matter they increase and enter into Matter in their passing hence. Then he went to Varuna, his father, and said, "Lord, teach me of the Brahman." But he said to him: "Energise (again) the conscious-energy in thee; for the Energy is Brahman."

*Taittiriya Upanishad*, III: 1, 2

The affirmation of a divine life upon earth and an immortal sense in mortal existence can have no base unless we recognise not only eternal Spirit as the inhabitant of this bodily mansion, the wearer of this mutable robe, but accept Matter of which it is made, as a fit and noble material out of which He weaves constantly His garbs, builds recurrently the unending series of His mansions.

Nor is this, even, enough to guard us against a recoil from life in the body unless, with the Upanishads, perceiving behind their appearances the identity in essence of these two extreme terms of existence, we are able to say in the very language of those ancient writings, "Matter also is Brahman," and to give its full value to the vigorous figure by which the physical universe is described as the external body of the Divine Being. Nor,—so far divided apparently are these two extreme terms,—is that identification convincing to the rational intellect if we refuse to recognise a series of ascending terms (Life, Mind, Supermind and the grades that link Mind to Supermind) between Spirit and Matter. Otherwise the two must appear as irreconcilable opponents bound together in an unhappy wedlock and their divorce the one reasonable solution. To identify them, to represent each in the terms of the other, becomes an artificial creation of Thought opposed to the logic of facts and possible only by an irrational mysticism.

If we assert only pure Spirit and a mechanical unintelligent substance or energy, calling one God or Soul and the other Nature, the inevitable end will be that we shall either deny God or else turn from Nature. For both Thought and Life, a choice then becomes imperative. Thought comes to deny the one as an illusion of the imagination or the other as an illusion of the senses; Life comes to fix on the immaterial and flee from itself in a disgust or a self-forgetting ecstasy, or else to deny its own immortality and take its orientation away from God and towards the animal. Purusha and Prakriti, the passively luminous Soul of the Sankhyas and their mechanically active Energy, have nothing in common, not even their opposite modes of inertia; their antinomies can only be resolved by the cessation of the inertly driven Activity into the immutable Repose upon which it has been casting in vain the sterile procession of its images. Shankara's wordless, inactive Self and his Maya of many names and forms are equally disparate and irreconcilable entities; their rigid antagonism can terminate only by the dissolution of the multitudinous illusion into the sole Truth of an eternal Silence.

The materialist has an easier field; it is possible for him by denying Spirit to arrive at a more readily convincing simplicity of statement, a real Monism, the Monism of Matter or else of Force. But in this rigidity of statement it is impossible for him to persist permanently. He too ends by positing an unknowable as inert, as remote from the known universe as the passive Purusha or the silent Atman. It serves no purpose but to put off by a vague concession the inexorable demands of Thought or to stand as an excuse for refusing to extend the limits of enquiry.

Therefore, in these barren contradictions the human mind cannot rest satisfied. It must seek always a complete affirmation; it can find it only by a luminous reconciliation. To reach that reconciliation it must traverse the degrees which our inner consciousness imposes on us and, whether by objective method of analysis applied to Life and Mind as to Matter or by subjective synthesis and illumination, arrive at the repose of the ultimate unity without denying the energy of the expressive multiplicity. Only in such a complete and catholic affirmation can all the multiform and apparently contradictory data of existence be harmonised. . . .

But when that rhythm has once been disturbed, it is necessary and helpful that man should test separately, in their extreme assertion, each of the two great opposites. It is the mind's natural way of returning more perfectly to the affirmation it has lost. On the road it may attempt to rest in the intervening degrees, reducing all things into the terms of an original Life-Energy or of sensation or of Ideas, but these exclusive solutions have always an air of unreality. They may satisfy for a time the logical reason which deals only with pure ideas, but they cannot satisfy the mind's sense of actuality. For the mind knows that there is something behind itself which is not the Idea; it knows, on the other hand, that there is something within itself which is more than the vital Breath. Either Spirit or Matter can give it for a time some sense of ultimate reality; not so any of the principles that intervene. . . .

It is therefore of good augury that after many experiments and verbal solutions we should now find ourselves standing to-day in the presence of the two that have alone borne for long the most rigorous tests of experience, the two extremes, and that at the end of the experience both should have come to a result which the universal instinct in mankind, that veiled judge, sentinel and representative of the universal Spirit of Truth, refuses to accept as right or as satisfying. In Europe and in India, respectively, the negation of the materialist and the refusal of the ascetic have sought to assert themselves as the sole truth and to dominate the conception of Life. In India, if the result has been a great heaping up of the treasures of the Spirit,—or of some of them,—it has also been a great bankruptcy of Life; in Europe, the fullness of riches and the triumphant mastery of this world's powers and possessions have progressed towards an equal bankruptcy in the things of the Spirit. Nor has the intellect, which sought the solution of all problems in the one term of Matter, found satisfaction in the answer that it has received. . . .

The denial of the materialist, although more insistent and immediately successful, more facile in its appeal to the generality of mankind, is yet less enduring, less effective finally than the absorbing and perilous refusal of the ascetic. For it carries within itself its own cure. Its most powerful element is the Agnosticism which, admitting the Unknowable behind all manifestation, extends the limits of the unknowable until it comprehends all that is merely unknown. Its premise is that the physical senses are our sole means of Knowledge and that Reason, therefore, even in its most extended and vigorous flights, cannot escape beyond their domain; it must deal always and solely with the facts which they provide or suggest; and the suggestions themselves must always be kept tied to their origins; we cannot go beyond, we cannot use them as a bridge leading us into a domain where more powerful and less limited faculties come into play and another kind of inquiry has to be instituted.

A premise so arbitrary pronounces on itself its own sentence of insufficiency. It can only be maintained by ignoring or explaining away all that vast field of evidence and experience which contradicts it, denying or disparaging noble and useful faculties, active consciously or obscurely or at worst latent in all human beings, and refusing to investigate supraphysical phenomena except as manifested in relation to matter and its movements and conceived as a subordinate activity of material forces. As soon as we begin to investigate the operations of mind and of supermind in themselves and without the prejudgment that is determined from the beginning to see in them only a subordinate term of Matter, we come into contact with a mass of phenomena which escape entirely from the rigid hold, the limiting dogmatism of the materialist formula. And the moment we recognise, as our enlarging experience compels us to recognise, that there are in the universe knowable realities beyond the range of the senses and in man's powers and faculties which determine rather than are determined by the material organs through which they hold themselves in touch with the world of the senses,—that outer shell of our true and complete existence, —the premise of materialistic Agnosticism disappears. We are ready for a large statement and an ever-developing enquiry.

But, first, it is well that we should recognise the enormous, the indispensable utility of the very brief period of rationalistic Materialism through which humanity has been passing. For that vast field of evidence and experience which now begins to reopen its gates to us, can only be safely entered when the intellect has been severely trained to a clear austerity; seized on by unripe minds, it lends itself to the most perilous distortions and misleading imaginations and actually in the past encrusted a real nucleus of truth with such an accretion of perverting superstitions and irrationalising dogmas that all advance in true knowledge was rendered impossible. It became necessary for a time to make a clean sweep at once of the truth and its disguise in order that the road might be clear for a new departure and a surer advance. The rationalistic tendency of Materialism has done mankind this great service. . . .

It is necessary, therefore, that advancing Knowledge should base herself on a clear, pure and disciplined intellect. It is necessary, too, that she should correct her errors sometimes by a return to the restraint of sensible fact, the concrete realities of the physical world. The touch of Earth is always reinvigorating to the son of Earth, even when he seeks a supraphysical Knowledge. It may even be said that the supraphysical can only be really mastered in its fullness—to its heights we can always reach—when we keep our feet firmly on the physical. "Earth is His footing," says the Upanishad whenever it images the Self that manifests in the universe. And it is certainly the fact that the wider we extend and the surer we make our knowledge of the physical world, the wider and surer becomes our foundation for the higher knowledge, even for the highest, even for the Brahmavidya.

In emerging, therefore, out of the materialistic period of human Knowledge we must be careful that we do not rashly condemn what we are leaving or throw away even one tittle of its gains, before we can summon perceptions and powers that are well grasped and secure, to occupy their place. Rather we shall observe with respect and wonder the work that Atheism has done for the Divine and admire the services that Agnosticism has rendered in preparing the illimitable increase of knowledge. In our world error is continually the handmaid and pathfinder of Truth; for error is really a half-truth that stumbles because of its limitations; often it is Truth that wears a disguise in order to arrive unobserved near to its goal. Well, if it could always be, as it has been in the great period we are leaving, the faithful handmaid, severe, conscientious, clean-handed, luminous within its limits, a half-truth and not a reckless and presumptuous aberration. . . .

Matter expresses itself eventually as a formulation of some unknown Force. Life, too, that yet unfathomed mystery, begins to reveal itself as an obscure energy of sensibility imprisoned in its material formulation; and when the dividing ignorance is cured which gives us the sense of a gulf between Life and Matter, it is difficult to suppose that Mind, Life and Matter will be found to be anything else than one Energy triply formulated, the triple world of the Vedic seers. Nor will the conception then be able to endure of a brute material Force as the mother of Mind. The Energy that creates the world can be nothing else than a Will, and Will is only consciousness applying itself to a work and a result.

What is that work and result, if not a self-involution of Consciousness in form and a self-evolution out of form so as to actualise some mighty possibility in the universe which it has created? And what is its will in Man if not a will to unending Life, to unbounded Knowledge, to unfettered Power? Science itself begins to dream of the physical conquest of death, expresses an insatiable thirst for knowledge, is working out something like a terrestrial omnipotence for humanity. Space and Time are contracting to the vanishing-point in its works, and it strives in a hundred ways to make man the master of circumstance and so lighten the fetters of causality. The idea of limit, of the impossible begins to grow a little shadowy and it appears instead that whatever man constantly wills, he must in the end be able to do; for the consciousness in the race eventually finds the means. It is not in the individual that this omnipotence expresses itself, but the collective Will of mankind that works out with the individual as a means. And yet when we look more deeply, it is not any conscious Will of the collectivity, but a super-conscious Might that uses the individual as a centre and means, the collectivity as a condition and field. What is this but the God in man, the infinite Identity, the multitudinous Unity, the Omniscient, the Omnipotent, who having made man in His own image, with the ego as a centre of working, with the race, the collective Narayana, the *viśvamānava* as the mould and circumscription, seeks to express in them some image of the unity, omniscience, omnipotence which are the self-conception of the Divine? "That which is immortal in mortals is a God and established inwardly as an energy working out in our divine powers." It is this vast cosmic impulse which the modern world, without quite knowing its own aim, yet serves in all its activities and labours subconsciously to fulfil.

## Chapter 3. The Two Negations[6]

### 2. The Refusal of the Ascetic

All this is the Brahman; this Self is the Brahman and the Self is fourfold.

Beyond relation, featureless, unthinkable, in which all is still.

*Mandukya Upanishad, 2,7*

And still there is a beyond.

For on the other side of the cosmic consciousness there is, attainable to us, a consciousness yet more transcendent, —transcendent not only of the ego, but of the Cosmos itself,—against which the universe seems to stand out like a petty picture against an immeasurable background. That supports the universal activity,—or perhaps only tolerates it; It embraces Life with Its vastness,—or else rejects it from Its infinitude.

If the materialist is justified from his point of view in insisting on Matter as reality, the relative world as the sole thing of which we can in some sort be sure and the Beyond as wholly unknowable, if not indeed non-existent, a dream of the mind, an abstraction of Thought divorcing itself from reality, so also is the Sannyasin, enamoured of that Beyond, justified from his point of view in insisting on pure Spirit as the reality, the one thing free from change, birth, death, and the relative as a creation of the mind and the senses, a dream, an abstraction in the contrary sense of Mentality withdrawing from the pure and eternal Knowledge.

[6] *Ibid.*, pp. 25-37.

What justification, of logic or of experience, can be asserted in support of the one extreme which cannot be met by an equally cogent logic and an equally valid experience at the other end? The world of Matter is affirmed by the experience of the physical senses which, because they are themselves unable to perceive anything immaterial or not organised as gross Matter, would persuade us that the suprasensible is the unreal. This vulgar or rustic error of our corporeal organs does not gain in validity by being promoted into the domain of philosophical reasoning. Obviously, their pretension is unfounded. Even in the world of Matter there are existences of which the physical senses are incapable of taking cognisance. Yet the denial of the suprasensible as necessarily an illusion or a hallucination depends on this constant sensuous association of the real with the materially perceptible, which is itself a hallucination. Assuming throughout what it seeks to establish, it has the vice of the argument in a circle and can have no validity for an impartial reasoning.

Not only are there physical realities which are suprasensible, but, if evidence and experience are at all a test of truth, there are also senses which are supraphysical and can not only take cognisance of the realities of the material world without the aid of the corporeal sense-organs, but can bring us into contact with other realities, supraphysical and belonging to another world—included, that is to say, in an organisation of conscious experiences that are dependent on some other principle than the gross Matter of which our suns and earths seem to be made.

Constantly asserted by human experience and belief since the origins of thought, this truth, now that the necessity of an exclusive preoccupation with the secrets of the material world no longer exists, begins to be justified by new-born forms of scientific research. The increasing evidences, of which only the most obvious and outward are established under the name of telepathy with its cognate phenomena, can not long be resisted except by minds shut up in the brilliant shell of the past, by intellects limited in spite of their acuteness through the limitation of their field of experience and enquiry, or by those who confuse enlightenment and reason with the faithful repetition of the formulas left to us from a bygone century and the jealous conservation of dead or dying intellectual dogmas.

It is true that the glimpse of supraphysical realities acquired by methodical research has been imperfect and is yet ill-affirmed; for the methods used are still crude and defective. But these rediscovered subtle senses have at least been found to be true witnesses to physical facts beyond the range of the corporeal organs. There is no justification, then, for scouting them as false witnesses when they testify to supraphysical facts beyond the domain of the material organisation of consciousness. Like all evidence, like the evidence of the physical senses themselves, their testimony has to be controlled, scrutinised and arranged by the reason, rightly translated and rightly related, and their field, laws and processes determined. But the truth of great ranges of experience whose objects exist in a more subtle substance and are perceived by more subtle instruments than those of gross physical Matter, claims in the end the same validity as the truth of the material universe. The worlds beyond exist: they have their universal rhythm, their grand lines and formations, their self-existent laws and mighty energies, their just and luminous means of knowledge. And here on our physical existence and in our physical body they exercise their influences; here also they organise their means of manifestation and commission their messengers and their witnesses.

But the worlds are only frames for our experience, the senses only instruments of experience and conveniences. Consciousness is the great underlying fact, the universal witness for whom the world is a field, the senses instruments. To that witness the worlds and their objects appeal for their reality and for the one world or the many, for the physical equally with the supraphysical we have no other evidence that they exist. It has been argued that this is no relation peculiar to the constitution of humanity and its outlook upon an objective world, but the very nature of existence itself; all phenomenal existence consists of an observing consciousness and an active objectivity, and the Action cannot proceed without the Witness because the universe exists only in or for the consciousness that observes and has no independent reality. It has been argued in reply that the material universe enjoys an eternal self-existence; it was here before life and mind made their appearance; it will survive after they have disappeared and no longer trouble with their transient strivings and limited thoughts the eternal and inconscient rhythm of the suns. The difference, so metaphysical in appearance, is yet of the utmost practical import, for it determines the whole outlook of man upon life, the goal that he shall assign for his efforts and the field in which he shall circumscribe his energies. For it raises the question of the reality of cosmic existence and, more important still, the question of the value of human life.

If we push the materialist conclusion far enough, we arrive at an insignificance and unreality in the life of the individual and the race which leaves us, logically, the option between either a feverish effort of the individual to snatch what he may from a transient existence, to "live his life," as it is said, or a dispassionate and objectless service of the race and the individual, knowing well that the latter is a transient fiction of the nervous mentality and the former only a little more long-lived collective form of the same regular nervous spasm of Matter. We work or enjoy under the impulsion of a material energy which deceives us with the brief delusion of life or with the nobler delusion of an ethical aim and a mental consummation. Materialism like spiritual Monism arrives at a Maya that is and yet is not,—is, for it is present and compelling, is not, for it is phenomenal and transitory in its works. At the other end, if we stress too much the unreality of the objective world, we arrive by a different road at similar but still more trenchant conclusions,—the fictitious character of the individual ego, the unreality and purposelessness of human existence, the return into the Non-Being or the relationless Absolute as the sole rational escape from the meaningless tangle of phenomenal life.

And yet the question cannot be solved by logic arguing on the data of our ordinary physical existence; for in those data there is always a hiatus of experience which renders all argument inconclusive. We have, normally, neither any definitive experience of a cosmic mind or supermind not bound up with the life of the individual body, nor, on the other hand, any firm limit of experience which would justify us in supposing that our subjective self really depends upon the physical frame and can neither survive it nor enlarge itself beyond the individual body. Only by an extension of the field of our consciousness or an unhoped-for increase in our instruments of knowledge can the ancient quarrel be decided.

The extension of our consciousness, to be satisfying, must necessarily be an inner enlargement from the individual into the cosmic existence. For the Witness, if he exists, is not the individual embodied mind born in the world, but that cosmic Consciousness embracing the universe and appearing as an immanent Intelligence in all its works to which either world subsists eternally and really as Its own active existence or else from which it is born and into which it disappears by an act of knowledge or by an act of conscious power. Not organised mind, but that which, calm and eternal, broods equally in the living earth and the living human body and to which mind and senses are dispensable instruments, is the Witness of cosmic existence and its Lord.

The possibility of a cosmic consciousness in humanity is coming slowly to be admitted in modern Psychology, like the possibility of more elastic instruments of knowledge, although still classified, even when its value and power are admitted, as a hallucination. In the psychology of the East it has always been recognised as a reality and the aim of our subjective progress. The essence of the passage over to this goal is the exceeding of the limits imposed on us by the ego-sense and at least a partaking, at most an identification with the self-knowledge which broods secret in all life and in all that seems to us inanimate.

Entering into that Consciousness, we may continue to dwell, like It, upon universal existence. Then we become aware—for all our terms of consciousness and even our sensational experience begin to change,—of Matter as one existence and of bodies as its formations in which the one existence separates itself physically in the single body from itself in all others and again by physical means establishes communication between these multitudinous points of its being. Mind we experience similarly, and Life also, as the same existence one in its multiplicity, separating and re-uniting itself in each domain by means appropriate to that movement. And, if we choose, we can proceed farther and, after passing through many linking stages, become aware of a supermind whose universal operation is the key to all lesser activities. Nor do we become merely conscious of this cosmic existence, but likewise conscious in it, receiving it in sensation, but also entering into it in awareness. In it we live as we lived before in the ego-sense, active, more and more in contact, even unified more and more with other minds, other lives, other bodies than the organism we call ourselves, producing effects not only on our own moral and mental being and on the subjective being of others, but even on the physical world and its events by means nearer to the divine than those possible to our egoistic capacity.

Real then to the man who has had contact with it or lives in it, is this cosmic consciousness, with a greater than the physical reality; real in itself, real in its effects and works. And as it is thus real to the world which is its own total expression, so is the world real to it; but not as an independent existence. For in that higher and less hampered experience we perceive that consciousness and being are not different from each other, but all being is a supreme consciousness, all consciousness is self-existence, eternal in itself, real in its works and neither a dream nor an evolution. The world is real precisely because it exists only in consciousness; for it is a Conscious Energy one with Being that creates it. It is the existence of material form in its own right apart from the self-illumined energy which assumes the form, that would be a contradiction of the truth of things, a phantasmagoria, a nightmare, an impossible falsehood.

But this conscious Being which is the truth of the infinite supermind, is more than the universe and lives independently in Its own inexpressible infinity as well as in the cosmic harmonies. World lives by That; That does not live by the world. And as we can enter into the cosmic consciousness and be one with all cosmic existence, so we can enter into the world-transcending consciousness and become superior to all cosmic existence. And then arises the question which first occurred to us, whether this transcendence is necessarily also a rejection. What relation has this universe to the Beyond?

For at the gates of the Transcendent stands that mere and perfect Spirit described in the Upanishads, luminous, pure, sustaining the world but inactive in it, without sinews of energy, without flaw of duality, without scar of division, unique, identical, free from all appearance of relation and of multiplicity,—the pure Self of the Adwaitins, the inactive Brahman, the transcendent Silence. And the mind when it passes those gates suddenly, without intermediate transitions, receives a sense of the unreality of the world and the sole reality of the Silence which is one of the most powerful and convincing experiences of which the human mind is capable. Here, in the perception of this pure Self or of the Non-Being behind it, we have the starting-point for a second negation,—parallel at the other pole to the materialistic, but more complete, more final, more perilous in its effects on the individuals or collectivities that hear its potent call to the wilderness,—the refusal of the ascetic.

It is this revolt of Spirit against Matter that for two thousand years, since Buddhism disturbed the balance of the old Aryan world, has dominated increasingly the Indian mind. Not that the sense of the cosmic illusion is the whole of Indian thought; there are other philosophical statements, other religious aspirations. Nor has some attempt at an adjustment between the two terms been wanting even from the most extreme philosophies. But all have lived in the shadow of the great Refusal and the final end of life for all is the garb of the ascetic. The general conception of existence has been permeated with the Buddhistic theory of the chain of

Karma and with the consequent antinomy of bondage and liberation, bondage by birth, liberation by cessation from birth. Therefore all voices are joined in one great consensus that not in this world of the dualities can there be our kingdom of heaven, but beyond, whether in the joys of the eternal Vrindavan or the high beatitude of Brahmaloka, beyond all manifestations in some ineffable Nirvana or where all separate experience is lost in the featureless unity of the indefinable Existence. And through many centuries a great army of shining witnesses, saints and teachers, names sacred to Indian memory and dominant in Indian imagination, have borne always the same witness and swelled always the same lofty and distant appeal,—renunciation the sole path of knowledge, acceptation of physical life the act of the ignorant, cessation from birth the right use of human birth, the call of the Spirit, the recoil from Matter.

For an age out of sympathy with the ascetic spirit—and throughout all the rest of the world the hour of the Anchorite may seem to have passed or to be passing—it is easy to attribute this great trend to the failing of vital energy in an ancient race tired out by its burden, its once vast share in the common advance, exhausted by its many-sided contribution to the sum of human effort and human knowledge. But we have seen that it corresponds to a truth of existence, a state of conscious realisation which stands at the very summit of our possibility. In practice also the ascetic spirit is an indispensable element in human perfection and even its separate affirmation cannot be avoided so long as the race has not at the other end liberated its intellect and its vital habits from subjection to an always insistent animalism.

We seek indeed a larger and completer affirmation. We perceive that in the Indian ascetic ideal the great Vedantic formula, "one without a second," has not been read sufficiently in the light of that other formula equally imperative, "All this is the Brahman." The passionate aspiration of man upward to the Divine has not been sufficiently related to the descending movement of the Divine leaning downward to embrace eternally Its manifestation. Its meaning in Matter has not been so well understood as Its truth in the Spirit. The reality which the Sannyasin seeks has been grasped in its full height, but not, as by the ancient Vedantins, in its full extent and comprehensiveness. But in our completer affirmation we must not minimise the part of the pure spiritual impulse. As we have seen how greatly Materialism has served the ends of the Divine, so we must acknowledge the still greater service rendered by Asceticism to Life. We shall preserve the truths of material Science and its real utilities in the final harmony, even if many or even if all of its existing forms have to be broken or left aside. An even greater scruple of right preservation must guide us in our dealing with the legacy, however actually diminished or depreciated, of the Aryan past.

# -3-

# Buddhist Mysticism

We now turn to the other great branch of Eastern mysticism, that which is enshrined in the religion of the Buddha. Buddha was born in northern India, probably about 483 B.C., and died at the age of eighty. We thus see that his religion preceded Christianity by nearly five hundred years. Buddha left no writings, and the earliest scriptures of the religion did not appear till some four centuries after his death. In these scriptures hundreds of thousands of words are put into his mouth, but we have no single sentence of which we can say with certainty that it is exactly what Buddha said. Nevertheless his main experience and ideas are without doubt embodied in these scriptures. The details of his life are also veiled in obscurity. Plenty of legends about his doings have reached us, from which one can sift out a certain amount of fairly reliable information. He belonged to the warrior caste and was of noble birth. He married and had a child. In early manhood, profoundly moved by the miseries of the human beings in the social environment in which he moved, he abandoned the life of luxury, abandoned his home, and "entered on the path of renunciation," determined to discover the secret which could free man from the sorrow of life. He tried extreme asceticism, nearly starving himself to death. Becoming convinced of the uselessness of this extremism, he adopted a "middle path" between too much and too little food, clothing, and the other usual material appurtenances of life. And this middle path later became a part of his ethical teaching. But "supreme enlightenment," which is the Buddhist phrase for the highest mystical consciousness, was still to seek. After a number of years of strenuous effort he reached the goal. Tempted at first to enjoy his own Nirvana without imparting his secret to the world, but being filled with compassion for suffering humanity, he returned to the world to teach men the truth he had found. Thus his religion was born. He founded the order of monks which is called the "Sangha" and which was to be the gateway through which all men who wished to do so could "enter on the path."

Since in this chapter we shall be concentrating solely on the mystical element in Buddhism, it is not necessary for us to discuss any of the details of the doctrines which became parts of the creed of the religion, nor the history of its sects and divisions. About the only historical fact we need as a more or less essential frame in which to set our picture of Buddhist mysticism concerns the distinction between the Hinayana and Mahayana schools. The former is apparently the earlier of the two. It is also called "southern" Buddhism because it is found in Ceylon, Burma, Thailand, and Cambodia, while the Mahayana or "northern" school became the faith of Tibet, China, and Japan. Mahayana means "greater vehicle," while Hinayana means "lesser vehicle." The terms were invented by the Mahayanists in order to magnify their own version of Buddhism and belittle the rival school. Consequently the term "Hinayana" is disliked by the southern Buddhists, who prefer to be called "Theravadins." But it seems that the name "Hinayana" is likely to stick, and it can, of course, be used as a label without any derogatory implications. The now much-talked-about school of Zen is a branch of the Mahayana. The Hinayana scriptures were in the Pali language and are included in what came to be called the Pali Canon. The Mahayanist writings were mostly in Sanskrit, Chinese, or Tibetan.

Buddhism is wholly the product of the Buddha's enlightenment experience, and therefore mysticism is the very essence of it. In this it is unlike Christianity, in which, as Professor E. A. Burtt has observed, mysticism is a minor strain. Buddha left no description of his experience, but there is any amount of indirect evidence, including the whole Buddhist tradition, that it must have been basically of the same kind as that which is described in the passage of the Mandukya Upanishad which we have quoted. It was, that is to say, "the unitary consciousness wherein all awareness of multiplicity has been completely obliterated." In other words, it was the undifferentiated unity which is the essence of all introvertive mysticism.

Buddha, however, interpreted his experience in a way utterly different from the way of the Vedanta, or of the Christian or Islamic West. He did not interpret it as being the self, either the individual self or the Universal Self. He did not interpret it as union with God. He appears to have repudiated the whole concept of a Supreme Being or First Cause of the universe, for which reason his religion is sometimes called atheistic.

What is perhaps even more remarkable is that he repudiated the concept of a self or soul. He applied to the notion of the self an analysis which is in essence identical with the famous skeptical argument of David Hume, so that in this respect he anticipated Hume by much more than two thousand years. There is, he admitted, a stream of consciousness consisting of sensations, thoughts, desires, and so on. He did not use this modern phraseology but expressed the same thought in the language of his time. The stream of consciousness is all that exists on the mental side of man. There is no I or soul or self which underlies and persists through the changes of consciousness. There is no personal identity in that sense. But he allowed to the mind the sort of continuing identity which we find in a wave passing across the water, or a fire which sweeps over a forest starting in one place and ending perhaps several miles away. Is it the "same" fire, or the "same" wave, all along its course? There is, according to Buddhism, no self-identical substance either in the flame or the wave or the human mind, but there is a flowing continuity. The Buddha taught, somewhat after the manner of Heraclitus, that "all things flow" and that there is no abiding reality, either in the material world or in the world of mind.

Buddha repudiated what we nowadays call metaphysics —for instance, problems about a first cause, or about the ultimate nature and origin of the world. He did not, however, argue his objection to such problems on the ground that they are meaningless—as the modern positivist does—but rather on the agnostic ground that no one will ever find the answers, and on the pragmatic ground that even if men did find the answers, such knowledge would be useless for the sole end which Buddhism sets out to reach, namely the getting rid of all sorrow and suffering.

In view of his evidently very skeptical turn of mind, we must inquire in what way he interpreted his mystical experience and made it the basis of a religion. In a sense one could say that he used it somewhat in the spirit of a modern psychiatrist, namely as a means for healing the sicknesses of both the mind and the body and of making men whole. We must say this somewhat guardedly, however. The notion of the Nirvana which Buddha was teaching men to reach cannot be treated as having no metaphysical or otherworldly implications. It is indeed a psychological state which is to bring peace of mind. But if Buddha were represented as not caring whether this state of mind corresponded to any objective truth about the world or not, or as not caring by what means it is induced—the sort of thing which hostile critics sometimes, whether with any justice or not, say about psychiatrists—this would gravely misrepresent Buddha's teaching. He is, however, represented in the scriptures as continually comparing himself to a physician. He does not claim that he can answer any ultimate questions. He is reported to have said of himself, "The Tathagata [Buddha] has no theories." But he claimed to be able to cure mankind of the universal disease of sorrow. Sorrow will be completely obliterated if one will follow his advice and attain the goal of supreme enlightenment and Nirvana. Nirvana is the end of sorrow and pain. It is ultimate peace. Moreover, Nirvana is only another name for the supreme enlightenment experience, so that it can be attained during this life and does not have to wait for death, although it does not cease at death. Permanent peace, therefore, the permanent end of sorrow, can be got now—at a price!

Nirvana, it must be said, is the one great Buddhist mystical idea. Buddhist mysticism simply means Nirvana. And Nirvana is the only mystical element in Buddhism, all other elements being rationalistic and skeptical. For this reason all the selections which follow in this chapter have for their subject matter, directly or indirectly, nothing except Nirvana. This is true in the most direct sense of the first four selections, which come from the Pali Canon. But in a slightly less direct way it is equally true of the remaining selections, which are Mahayanist. All of them turn about the Nirvanic experience as their center, and they would mean nothing at all without it.

Although Nirvana can be attained in this life, and although the Buddha himself lived in the Nirvanic consciousness for fifty-odd years till his death, nevertheless Nirvana passes beyond death. Buddha, whose ideas were revolutionary in all other ways, accepted from Indian tradition a belief in reincarnation. It will be asked how belief in that theory

is possible if, as Buddha maintained, there is no permanent
soul to be reincarnated. The answer is not difficult to see.
It is implicit in the comparison between the stream of consciousness and the wave passing over the water or the flame
passing over the forest. If there is a continuity in the
stream of consciousness through a man's life there is in
principle no reason why the "same" stream should not continue through repeated lives—it will remain the "same" in the
sense in which the wave or the flame remains the same.
But Buddha, like other Indians, believed that ahead of every
man there stretches after this life a series of births and
deaths which will last through thousands of millions of
years into a future to which there is no discernible end. And
as Buddha maintained that life is necessarily and incurably
sorrowful the prospect for every human being is nothing but
literally endless misery unless some way of escape can be
found. And here the Buddha seems to have accepted from
his predecessors the idea that one finds in the Upanishads:
that whoever attains the unitary consciousness, and can hold
onto it, will never be reborn and has succeeded in breaking
the otherwise endless chain of reincarnate lives.

In that case, we naturally ask, what happens to the enlightened man after death? He has attained Nirvana even while
alive, and there is a special name for the final Nirvana into
which he enters when he dies. It is called parinirvana. But
we cannot remain content with only a word. What is parinirvana?

Early European travelers in India, missionaries and others,
brought back to the West the view that final Nirvana means
nothing except total annihilation. It was called peace, but this
could mean nothing except the peace of the grave. It is certain that this view is completely mistaken. Nirvana is not
annihilation but a state of positive bliss. Is it anything like
the Christian idea of heaven—in so far as that can be said
to possess any definite content? The great difference between
heaven and Nirvana seems to be this: that heaven is thought
to include the everlasting existence of the individual human
soul as an individual while Nirvana is the paradox that the
separate individuality of a man perishes but yet this is not
his annihilation. I shall take up this matter again at a suitable
point later.

Let us turn now to the first group of four selections. They
constitute a group because they are all from Hinayana sources.

# Hinayana Selections

### Nirvana[1]

There is, monks, that plane where there is neither extension nor . . . motion nor the plane of infinite ether . . . nor that of neither-perception-nor-non-perception, neither this world nor another, neither the moon nor the sun. Here, monks, I say that there is no coming or going or remaining or deceasing or uprising, for this is itself without support, without continuance, without mental object—this is itself the end of suffering.

There is, monks, an unborn, not become, not made, uncompounded, and were it not, monks, for this unborn, not become, not made, uncompounded, no escape could be shown here for what is born, has become, is made, is compounded. But because there is, monks, an unborn, not become, not made, uncompounded, therefore an escape can be shown for what is born, has become, is made, is compounded.

### Commentary

The first paragraph warns us that Nirvana is wholly inconceivable in terms of any ordinary empirical characters. It is, like the Self of the Upanishads, "not this, not that." It is plainly mystical and paradoxical.

The second paragraph is of great importance. There can be little doubt that it truly represents Buddha's thought. His teaching has already been likened to the flux-philosophy of Heraclitus. All things flow. Nothing is permanent, and there is no underlying "substance" of things. And many accounts of Buddhism give the impression that this flux-philosophy is the whole of Buddha's thought. This is a grave mistake. Nirvana is not part of the flux. Nirvana stands in contrast to samsara—though it is true, as we shall see, that this distinction is again annulled in some branches of the Mahayana. Samsara is the fleeting world of temporal events. From the human point of view it is the endless round of reincarnate lives. In the world of samsara everything is compounded of parts, and is therefore subject to dissolution, and everything which arises is produced by some cause. But Nirvana is not compounded, and is not produced

[1] From Udāna, 80-81. Quoted from *Buddhist Texts Through the Ages*, edited by E. Conze and others. Oxford: Bruno Cassirer (Publishers), Ltd., 1954, pp. 94-95; New York: Philosophical Library, 1954.

by any causes. Causes and effects lie in the stream of time. Nor should we say that Nirvana is permanent, since this means "enduring through time." But Nirvana is in what Eckhart would call "the eternal Now." It is only because there is this "unborn" reality that an escape from samsara is possible.

This passage and others like it show plainly that Nirvana is not to be thought of as a mere subjective state of mind, or of being, at which the aspirant arrives. It is trans-subjective and transcendent of any individual mind. This is what distinguishes it from the prescriptions for "peace of mind" which might be given by the kind of psychotherapist who has no ultimate convictions or principles. This is perhaps why Buddhism is rightly called a religion although it does not admit the existence of a God in the popular Western sense. Nirvana is the Buddhist version of the Eternal.

It is implied in this selection and specifically stated in the next selection that Nirvana is not "produced." But the reader will ask whether the spiritual exercises, the exercises of meditation and concentration, the breathing exercises, which Buddhists are recommended to undertake, are not intended to "produce" Nirvana in them. The reply is, No. Nirvana is an eternal principle which is not produced. Moreover, it is something superindividual. A man does not arrive at his own private Nirvana. There is but one Nirvana in which individual men can indeed come to participate. And if we like to say that the physicospiritual exercises which a man uses produce his participation in Nirvana, we can do so. But they do not produce Nirvana.

It may be asked whether, after all, Buddha has not become a metaphysician. He began by repudiating certain kinds of questions—for instance, whether the world has existed through infinite time or whether it had a beginning—which in our modern jargon we are inclined to label metaphysical. But now in these statements about Nirvana he seems to posit something of the nature of a transcendental Absolute. And is not this a lapse into metaphysics? To answer this question we must ask what is the meaning of "metaphysics." It would, I think, be right to say that a metaphysical question is one which could never be answered by any empirical evidence or criteria. On this basis most modern thinkers would doubtless class the Buddha's Nirvana as metaphysical. But it would not be so to Buddha, because he would not, like most modern empiricists, identify experience with sense-experience. The Buddhist adept claims to have direct experience of Nirvana in this life and without waiting for another life. Therefore for Buddha the conception of Nirvana is not metaphysical but empirical.

### Nirvana[2]

"Revered Nagasena, is Nirvana uncompounded?"

"Yes, sire, Nirvana is uncompounded; it is made by nothing at all. Sire, one cannot say of Nirvana that it arises or that it does not arise or that it is to be produced or that it is past or future or present, or that it is cognizable by the eye, ear, nose, tongue or body."

"If, revered Nagasena, Nirvana neither arises nor does not arise and so on, as you say, well then, revered Nagasena, you indicate Nirvana as a thing that is not; Nirvana is not."

"Sire, Nirvana is."

### Commentary

This selection repeats the meaning of the first in somewhat different words. The point of reproducing it here lies in the fact that it comes from a different Hinayana source, *The Questions of King Milinda*, which belongs to a later age. The speaker is no longer Buddha but the monk Nagasena. The questions are put to him by the skeptical Bactrian king who is under the influence of Greek culture. The selection therefore re-emphasizes the truths of the former selection in a different age and cultural framework, showing that what is said about Nirvana in the first selection is not exceptional but is an accepted part of Buddhist thought.

### The Great Decease[3]

Then The Blessed One addressed the priests:—

"And now, O priests, I take my leave of you; all the constituents of being are transitory; work out your salvation with diligence."

And this was the last word of The Tathāgata.

Thereupon The Blessed One entered the first trance; and

[2] Conze, *op. cit.* Quoted in *The Teachings of the Compassionate Buddha*, edited by E. A. Burtt. New York: New American Library (Mentor Books), 1955, p. 115.

[3] From the Mahā-Parinibbana-Sutta of the Digha-Nikāya. Quoted from H. C. Warren, *Buddhism in Translations* (No. 3 in the Harvard Oriental Series). Cambridge: Harvard University Press, 1896, Vol. 3, pp. 109-10.

rising from the first trance, he entered the second trance; and rising from the second trance, he entered the third trance; and rising from the third trance, he entered the fourth trance; and rising from the fourth trance, he entered the realm of the infinity of space; and rising from the realm of the infinity of space, he entered the realm of the infinity of consciousness; and rising from the realm of the infinity of consciousness, he entered the realm of nothingness; and rising from the realm of nothingness, he entered the realm of neither perception nor yet non-perception; and rising from the realm of neither perception nor yet non-perception, he arrived at the cessation of perception and sensation.

Thereupon the venerable Ānanda spoke to the venerable Anuruddha as follows:—

"Reverend Anuruddha, The Blessed One has passed into Nirvana."

"Nay, brother Ānanda, The Blessed one has not passed into Nirvana; he has arrived at the cessation of perception and sensation."

Thereupon The Blessed One rising from the cessation of his perception and sensation, entered the realm of neither perception nor yet non-perception; and rising from the realm of neither perception nor yet non-perception, he entered the realm of nothingness; and rising from the realm of nothingness, he entered the realm of the infinity of consciousness; and rising from the realm of the infinity of consciousness, he entered the realm of the infinity of space; and rising from the realm of the infinity of space, he entered the fourth trance; and rising from the fourth trance, he entered the third trance; and rising from the third trance, he entered the second trance; and rising from the second trance, he entered the first trance; and rising from the first trance, he entered the second trance; and rising from the second trance, he entered the third trance; and rising from the third trance, he entered the fourth trance; and rising from the fourth trance, immediately The Blessed One passed into Nirvana.

## Commentary

This is the traditional account of the Buddha's entrance into Nirvana. As such it is entitled to be reproduced here. But it is doubtful whether it really throws any light on the nature of Nirvana. How, in the first place, could anyone ever come to know through what stages the Buddha passed at death? The account reads, to me at least, as if it were a very unreal and artificial construction invented in later times by scholars or monks with a taste for the grandiose and verbose, and perhaps with the motive of trying to magnify the greatness of the experiences of the founder of religion. On the other hand Mr. E. Conze, an excellent authority, in his book *Buddhism: Its Essence and Development,* seems to take this material quite seriously as an account of the stages through which any good Buddhist, if he really reaches the goal, will pass.

## Is Nirvana Annihilation or Not-annihilation?[4]

Thus have I heard.

On a certain occasion The Blessed One was dwelling at Sāvatthi in Jetavana monastery in Anāthapindika's Park. Then drew near Vaccha, the wandering ascetic, to where The Blessed One was; and having drawn near, he greeted The Blessed One; and having passed the compliments of friendship and civility, he sat down respectfully at one side. And seated respectfully at one side, Vaccha, the wandering ascetic, spoke to The Blessed One as follows:—

"How is it, Gotama? Does Gotama hold that the saint exists after death?"

"Nay, Vaccha. I do not hold that the saint exists after death."

"But how is it, Gotama? Does Gotama hold that the saint does not exist after death?"

"Nay, Vaccha. I do not hold that the saint does not exist after death."

"But has Gotama any theory of his own?"

"The Tathāgata, O Vaccha, is free from all theories. . . ."

"But Gotama, where is the priest reborn who has attained to this deliverance for his mind?"

"Vaccha, to say that he is reborn would not fit the case."

"Then, Gotama, he is not reborn."

"Vaccha, to say that he is not reborn would not fit the case."

"When I say to you, 'But, Gotama, where is the priest reborn who has attained to this deliverance for his mind?' you reply, 'Vaccha, to say that he is reborn would not fit the case.' And when I say to you, 'Then, Gotama, he is not reborn,' you reply, 'Vaccha, to say that he is not reborn would not fit the case.' . . . Gotama, I am at a loss what to think

4 From the Majjhima-Nikāya, Sutta 72. Quoted from *ibid.,* pp. 123-26.

in this matter, and I have become greatly confused, and the faith in Gotama inspired by a former conversation has now disappeared."

"Enough, O Vaccha! Be not at a loss what to think in this matter, and be not greatly confused. Profound, O Vaccha, is this doctrine, recondite, and difficult of comprehension, good, excellent, and not to be reached by mere reasoning, subtle, and intelligible only to the wise."

## Commentary

This is of central importance because it purports to show the answer which Buddha himself is traditionally supposed to have given to the question whether Nirvana is annihilation. Buddha's reply is that it is equally incorrect to say that he who attains Nirvana exists after death and to say that he does not exist. The essential point is that Buddha refuses to accept the alternatives posed by the logician's "either—or." The laws of logic—in this case the law of excluded middle —are no doubt valid for the space-time world, the world of samsara, but they have no application to the mystical experience of Nirvana. Mystical experience is paradoxical and "beyond logic," just as it is beyond space and time.

We are therefore left still wondering what to think about Nirvana. Can anything further be said? At the risk of being grossly presumptuous in attempting what the Buddha said cannot be done, I shall try to throw at least a little further light on this problem.

Does the person in Nirvana cease to exist? I believe the answer is that he does cease to exist as a separate and finite individual, but that he still exists in the sense that he has become infinite, or has passed into the infinite consciousness. He is no longer this individual as distinct from that. The separateness of individuals is what constitutes finitude. In the mystical consciousness what we have is the undifferentiated unity in which all divisions, and therefore the division between "I" and "you" and "he" and "she," are lost. Yet this is not annihilation. I cease to be I but I do not become extinct. My being has not shrunk to zero, which would be what annihilation means. On the contrary, my being has expanded to infinity.

If this seems absurd to the reader, let him reflect that human beings even in our own time and civilization have actually experienced it. One case, that of Tennyson, has already been quoted. He said: "All at once, as it were out of the intensity of the consciousness of individuality, individuality itself seemed to fade away into boundless being—the loss of personality (if so it were) *seeming no extinction but the only true life*" (my italics).

I suggest that this modern experience gives us the key to what Nirvana is. Tennyson obtained a momentary glimpse of Nirvana. Individuality fades away into "boundless being"—that is, into the Infinite. Yet this is not extinction but rather "the only true life." And in the final selection of this book we find Arthur Koestler saying the very same thing in different words. If the reader wishes to see that piece of additional evidence now, he can turn at once to page 232.

## Mahayana Selections

So far as the purely mystical element of Buddhism is concerned, there is no important difference between Hinayana and Mahayana. For the only properly mystical element in Buddhism is Nirvana, and Nirvana must be conceived as having the same nature in both. The differences lie in the respective matrices of interpretative belief, moral ideas, and emotional atmosphere in which the experience of Nirvana is embedded. Strictly speaking, therefore, we need not, in a book devoted to mysticism, lay any emphasis on the differences. But to ignore them wholly here would be being, if one may use the expression, *too* logical. Nevertheless we can reduce our discussion of them to a minimum. To begin with the emotional differences, the Mahayanists consider their version of Buddhism to be the "larger vehicle" because it is likely to carry more people to the far shore of Nirvana than the "little" vehicle of the Hinayana. This, in effect, means that the Mahayana is supposed to be more broadly popular in the sense of finding a place for all types of men and for simple-minded people, while the Hinayana is really suitable only for the few. There is therefore about the Mahayana a certain emotional warmth and friendliness which is not so evident in the dry and austere, not to say arid, formulas of southern Buddhism—although, as anyone knows who has traveled in southern Buddhist lands, the Hinayana too somehow manages to adapt itself to the common people. But in its aspect of a more popular religion, the Mahayana—a critic may think—allows to grow up on its soil a rank growth of superstitious usages. On the other hand, nothing could be more abstruse than the philosophical writings of the intellectual leaders of the Mahayana such as Nagarjuna, Asanga, and Vasubandhu.

As to the differences of philosophical belief between the two schools, these consist, at the lower end of the intellectual scale, in the influx of popular beliefs in the Mahayana, and at the upper end of the scale in a great development of metaphysics—a little of which will appear in the following selections—as distinguished from the antimetaphysical bias of the Hinayana and apparently of the Buddha himself.

The moral differences between the two schools are perhaps the most important. The northern school accuses the Hinayanists of selfishly pursuing each man his own salvation in Nirvana—inevitably leaving the vast majority of human beings without hope. The Mahayanists therefore developed the ideal of the Bodhisattva. The Bodhisattva is one who, having himself attained supreme enlightenment, nevertheless refuses to enter his final Nirvana till all other beings have been saved. He therefore voluntarily comes back to earth in ever-renewed cycles of reincarnations for the purpose of helping all other beings to achieve the supreme goal.

We may now proceed to our selections. The first comes from a famous treatise called *The Awakening of Faith*, attributed to Ashvagosha. Most of this treatise is unsuitable for inclusion in the book, not being easily intelligible save to a professional Buddhist scholar. I extract merely a few paragraphs which show the relationship of Buddhist mysticism to universal mysticism.

FROM *The Awakening of Faith*[5]

First as to the unfolding of the true principle. The mind has two doors from which issue its activities. One leads to a realization of the mind's Pure Essence, the other leads to the differentiations of appearing and disappearing, of life and death. Through each door pass all the mind's conceptions so interrelated that they never have been separated and never will be.

What is meant by the Pure Essence of Mind? It is the ultimate purity and unity, the all-embracing wholeness, the quintessence of Truth. Essence of Mind belongs to neither death nor rebirth, it is uncreated and eternal. The concepts

---

5 Dwight Goddard, ed., *A Buddhist Bible*. New York: E. P. Dutton & Co., Inc., revised and enlarged edition, 1952, pp. 362-63.

of the conscious mind are being individualized and discriminated by false imaginations. If the mind could be kept free from discriminative thinking there would be no more arbitrary thoughts to give rise to appearances of form, existences and conditions.

## Commentary

The metaphor of the two doors of the mind means that the mind can look outward into the space-time world of samsara, "the differentiations of appearing and disappearing"—i.e., the world of becoming; or inward into itself—what we have called introversion—toward Mind-Essence.

Mind-Essence is the key concept of Ashvagosha's treatise. As explained in the second paragraph, "it is the ultimate purity and unity" which is reached if the mind is "kept free from discriminative thinking." In other words, it is undifferentiated, since there is in it no discrimination or distinction between one thing and another. Thus this Buddhist treatise joins hands with the introvertive mysticism of all other cultures.

The undifferentiated unity is interpreted as being the Pure Essence of Mind. We see in this a return toward the Upanishadic concept of the Universal Self. How is this to be rendered consistent with the fundamental Buddhist repudiation of the concept of the soul or self? The suggestion has been put forward that Buddha's repudiation of the self was only meant to deny the existence of a separate individual self and not to deny the Universal Self. That the historical Buddha would have admitted this seems highly doubtful, but Mahayana Buddhists are not likely to think this important. They have been quite willing to develop their own doctrine. The following also comes from *The Awakening of Faith*.[6]

Again, if we are to distinguish different aspects of Mind-Essence, there is an emptiness aspect of its invariable Essence for it can unfold its primal reality. And there is a non-emptiness aspect, for it has its own substantiality possessing all sorts of merits of a non-intoxicant nature, that is, that it exists in its own right. The first is an aspect of negation, the second an aspect of affirmation. From the very beginning Mind-Essence has never given any mutual response to any contaminated conceptions of differentiations,

6 *Ibid.*, pp. 363-64.

it has ever been free from discriminations among thoughts or phenomena, for it is perfect unity, perfect purity. It should be clearly understood that the true nature of Mind-Essence does not belong to any individualized conception of phenomena or of non-phenomena; nor of the absence of phenomena, nor of the absence of non-phenomena; nor of unity or of disunity; nor of the absence of unity or of disunity; in other words, it has no particularizing consciousness, it does not belong to any kind of describable nature. Individuations and the consciousness of them come into being only as sentient beings cherish false imaginations of differences and the mind makes discriminations among them, thought after thought rising with no mutual response among them, resulting in confusion and conflict and suffering. This is what is meant when speaking of Mind-Essence as being empty. But if the Truth is fully understood it will be seen that the conception of emptiness as it relates to Mind-Essence is itself "empty." If the mind can be kept free from false imaginations there can be no conceivable meaning to the term "emptiness."

On the other hand, Mind-Essence is by no means to be thought of as being empty of its own perfectly universalized nature.

## Commentary

Mind-Essence has two aspects. Since it has been reached by emptying the mind of all multiplicity, it is Emptiness. On the other hand, it has its own positive reality. This is the positive-negative paradox, which we have already met in another context. To use the usual metaphors, it is both darkness and light. It is the "dazzling obscurity" of Dionysius the Areopagite and of Henry Suso.

Mind-Essence, in so far as it exists at least potentially in every individual, is the same as Eckhart's "apex of the soul," to which we shall come in Chapter 6. In so far as it transcends all individuality, being, as was said in the previous selection, "uncreated and eternal," it can be equated with Eckhart's "Godhead." Eckhart's metaphors describing the Godhead as "barren," "desert," etc., mean the same as what is here called Emptiness.

The latter part of this selection re-emphasizes "the absence of all individualized phenomena or non-phenomena," i.e., from this ultimate unity—what the Mandukya Upanishad called "the unity from which all awareness of multiplicity has been obliterated."

The following is our last selection from *The Awakening of Faith.*[7]

Then there is the appearing and dis-appearing aspect of Mind-Essence, that we think of as birth and death. In this connection we think of Mind-Essence as the Womb of Tathagata, but in fact nothing comes forth and nothing returns and there is no Womb of Tathagata, for the nature of appearing and disappearing coincides with the nature of non-appearing and non-disappearing. The pure Essence of Mind is neither unity nor plurality and yet we conceive it as the inconceivable Alaya-vijnana, the "storage" or Universal Mind. This Alaya consciousness embraces two significant aspects which can both receive and give forth all definitive concepts. The one aspect is that of Enlightenment, the other that of Ignorance.

## Commentary

There is here the hint of a new phase of the mystical consciousness later to be exhibited further. There is the suggestion that the space-time world of samsara is produced out of Mind-Essence—that Mind-Essence is, in other words, the creative source of the world. Mind-Essence is the Womb of the Tathagata because the womb, though empty, creates life. But of course there is the usual paradox. Although Mind-Essence is the Womb from which everything comes forth, yet "in fact nothing comes forth, and nothing returns and there is no Womb of the Tathagata." This paradox will be further developed in later sections of this book.

In other parts of Ashvagosha's treatise a much shallower explanation of the origin of the cosmic multiplicity is put forward—finite things do not really exist at all, being produced "by false imaginations." It is only we who are under the illusion that there is a world of multiplicity. This is the Mahayana version of a persistent theme of Indian philosophy. The theory that the world of finite things does not exist at all but that it is only we who, because of ignorance, imagine it to exist is one which cannot possibly be rendered philosophically respectable. If I imagine the world to exist I myself must exist to have this imagination, as Descartes showed—even if "I" am only a stream of consciousness. Moreover, if the world consists of "false imaginations," these false imaginations really exist. The paradox that the world arises through the Self-differentiation of the undifferentiated is the true mystical solution of the problem of creation.

## The Prajna-Paramita Texts

We now come to some selections which give expression to what Professor Heinrich Zimmer calls "a bold and stunning paradox." All mysticism contains implicitly or explicitly the basic paradox that, since all distinctions disappear in the mystical consciousness, that consciousness is on the one hand completely empty, pure nothing, yet is on the other hand the highest pinnacle of existence, the supreme light of life, the ultimate reality of the universe. But only Mahayana Buddhism, so far as I know, carries that paradox through to the last possible degree of conceivable or inconceivable paradoxicality. This is what we are now to study. The essence of this final paradox lies in a thought which is quite simple. Nirvana, which, as we have seen, is nothing other than the introvertive mystical consciousness, is therefore the disappearance of all distinctions. But in saying this we are likely to leave standing one great and final distinction, the distinction between Nirvana itself and its opposite, samsara, or between eternity and time, this world and the other world. But, since in Nirvana absolutely *all* duality must be abolished, it follows that to one who has truly entered into Nirvana the duality of Nirvana and samsara must also have disappeared. And since Nirvana is the ultimate truth of the world, it follows that there is in reality no difference between Nirvana and samsara. In that case both Nirvana and samsara are seen to be empty nothingness. There are no such realities. There is no such thing as Nirvana. And since there are now no realities at all, we must also say that there is not, and never was, any such being as Buddha, or any such religion as Buddhism! This is the length to which Buddhism pushed the paradox of all mysticism, that the mystical consciousness is both full and empty, both something and nothing.

In case it should be thought that this is either a silly joke or else a *reductio ad absurdum* of mysticism I shall try to show, in the commentary at the end, what I believe to be the serious practical upshot of this "bold and stunning paradox." But meanwhile I should like to quote Professor Zimmer on the subject. He speaks of certain "strange esoteric texts" of the Mahayana, and proceeds: "They are named *'Prajna Paramita:* The Accomplishment of Transcendental Wisdom.' And they are a series of most curious dialogues, conducted in a sort of conversation cycle of Buddhas and Bodhisattvas—mostly legendary beings, superhuman saviors, without a single merely human, still half-bewildered aspirant to enlightenment, among them.

"The Illumined Ones behave in a way that should be rather shocking and confusing to any sound thinker, who, from habit and firm determination, is resolved to keep his feet on the ground. In a sort of mocking conversation, these Buddhas and Bodhisattvas entertain themselves with enigmatical statements of the unstatable truth. They delight in declaring, time and again, that there is no such thing as Buddhism, no such thing as Enlightenment, nothing remotely resembling the extinction of Nirvana, setting traps for each other and trying to trick each other into assertions that might imply—even remotely—the reality of such conceptions. Then, most artfully, they always elude the cleverly placed hazards and hidden pitfalls—and engage in a glorious trans-Olympian laugh; for the merest hint of a notion of Nirvana would have betrayed a trace of the vestige of the opposite attitude, samsara, and the clinging to individual existence." [8]

From these prajna-paramita texts the following selections are taken.

### FROM *Maha-Prajna-Paramita-Hridaya*[9]

Thus, O Sariputa, all things having the nature of emptiness have no beginning and no ending. They are neither faultless nor not faultless; they are neither perfect nor imperfect. In emptiness there is no form, no sensation, no perception, no discrimination, no consciousness. There is no eye, no ear, no nose, no tongue, no sensitiveness to contact, no mind. There is no sight, no sound, no smell, no taste, no touch, no mental process, no object, no knowledge, no ignorance. There is no destruction of objects, there is no cessation of knowledge, no cessation of ignorance. There is no Noble Four-fold Truths; no pain, no cause of pain, no cessation of pain, no Noble Path leading to the cessation of

pain. There is no decay and no death, and no destruction of
the notion of decay and death. There is no knowledge of
Nirvana, there is no obtaining of Nirvana, there is no not
obtaining of Nirvana.

### Commentary

The nearest thing to this kind of language which is known
to me in Christendom, or elsewhere than in Buddhism, will
be found in the passage in which Dionysius the Areopagite
denies that any words, positive or negative, apply to God.
This will be found on page 137.

FROM *the Diamond Sutra*[10]

Then the Lord Buddha addressed the assembly. . . .
Though the sentient beings thus to be delivered by me are
innumerable and without limit yet, in reality, there are no
sentient beings to be delivered. And why, Subhuti? Because,
should there exist in the minds of Bodhisattva–Mahasattvas
such arbitrary conceptions of phenomena as the existence of
one's own ego-selfness, the ego-selfness of another, self-ness
as divided into an infinite number of living and dying beings,
or selfness as unified into one Universal Self existing
eternally, they would be unworthy to be called Bodhisattva–
Mahasattvas. . . .

The Lord Buddha continued:—Do not think, Subhuti,
that the Tathagata would consider within himself:—I will
deliver human beings. That would be a degrading thought.
Why? Because really there are no sentient beings to be delivered by the Tathagata. Should there be any sentient beings
to be delivered by the Tathagata, it would mean that the
Tathagata was cherishing within his mind arbitrary conceptions of phenomena such as one's own self, other selves, living beings and an universal self. Even when the Tathagata
refers to himself, he is not holding in his mind any such
arbitrary thought. Only terrestrial human beings think of
selfhood as being a personal possession. Subhuti, even the
expression "terrestrial beings" as used by the Tathagata does
not mean that there are any such beings. It is used only as a
figure of speech. . . .

What think you, Subhuti? Has the Tathagata attained anything that can be described as Anuttara-samyak-sambodhi

10 *Ibid.*, pp. 88, 91-92, 102, 103.

[the real true enlightenment of the Buddha himself]? Has he ever given you any such teaching?

Subhuti replied:—As I understand the teaching of the Lord Buddha, there is no such thing as Anuttara-samyak-sambodhi, nor is it possible for the Tathagata to teach any fixed Dharma. And why? Because the things taught by the Tathagata are, in their essential nature, inconceivable and inscrutable; they are neither existent nor non-existent; they are neither phenomena nor noumena. . . .

The Lord said:—Subhuti, if any disciple were to say that the Tathagata is now coming or now going, or is now sitting up or is now lying down, he would not have understood the principle that I have been teaching. And why? Because while the word, Tathagata, means "He who has thus come" and "He who has thus gone," the true Tathagata is never coming from anywhere, nor is he going anywhere. The name, Tathagata, is merely a word.

And the last words of the Lankavatra Sutra, speaking of the beings who are awaiting salvation, are:

If they only realised it, they are already in the Tathagata's Nirvana for, in Noble Wisdom, all things are in Nirvana from the beginning.[11]

## Commentary

From the theoretical point of view these quotations may be considered simply as expressions of the inscrutability of Nirvana. If Nirvana is ineffable, one way of saying this is to pile up lists of words, phrases, sentences which cannot be used of it. It cannot be called Nirvana nor non-Nirvana, etc. The quotations above merely draw out the last ounce of paradox, and doubtless of humor, which can be drawn from this situation. And if the logician insists that paradox means logical contradiction and that what is self-contradictory, whether it is a square circle or a Nirvana which is non-Nirvana, cannot exist, it may be said that the purport of these selections is to agree with him heartily. But the Buddhist mystic, or any mystic, adds that there is nevertheless something which is beyond all logic, and beyond all existence.

But apart from theory we may also ask what is the practi-

11 *Ibid.*, p. 356.

cal upshot of these passages. Have they a serious meaning for us? Professor Zimmer in his account of the matter suggests that these Buddhas and Bodhisattvas perhaps end their dialogues with a roar of "trans-Olympian laughter." Certainly the element of humor is there. Certainly a Buddha ought to be able to laugh at himself. But I think there is a deeper meaning in these texts. They are not mere jokes. The essential point is that since all distinctions disappear in Nirvana, the distinction between Nirvana and samsara must also disappear. Nirvana and samsara are thus identically the same thing. The practical meaning of this is that we should not seek Nirvana *in another world*. We must find it here in this world. Instead of escaping from this world, turning our backs on it, fleeing from samsara to Nirvana, we should endeavor rather to bring Nirvana down onto this earth. Nirvana is not something to be sought outside samsara, but in it.

How is this to be done? I fear that I am wading out of my depth. Yet I shall struggle on a few steps. We began in the first chapter of this book by distinguishing two quite different kinds of consciousness, the sensory-intellectual consciousness and the mystical. The former is samsara, the latter Nirvana. Most mystics never get beyond the stage of passing back and forth from the one to the other. Most of their lives they live in the everyday world of sense and intellect, but every now and then they have what they call a "mystical experience." Their two lives are thus kept separate, although no doubt the mystical life deeply influences the sensory-intellectual life. But it seems that there is a stage beyond this in which the two kinds of consciousness are somehow integrated together, coalesce, and become one. The tradition is that the Buddha, having attained enlightenment in early manhood, remained always in Nirvana while continuing to work actively in the world. In Christian mysticism such a state is well known under a variety of names —e.g., "the unitive state," or the state of "deification." Ruysbroeck and St. Teresa and several others seem to have risen to that ultimate perfection. At the time when St. Teresa wrote her autobiography she was frequently passing in and out of trances and raptures. Between the raptures she was without the mystical vision. But later in life, when she came to write her book called *The Interior Castle,* something rather mysterious had happened; a change had come over her. She no longer alternated between trance and waking life. Her mystical illumination was no longer intermittent but a steady light persisting through her daily tasks. This is described in our final selection from St. Teresa on page 184.

The ideas which we are discussing have deeply influenced Zen Buddhism and are a part of it. When asked what would happen if a man suddenly had a satori (the Japanese word for enlightenment) while chopping wood, Suzuki replied, "He would go on chopping wood." This subject will be further discussed in the commentary at the end of the next selection.

## D. T. Suzuki: ZEN

Zen Buddhism is a branch of the Mahayana. It is a mistake to think of it as if it were something quite unique and different from any other kind of Buddhism. Its fundamental experience, "satori," is the same as the enlightenment experience in all Buddhism. And most of its doctrines and ideas are shared with other Mahayanists. The way in which it chiefly differs from other forms of Buddhism is not in regard to its goal or its doctrines but in regard to the techniques by means of which enlightenment is sought. These include various kinds of paradoxical questions or enigmas (koans), and even acts of physical violence, which are apparently intended as a kind of shock treatment aimed at jolting the aspirant out of his intellectual understanding of the world into the mystical consciousness. The Western, European or American, aspirant to mystical consciousness has at his disposal various more normal methods—for instance, the Yoga disciplines, or those which have been used in Christian circles. One would suppose that the Zen techniques were precisely those which are for the Western mind the most unsuitable and the least likely to succeed. And it is difficult not to think that the present craze for Zen in America is based at least by some of its followers on a kind of empty-minded foolishness, a mere running after strange things, rather than on any serious seeking for the mystic goal.

These remarks are not intended to be derogatory of Zen Buddhism, which is, for those who are able to benefit by its methods and for whom it is suited, one of the great forms of mysticism. For it the reader of these lines should, like the writer of them, entertain a deep respect.

There are other ways in which, besides its unusual techniques, Zen stands out from other forms of Buddhism; but they are mostly matters of atmosphere and affective tone rather than of doctrine or goal. Zen tends to be down-to-earth and practical, not dreamy or otherworldly. It is also remarkable for its sturdy self-reliance and refusal to follow tradition blindly, even the tradition of the Buddha himself. If the Zen Buddhist expresses a certain opinion, he is not likely to be much abashed by being told that the Buddha thought otherwise.

I have chosen a selection in which the peculiar techniques and eccentricities of Zen, though mentioned, are not emphasized. Much of Professor Suzuki's writing, though put in a Zen framework, might just as well be regarded as an expository of Buddhist philosophy in general.

### Satori, or Enlightenment [12]

The essence of Zen Buddhism consists in acquiring a new viewpoint on life and things generally. By this I mean that if we want to get into the inmost life of Zen, we must forgo all our ordinary habits of thinking which control our everyday life, we must try to see if there is any other way of judging things, or rather if our ordinary way is always sufficient to give us the ultimate satisfaction of our spiritual needs. If we feel dissatisfied somehow with this life, if there is something in our ordinary way of living that deprives us of freedom in its most sanctified sense, we must endeavour to find a way somewhere which gives us a sense of finality and contentment. Zen proposes to do this for us and assures us of the acquirement of a new point of view in which life assumes a fresher, deeper, and more satisfying aspect. This acquirement, however, is really and naturally the greatest mental cataclysm one can go through with in life. It is no easy task, it is a kind of fiery baptism, and one has to go through the storm, the earthquake, the overthrowing of the mountains, and the breaking in pieces of the rocks.

This acquiring of a new point of view in our dealings with life and the world is popularly called by Japanese Zen students "satori" (*wu* in Chinese). It is really another name for Enlightenment (*anuttara-samyak-sambodhi*), which is the word used by the Buddha and his Indian followers ever since his realization under the Bodhi-tree by the River Nairanjana. There are several other phrases in Chinese designating this spiritual experience, each of which has a special connotation, showing tentatively how this phenomenon is in-

[12] D. T. Suzuki, *Essays in Zen Buddhism*. London: Rider & Co. Quoted from *Zen Buddhism*, edited by William Barrett. New York: Doubleday & Company, Inc. (Anchor Books), 1956, pp. 84-85.

terpreted. At all events there is no Zen without satori, which is indeed the Alpha and Omega of Zen Buddhism. Zen devoid of satori is like a sun without its light and heat. Zen may lose all its literature, all its monasteries, and all its paraphernalia; but as long as there is satori in it, it will survive to eternity. I want to emphasize this most fundamental fact concerning the very life of Zen; for there are some even among the students of Zen themselves who are blind to this central fact and are apt to think when Zen has been explained away logically or psychologically, or as one of the Buddhist philosophies which can be summed up by using highly technical and conceptual Buddhist phrases, Zen is exhausted, and there remains nothing in it that makes it what it is. But my contention is, the life of Zen begins with the opening of satori (*kai wu* in Chinese).

Satori may be defined as an intuitive looking into the nature of things in contradistinction to the analytical or logical understanding of it. Practically, it means the unfolding of a new world hitherto unperceived in the confusion of a dualistically-trained mind. Or we may say that with satori our entire surroundings are viewed from quite an unexpected angle of perception. Whatever this is, the world for those who have gained a satori is no more the old world as it used to be; even with all its flowing streams and burning fires, it is never the same one again. Logically stated, all its opposites and contradictions are united and harmonized into a consistent organic whole. This is a mystery and a miracle, but according to the Zen masters such is being performed every day. Satori can thus be had only through our once personally experiencing it.

Its semblance or analogy in a more or less feeble and fragmentary way is gained when a difficult mathematical problem is solved, or when a great discovery is made, or when a sudden means of escape is realized in the midst of most desperate complications; in short, when one exclaims "Eureka! Eureka!" But this refers only to the intellectual aspect of satori, which is therefore necessarily partial and incomplete and does not touch the very foundations of life considered one indivisible whole. Satori as the Zen experience must be concerned with the entirety of life. For what Zen proposes to do is the revolution, and the revaluation as well, of oneself as a spiritual unity. The solving of a mathematical problem ends with the solution, it does not affect one's whole life. So with all other particular questions, practical or scientific, they do not enter the basic life-tone of the individual concerned. But the opening of satori is the remaking of life itself. When it is genuine—for there are many simulacra of it—its effects on one's moral and spiritual life are revolutionary, and they are so enhancing, purifying, as well as exacting. When a master was asked what constituted Buddhahood, he answered, "The bottom of a pail is broken through." From this we can see what a complete revolution is produced by this spiritual experience. The birth of a new man is really cataclysmic. . . .

### Chief Characteristics of Satori [13]

1. *Irrationality.* By this I mean that satori is not a conclusion to be reached by reasoning, and defies all intellectual determination. Those who have experienced it are always at a loss to explain it coherently or logically. When it is explained at all, either in words or gestures, its content more or less undergoes a mutilation. The uninitiated are thus unable to grasp it by what is outwardly visible, while those who have had the experience discern what is genuine from what is not. The satori experience is thus always characterized by irrationality, inexplicability, and incommunicability.

Listen to Tai-hui once more: "This matter [i.e. Zen] is like a great mass of fire; when you approach it your face is sure to be scorched. It is again like a sword about to be drawn; when it is once out of the scabbard, someone is sure to lose his life. But if you neither fling away the scabbard nor approach the fire, you are no better than a piece of rock or of wood. Coming to this pass, one has to be quite a resolute character full of spirit." There is nothing here suggestive of cool reasoning and quiet metaphysical or epistemological analysis, but of a certain desperate will to break through an insurmountable barrier, of the will impelled by some irrational or unconscious power behind it. Therefore, the outcome also defies intellection or conceptualization.

2. *Intuitive insight.* That there is noetic quality in mystic experiences has been pointed out by James in his *The Varieties of Religious Experience,* and this applies also to the Zen experience known as satori. Another name for satori is "ken-sho" (*chien-hsing* in Chinese) meaning "to see essence or nature," which apparently proves that there is "seeing" or "perceiving" in satori. That this seeing is of quite a different quality from what is ordinarily designated as knowledge need not be specifically noticed. Hui-k'e is reported to have made this statement concerning his satori which was

[13] *Ibid.,* pp. 103-8.

confirmed by Bodhidharma himself: "[As to my satori], it is not a total annihilation; it is knowledge of the most adequate kind; only it cannot be expressed in words." In this respect Shen-hui was more explicit, for he says that "the one character *chih* (knowledge) is the source of all mysteries."

Without this noetic quality satori will lose all its pungency, for it is really the reason of satori itself. It is noteworthy that the knowledge contained in satori is concerned with something universal and at the same time with the individual aspect of existence. When a finger is lifted, the lifting means, from the viewpoint of satori, far more than the act of lifting. Some may call it symbolic, but satori does not point to anything beyond itself, being final as it is. Satori is the knowledge of an individual object and also that of Reality which is, if I may say so, at the back of it.

3. *Authoritativeness.* By this I mean that the knowledge realized by satori is final, that no amount of logical argument can refute it. Being direct and personal it is sufficient unto itself. All that logic can do here is to explain it, to interpret it in connection with other kinds of knowledge with which our minds are filled. Satori is thus a form of perception, an inner perception, which takes place in the most interior part of consciousness. Hence the sense of authoritativeness, which means finality. So, it is generally said that Zen is like drinking water, for it is by one's self that one knows whether it is warm or cold. The Zen perception being the last term of experience, it cannot be denied by outsiders who have no such experience.

4. *Affirmation.* What is authoritative and final can never be negative. For negation has no value for our life, it leads us nowhere; it is not a power that urges, nor does it give one a place to rest. Though the satori experience is sometimes expressed in negative terms, it is essentially an affirmative attitude towards all things that exist; it accepts them as they come along regardless of their moral values. Buddhists call this *kshanti*, "patience," or more properly "acceptance," that is, acceptance of things in their suprarelative or transcendental aspect where no dualism of whatever sort avails.

Some may say that this is pantheistic. The term, however, has a definite philosophic meaning and I would not see it used in this connection. When so interpreted the Zen experience exposes itself to endless misunderstandings and "defilements." Tai-hui says in his letter to Miao-tsung: "An ancient sage says that the Tao itself does not require special disciplining, only

let it not be defiled. I would say: To talk about mind or
nature is defiling; to talk about the unfathomable or the mysterious is defiling; to practise meditation or tranquillization is
defiling; to direct one's attention to it, to think about it is defiling; to be writing about it thus on paper with a brush is especially defiling. What then shall we have to do in order to get
ourselves oriented, and properly apply ourselves to it? The
precious vajra sword is right here and its purpose is to cut off
the head. Do not be concerned with human questions of right
and wrong. All is Zen just as it is, and right here you are to
apply yourself." Zen is Suchness—a grand affirmation.

5. *Sense of the Beyond*. Terminology may differ in different
religions, and in satori there is always what we may call a
sense of the Beyond; the experience indeed is my own but
I feel it to be rooted elsewhere. The individual shell in which
my personality is so solidly encased explodes at the moment
of satori. Not, necessarily, that I get unified with a being
greater than myself or absorbed in it, but that my individuality, which I found rigidly held together and definitely kept
separate from other individual existences, becomes loosened
somehow from its tightening grip and melts away into something indescribable, something which is of quite a different
order from what I am accustomed to. The feeling that follows is that of a complete release or a complete rest—the
feeling that one has arrived finally at the destination. "Coming home and quietly resting" is the expression generally used
by Zen followers. The story of the prodigal son in the
*Saddharmapundarika*, in the *Vajra-samadhi*, and also in the
New Testament points to the same feeling one has at the
moment of a satori experience.

As far as the psychology of satori is considered, a sense of
the Beyond is all we can say about it; to call this the Beyond,
the Absolute, or God, or a Person is to go further than the
experience itself and to plunge into a theology or metaphysics. Even the "Beyond" is saying a little too much. When a
Zen master says, "There is not a fragment of a tile above my
head, there is not an inch of earth beneath my feet," the expression seems to be an appropriate one. I have called it
elsewhere the Unconscious, though this has a psychological
taint.

6. *Impersonal Tone*. Perhaps the most remarkable aspect of
the Zen experience is that it has no personal note in it as is
observable in Christian mystic experiences. There is no reference whatever in Buddhist satori to such personal and frequently sexual feelings and relationships as are to be gleaned
from these terms: flame of love, a wonderful love shed in

the heart, embrace, the beloved, bride, bridegroom, spiritual matrimony, Father, God, the Son of God, God's child, etc. We may say that all these terms are interpretations based on a definite system of thought and really have nothing to do with the experience itself. At any rate, alike in India, China, and Japan, satori has remained thoroughly impersonal, or rather highly intellectual.

Is this owing to the peculiar character of Buddhist philosophy? Does the experience itself take its colours from the philosophy or theology? Whatever this is, there is no doubt that in spite of its having some points of similitude to the Christian mystic experience, the Zen experience is singularly devoid of personal or human colourings. Chao-pien, a great government officer of the Sung dynasty, was a lay-disciple of Fach'uan of Chiang-shan. One day after his official duties were over, he found himself leisurely sitting in his office, when all of a sudden a clash of thunder burst on his ear, and he realized a state of satori. The poem he then composed depicts one aspect of the Zen experience:

> "Devoid of thought, I sat quietly by the desk in my
>     official room,
> With my fountain-mind undisturbed, as serene as
>     water;
> A sudden clash of thunder, the mind-doors burst
>     open,
> And lo, there sitteth the old man in all his homeli-
>     ness."

This is perhaps all the personal tone one can find in the Zen experience, and what a distance between "the old man in his homeliness" and "God in all his glory," not to say anything about such feelings as "the heavenly sweetness of Christ's excellent love," etc.! How barren, how unromantic satori is when compared with the Christian mystic experiences!

Not only satori itself is such a prosaic and non-glorious event, but the occasion that inspires it also seems to be unromantic and altogether lacking in supersensuality. Satori is experienced in connection with any ordinary occurrence in one's daily life. It does not appear to be an extraordinary phenomenon as is recorded in Christian books of mysticism. Someone takes hold of you, or slaps you, or brings you a cup of tea, or makes some most commonplace remark, or recites some passage from a sutra or from a book of poetry, and when your mind is ripe for its outburst, you come at once to satori. There is no romance of love-making, no voice of the

Holy Ghost, no plenitude of Divine Grace, no glorification of any sort. Here is nothing painted in high colours, all is grey and extremely unobtrusive and unattractive.

7. *Feeling of Exaltation.* That this feeling inevitably accompanies satori is due to the fact that it is the breaking-up of the restriction imposed on one as an individual being, and this breaking up is not a mere negative incident but quite a positive one fraught with signification because it means an infinite expansion of the individual. The general feeling, though we are not always conscious of it, which characterizes all our functions of consciousness, is that of restriction and dependence, because consciousness itself is the outcome of two forces conditioning or restricting each other. Satori, on the contrary, essentially consists in doing away with the opposition of two terms in whatsoever sense—and this opposition is the principle of consciousness as before mentioned, while satori is to realize the Unconscious which goes beyond the opposition.

To be released of this, therefore, must make one feel above all things intensely exalted. A wandering outcast maltreated everywhere not only by others but by himself finds that he is the possessor of all the wealth and power that is ever attainable in this world by a mortal being—if this does not give him a high feeling of self-glorification, what could? Says a Zen master, "When you have satori you are able to reveal a palatial mansion made of precious stones on a single blade of grass; but when you have no satori, a palatial mansion itself is concealed behind a simple blade of grass."

Another Zen master, evidently alluding to the *Avatamsaka*, declares: "O monks, lo and behold! A most auspicious light is shining with the utmost brilliancy all over the great chilio-cosm, simultaneously revealing all the countries, all the oceans, all the Sumerus, all the suns and moons, all the heavens, all the lands—each of which number as many as hundreds of thousands of kotis. O monks, do you not see the light?" But the Zen feeling of exaltation is rather a quiet feeling of self-contentment; it is not at all demonstrative, when the first glow of it passes away. The Unconscious does not proclaim itself so boisterously in the Zen consciousness.

8. *Momentariness.* Satori comes upon one abruptly and is a momentary experience. In fact, if it is not abrupt and momentary, it is not satori. This abruptness (*tun*) is what characterizes the Hui-neng school of Zen ever since its proclamation late in the seventh century. His opponent Shen-hsiu was insistent on a gradual unfoldment of Zen consciousness. Hui-neng's followers were thus distinguished as strong upholders

of the doctrine of abruptness. This abrupt experience of satori, then, opens up in one moment (*ekamuhurtena*) an altogether new vista, and the whole existence is appraised from quite a new angle of observation.

## Commentary

This selection may give the reader the impression that Zen satori is something quite different from the introspective mystical consciousness which we have been discussing, and illustrating, in this book. In spite of appearances, I do not believe this is so. What I think chiefly gives this impression is the fact that Professor Suzuki seems in many places to mean that in satori the mind does not cease to be aware of objects in the world but includes them in its consciousness. For example, he says "satori is the knowledge of individual object and also that of Reality which, if I may say so, is at the back of it." And in the middle of satori "lo, there sitteth the old man in all his homeliness." How, it will be asked, can this be the same as the experience described in the Mandukya Upanishad, in which "awareness of the world and of multiplicity is completely obliterated"? But I do not think there is any inconsistency. I quoted on page 88 Suzuki's remark that if a man were chopping wood at the time he had a satori, he would go on chopping wood. And it was pointed out that the message of the Prajna-Paramita to the effect that Nirvana and samsara are not opposites, but that Nirvana is to be found in samsara, deeply influenced Zen and is a part of it. We saw too that there is a final stage of the mystical life in which the sensory-intellectual consciousness and the mystical consciousness have become integrated and that this stage, called by Christian mystics the "unitive life," was reached both by the Buddha and by many Christian mystics. It seems likely, therefore, that this is what we have in the most highly developed Zen satori.

Suzuki gives "irrationality" as one of the characteristics of satori. I think he means nonrationality, being beyond reason, beyond understanding. He may be unaware of the undesirable nuances of thought and feeling usually conveyed in English by the word "irrationality." I suspect also that by the word "momentariness" (the eighth characteristic of satori) what he really means is "suddenness." The Buddha's enlightenment may have come suddenly, but it was not momentary in the sense of lasting only a moment. On the contrary, it lasted half a century.

## Eugen Herrigel: ZEN

In introducing the extracts which follow it is not necessary to add much to what has already been said about Zen in the preceding section. Eugen Herrigel's *The Method of Zen* is at the moment of writing the most recent book on the subject, having been published in 1960. It is also certainly one of the most profound treatments of it in existence. What Herrigel says of the koan exercise and of the satori experience may profitably be set alongside the Suzuki extract for purposes of comparison and supplementation. Herrigel is a past master in the art of delicate and subtle psychological introspection and description. By means of subtle hints and suggestive analogies he contrives to create in us something of the feel of those experiences which at the same time he declares to be indescribable.

Herrigel, a German professor who taught philosophy in the University of Tokyo, later underwent six years' rigorous training under a Zen master. He died in 1955. Out of the great quantity of notes which he left behind him his editors selected the material that constitutes the book from which our extracts are taken.

### The Koan[14]

The subject for meditation is the koan. It requires a supreme mental effort and permits of no lazy daydreaming. Here are a few examples of koans:

Show me your original face before you were born.

If you meet someone in the street who has attained to the truth, you must pass him neither speaking nor in silence. How would you meet him?

The priest Shusan held his staff before the eyes of the assembled monks and said: "If you call this a stick, it is disgusting. If you don't call it a stick, it is wrong. What will you call it?"

Hakuin held his hand up in the air and told his pupils to listen to the sound it made. What was it like?

[14] Eugen Herrigel, *The Method of Zen*, edited by Hermann Tausend, translated by R.F.C. Hull. Toronto: McClelland and Stewart; 1960. New York: Pantheon Books, Inc., 1960, pp. 39-52.

With the help of this last koan I will try, as best I may, to show what course the meditant follows, and what is the point of the exercise.

For hours, days, and weeks the pupil meditates on his task. Sunk in profound concentration, he thinks the problem through in all possible directions. One thing is clear; since only two hands striking together can produce a sound, the answer can only be: No one, with the best will in the world, can hear the sound of one hand. But the solution cannot be as simple as that. Would it not be more cautious to say: A single hand does not emit a sound that is perceptible to the human ear? But that does not get him any further. Obviously, the point is not the sound and its audibility, which are thrown in just to make the problem more complicated. The point is obviously: What is the significance of one hand in contradistinction to two? Is not this the same as the fundamental distinction between unity and duality? The hand must be a symbol of the principle: "One without a second." This solution recommends itself to the pupil because it is a distinction that plays a crucial role in Buddhism and is so often discussed.

Having found such an admirable solution, the pupil hurries off to the Master. He has the right to ask him one question a day. He propounds his solution with pride and enthusiasm. The Master hears him out, shakes his head, and sends the bewildered pupil back to the meditation hall without a word. But it sometimes happens that he does not let the pupil utter a word and sends him away when he has scarcely opened the door. The pupil, thrown back on himself, begins to concentrate anew. He will distinguish himself yet, astonish the Master. Meditating doggedly, he tries to force a solution. But however he twists and turns it, he can come to no other conclusion. Why, then, did the Master dismiss him? Perhaps he only expressed himself badly? He turns the formulation over in his mind. Once more he goes to the Master, who dismisses him again, this time with evident disapproval. But again the pupil fails to discover where he has gone wrong. He now gets into a state. If he is so far from the solution, will he ever be able to reach the goal? He pulls himself together. It is a matter of life and death! With passionate energy he throws himself on the problem, not with the discriminating intellect, but with the combined forces of body, soul, and spirit, so that it never lets him alone. It torments him during recreation, at mealtimes, at his daily work. It pursues him even in sleep. No need now to force himself to think about it! Even when he wants distraction, *it* goes on thinking in him. All in vain; the solution just will not come. He doubts his own ability, begins to despair, and does not know where to turn. He is saved from utter despair only by the Master's admonition that he is to increase the concentration until he is no longer disturbed by moody thoughts. He must learn to wait, patiently and trustfully, until the solution is ripe and comes of its own accord, without being forced.

So now he sets about it a different way. It is no longer necessary to analyze the problem and think it out: he has done enough of that already. He no longer thinks in a circle, of this or that, of one hand or two hands, of principles and suchlike; he does not even think about the solution in order to force it, and yet he is constantly related to it in an extraordinary spiritual tension. He longs for it like a man thirsting for a quenching drink. But he behaves like a man who is trying to remember something. He feels like a person who is seeking something he has forgotten, something he has to remember at any cost, because his life depends on it.

In this state of spiritual tension, it may happen that the solution will suddenly come to him, quite unexpectedly. Or else a shout, a loud noise, or, in obstinate cases—as used to be done in earlier times—a painful blow will bring the tension to bursting point. How exciting is this moment! The pupil trembles, breaks out in a sweat. But rapturous too: what he has sought in vain comes to him in a flash. He now sees clearly where everything was a tangle before; he can see the wood in spite of the trees. The scales fall from his eyes. He feels saved. The moment is brief, like a flash of lightning, yet profoundly impressive. No wonder he cannot grasp it.

### Satori

In this frame of mind he goes to the Master. . . .

The Master looks through him at once. Possibly he knew, as soon as the pupil opened the door, that this was the real thing: *satori*, enlightenment. . . .

What has happened? The pupil has not found any new interpretation, any new thought. Rather, in a flash of enlightenment, he has come to the solution as if a new, spiritual eye had been let into his head. The things he sees are no different from before, he just sees them differently. . . .

This new vision cannot be compared to anything and is, strictly speaking, indescribable.

But is there no hope even of hinting at its character-istics? . . .

I will try. . . .

The first characteristic, it seems to me, of the new way of seeing is that all things are of equal importance in its sight, the most trivial as well as the most significant by ordinary human standards. They all seem to have acquired an abso-lute value, as if they had become transparent, revealing a re-lationship which does not obtain in the ordinary field of vision. This relationship is not horizontal, linking one thing to another and so remaining within the world of objects, but vertical: it plumbs each single thing to its very depths, to the point of origination. Things are thus seen, . . . from the origin, out of the "being" which manifests itself in them. To that extent they are all of equal rank, all possessing the illustrious patents of their origin. They are not objects iso-lated in themselves; they point beyond themselves, to the common ground of their being, and yet this ground can be perceived only through them, through what exists, although it is the origin of all existence.

. . . There is not the slightest trace of reflection in this way of seeing. . . . Rather, the vision comes upon you like a flash of lightning, at a single stroke. It is so physically clear that it brings with it absolute certainty, so that you instantly "see" and understand that things *are* by virtue of what they are *not*, and that they owe their being to this not-being which is their ground and origin.

Perhaps an anecdote, often used as a koan, will explain what is meant:

One day as Hyakujo stepped out of the house with his Master, Baso, they saw a flight of wild geese. Baso asked: "Where are they flying?" "They have already flown away, Master." Suddenly Baso seized Hyakujo by the nose and twisted it. Overcome by pain, Hyakujo cried out: "Oh, oh!"

"You say they have flown away," said Baso, "but they have all been here from the beginning."

Then Hyakujo's back ran with sweat, and he had *satori*.

The difference between these two statements is so enor-mous that they cannot be reconciled with one another. "They have flown away" is a self-evident statement of ordinary com-mon sense. . . .

Baso sees quite differently.

. . . With the "third" eye, which is acquired only when one is "reborn," you see just this existence of something that is, the ground of its being. Therefore the statement must be: "They have always been here"—naturally not at this point of space, as space and time have no part in this vision. What is bound to appear senseless, perverse, a poor joke, is thus in reality a quite simple statement of fact—a fact which Baso sees as clearly and as corporeally as Hyakujo sees the fact that the geese have flown away. Neither of these facts refutes the other, as they belong to totally different dimensions, and Hyakujo would never have been able to find the solution by prolonged reflection. Only at the moment of acute pain, which stopped him from thinking, did he find the solution through *satori*.

. . . You must not imagine that you can adopt Baso's standpoint and project something meaningful, possibly even profound, into his statement. That is not the point at all: everything depends on your "seeing," as Baso did. . . .

. . . What applies to each and every thing applies also to the so-called ego. In this vision the ego, too, becomes transparent, even to the ultimate depths in which it is grounded. Here we may recall the koan: Show me your original face before you were born—that is, before you existed as an individual ego, as this particular person, in the world of multiplicity and oppositeness.

. . . What you then experience in regard to your own ego is not transferred by analogy to other egos, still less to things; all these other forms are directly experienced too, each by itself, from the origin.

# -4-

# Taoist Mysticism

The Chinese people have not been much given to mysticism, the down-to-earth practical moralisms of Confucius being a better expression of their temperament and genius. They absorbed Buddhist mysticism and modified it in their own way. In their hands it became Ch'an or, in the Japanese language, Zen. The only mysticism which originated in China is found in Taoism. The traditional founder of Taoism was Lao-Tzu, but actually the movement originated among hermits whose names are unrecorded, but who lived in remote valleys at a much earlier date. Doubts have been raised whether Lao-Tzu was a historical individual at all; but assuming that he was, he seems to have been born about 570 B.C. There were other Taoist writers besides Lao-Tzu, of whom the best known is Chuang Tzu. But here we shall confine ourselves to the poems of Lao-Tzu.

His book is called the *Tao Tê Ching*. Many of the poems in it seem to concern practical, moral, and political affairs and have little or no mystical content. For our selection I have picked out those in which the mystical import seems most plain and undeniable. The translations are those made by Doctor R. B. Blakney in the volume *Lao Tzu* in this series. Doctor Blakney writes, "The Chinese mystics were original and to the point in their writings, but their point was identical with that of the great mystics elsewhere."

The central mystical idea of the poems is the Tao. This word literally means "way." Some translators retain the Chinese word Tao as a sort of technical term. Others, including our translator, use the English with a capital and call it "the Way." The Chinese word has, I understand, several meanings. It may mean the way of life in a quite non-mystical sense. It may also mean the way of the universe, the laws and operations of the universe. It may also have a mystical meaning. All these three meanings seem to be here intentionally blended or even identified in the one concept.

Perhaps the easiest way to seize the mystical meaning, which is alone what is important to us in this book, is to read poem No. 4, which is the second poem printed in this selection. The Way, it says, is a void which is never filled but out of which all things come. The Way, thus conceived, is the source of the world—corresponding to the Brahman of Hindu thought, or the womb of the Tathagata in Buddhism, or the Absolute of Western thinkers. "A deep pool it is, Never to run dry." In the last chapter I contrasted the view, found in *The Awakening of Faith*, that the world of finite objects is due to "false imaginations" with the far profounder view that the Emptiness, the undifferentiated void, produces the world of things out of itself by a process of self-differentiation. Suzuki has put the paradox boldly. "Sūnyata (the Void)," he says, "is a reservoir of infinite possibilities and not just mere emptiness. Differentiating itself and yet remaining in itself undifferentiated . . . we may say that it is a creation out of nothing." This seems certainly to be the meaning of poem No. 4 of Lao-Tzu. In the last three lines of the poem the point is made that the Tao is even "prior to God." If there is a being who is rightly called God, then that being has come out of the Emptiness. God is one of the differentiations into which the emptiness of the Tao divides itself. We shall find this the same thought in Meister Eckhart. According to him the Godhead is an empty void—in his words, a "barren desert"—which differentiates itself into the three Persons of the Trinity.

In poem No. 11 the dependence of all things on the void is again taught. In poem No. 16 we hear of the "ultimate emptiness" of which it is asserted that it "is the stillness," a metaphor for the mystical consciousness with which we are already familiar.

Enough has been said to put the key to the understanding of these poems in the reader's hand. With this key he can very easily unlock for himself the meaning of the rest of the poems selected.

It is noteworthy that there is no direct description, or even mention, of mystical *experience* in Lao-Tzu. The nearest approach to it comes in poem No. 48, which could be read as a reference to the method of attaining mystical consciousness by emptying the self of sensations, images, thoughts, etc. This may be what is meant by saying that the Way is reached by loss—though I do not feel sure of this interpretation. Since there is no direct description of the mystical experience, what we have in the poems is what on page 9 I termed "mystical ideas"—theoretical-intellectual or philosophical statements which must have been derived from someone's mystical experience. And one cannot doubt that the author or authors of the *Tao Tê Ching* had the mystical consciousness and could not have originated these poems without it. But as is often the case with mystics, they do not speak of themselves nor of their own inner lives.

## Lao-Tzu[1]

### 1

There are ways but the Way is uncharted;
There are names but not nature in words:
Nameless indeed is the source of creation
But things have a mother and she has a name.

The secret waits for the insight
Of eyes unclouded by longing;
Those who are bound by desire
See only the outward container.

These two come paired but distinct
By their names.
Of all things profound,
Say that their pairing is deepest,
The gate to the root of the world.

### 4

The Way is a void,
Used but never filled:
An abyss it is,
Like an ancestor
From which all things come.

[1] *Lao Tzu, The Way of Life: Tao Tê Ching*, translated by R. B. Blakney. New York: New American Library (Mentor Books), 1955, pp. 53-101, *passim*.

It blunts sharpness,
Resolves tangles;
It tempers light,
Subdues turmoil.

A deep pool it is,
Never to run dry!
Whose offspring it may be
I do not know:
It is like a preface to God.

## 11

Thirty spokes will converge
In the hub of a wheel;
But the use of the cart
Will depend on the part
Of the hub that is void.

With a wall all around
A clay bowl is molded;
But the use of the bowl
Will depend on the part
Of the bowl that is void.

Cut out windows and doors
In the house as you build;
But the use of the house
Will depend on the space
In the walls that is void.

So advantage is had
From whatever is there;
But usefulness rises
From whatever is not.

## 16

Touch ultimate emptiness,
Hold steady and still.

All things work together:
I have watched them reverting,
And have seen how they flourish
And return again, each to his roots.

This, I say, is the stillness:
A retreat to one's roots;
Or better yet, return
To the will of God,
Which is, I say, to constancy.
The knowledge of constancy
I call enlightenment and say
That not to know it
Is blindness that works evil.

But when you know
What eternally is so,
You have stature
And stature means righteousness
And righteousness is kingly
And kingliness divine
And divinity is the Way
Which is final.

Then, though you die,
You shall not perish.

### 21

The omnipresent Virtue will take shape
According only to the Way.
The Way itself is like some thing
Seen in a dream, elusive, evading one.
In it are images, elusive, evading one.
In it are things like shadows in twilight.
In it are essences, subtle but real,
Embedded in truth.

From of old until now,
Under names without end,
The First, the Beginning is seen.
How do I know the beginning of all,
What its nature may be?
By these!

### 25

Something there is, whose veiled creation was
Before the earth or sky began to be;
So silent, so aloof and so alone,

It changes not, nor fails, but touches all:
Conceive it as the mother of the world.

I do not know its name;
A name for it is "Way";
Pressed for designation,
I call it Great.
Great means outgoing,
Outgoing, far-reaching,
Far-reaching, return.

The Way is great,
The sky is great,
The earth is great,
The king also is great.
Within the realm
These four are great;
The king but stands
For one of them.

Man conforms to the earth;
The earth conforms to the sky;
The sky conforms to the Way;
The Way conforms to its own nature.

### 34

O the great Way o'erflows
And spreads on every side!
All being comes from it;
No creature is denied.
But having called them forth,
It calls not one its own.
It feeds and clothes them all
And will not be their lord.

Without desire always,
It seems of slight import.
Yet, nonetheless, in this
Its greatness still appears:
When they return to it,
No creature meets a lord.

The Wise Man, therefore, while he is alive,
Will never make a show of being great:
And that is how his greatness is achieved.

### 37

The Way is always still, at rest,
And yet does everything that's done.
If then the king and nobles could
Retain its potency for good,
The creatures all would be transformed.

But if, the change once made in them,
They still inclined to do their work,
I should restrain them then
By means of that unique
Original simplicity
Found in the Virgin Block,
Which brings disinterest,
With stillness in its train,
And so, an ordered world.

### 39

These things in ancient times received the One:

The sky obtained it and was clarified;
The earth received it and was settled firm;
The spirits got it and were energized;
The valleys had it, filled to overflow;
All things, as they partook it came alive;
The nobles and the king imbibed the One
In order that the realm might upright be;
Such things were then accomplished by the One.

Without its clarity the sky might break;
Except it were set firm, the earth might shake;
Without their energy the gods would pass;
Unless kept full, the valleys might go dry;
Except for life, all things would pass away;
Unless the One did lift and hold them high,
The nobles and the king might trip and fall.

The humble folk support the mighty ones;
They are base on which the highest rest.
The nobles and the king speak of themselves
As "orphans," "desolate" and "needy ones."
Does this not indicate that they depend
Upon the lowly people for support?

Truly, a cart is more than the sum of its parts.

Better to rumble like rocks
Than to tinkle like jade.

### 40

The movement of the Way is a return;
In weakness lies its major usefulness.
From What-is all the world of things was born
But What-is sprang in turn from What-is-not.

### 48

The student learns by daily increment.
The Way is gained by daily loss,
Loss upon loss until
At last comes rest.

By letting go, it all gets done;
The world is won by those who let it go!
But when you try and try,
The world is then beyond the winning.

# -5-

# Plotinus

Plotinus was undoubtedly one of the greatest mystics the world has seen. Yet he was not primarily a mystic but rather an intellectual and a philosopher. In the ancient world he stands as the chief representative of Neo-Platonism. His philosophy is basically that of Plato modified and changed in certain ways which do not concern us here. By far the greater part of his writing is concerned with the exposition and defense of his version of Platonism, and only a comparatively small portion is given over to a description of his mystical experiences. A majority of mystics have not been philosophers or in any real sense intellectuals at all. The combination in one person of supremely great mystical illumination with supremely great intellectual power is very rare. One thinks of the Buddha, and of Eckhart, and of Plotinus. There may be others, but I am far from being sure who they are.

Plotinus was born in Egypt about 205 A.D. He attended the University of Alexandria. He made an attempt to journey to India, but failed to get there. This attempt to reach what one may fairly call the great world-reservoir of mysticism is very significant. No doubt the fame of Indian mysticism had long been rumored abroad in the Western world, and Plotinus wished to drink at the source. His mysticism has a markedly Indian tinge, belongs as much to the East as to the West, and has not yet taken on the peculiar stamp of the Western theistic religions which we find especially in Christian mysticism and Sufism.

Later in life Plotinus left Egypt and settled in Rome. He there became a famous and honored teacher. Among his listeners were senators and other highly placed personages. The Emperor Gordianus was his friend. Certainly one does not measure the greatness of a man's spirituality by his capacity for attracting friends among powerful worldlings. More often the greatest spirits have been poor and humble, unhonored and outcast. But it is doubtful whether Plotinus attracted great personages because of his mysticism. Perhaps most of them were not even aware of it. He is more likely to have been honored in Rome as a representative of Greek philosophy. He died in Rome in 270 A.D.

Plotinus, though well aware of the existence of Christianity, did not become a Christian. Indeed, he cannot be said to have adopted any religion. He interpreted his mysticism in terms of a philosophy, not of any theological system. He was a religious spirit in the sense in which, as explained in Chapter 1, all mysticism can be called religious, namely because it carries with it the feeling of the sacred and of a transcendental reality. But he is living proof of the fact that mysticism is not a religious phenomenon in the conventional sense that it must appear in the framework of some specific religious system, such as Christianity, Hinduism, Buddhism, or Islam.

The world system into which Plotinus fits his mysticism is a kind of pantheistic emanationism. It is because of this fact that his affinities lie with the East rather than with the West. The supreme source of the world, according to Plotinus, is the One. The One is pure unity destitute of any multiplicity, wholly undifferentiated. It is the undifferentiated unity of the mystic. One might identify it with the One of the Upanishads with certain provisos. It is not, like the Upanishadic One, identified with the Self, nor is it the "pure consciousness" of the Vedanta. It is not conscious in any sense. It has no characteristics whatever except its oneness. Plotinus sometimes calls it God, but this is not intended to imply personality. It is God only in the sense that it is at once the source of the world and the goal of aspiration. The world flows from it and the soul seeks to return to it.

But the relation of the One to the world in Plotinus is quite different from the relation of God to the world as conceived in the theistic religions of the West. In Christianity, Judaism, and Islam, God is said to "create" the world. But for Plotinus the world is an "emanation" or "manifestation" of the One, or rather it is a series of emanations. From the point of view of philosophical analysis, it is extremely difficult to pinpoint the exact difference between "creation" and "emanation." Both are somewhat vague concepts. Both are, in fact, no more than metaphors. But the essence of the matter seems to be in the fact that for the Western theistic mind the world, after it has been created, is a wholly different "substance" from God, having its own independent existence. God and the world are two separate existences. God never becomes the world, nor does anything in the world become God. In no sense can it be said that the world is a "form" of God, a shape or disguise which God has assumed, a transformation of himself into something else. But this is precisely what, according to the theory of manifestation, the world is. God has transformed himself into the world, which, accordingly, is not a different substance from God but the same substance in another form. This view may be called pantheistic, the creation theory theistic.

Basically the major tradition of the Vedanta is emanationist, although no word corresponding to "emanation" is used. But according to the Upanishads "all this is Brahman." "All this" means the world around us. It is God. But the world is a multiplicity, whereas Brahman, as it is in itself, is wholly undifferentiated. Plainly, therefore, the world is Brahman somehow transformed into a multiplicity. Indian thought struggles with the monstrous problem how the One becomes the Many. But the detail of this is not our business here. The present point is simply that the Vedanta and the Plotinian philosophy stand together as two different versions of manifestationism over against the creationism of the theistic West.

According to Plotinus the cosmos arises out of the One by a series of emanations, or descending steps. Each step is further away from the divine One than the previous step. Each step in the emanation series is a step downward in point of value, away from the good and toward the evil, although pure evil is beyond all emanations and is pure non-being. The first emanation from the One is called Intelligence. This is not the intelligence of any finite or personal being. It may be called the Mind of God since it is the first emanation from God. The One itself is not Mind, but its first emanation is. Intelligence is timeless and spaceless. It is the pure contemplation of the Platonic forms or "ideas."

Out of Intelligence proceeds the second emanation, which is called Soul. This does not primarily mean the souls of individual finite beings. It is rather the World Soul, although individual souls are parts of it. The final emanation which proceeds out of Soul is matter. Below the level of the material world is nothing, pure non-being. The whole system is likened to the rays which proceed outward from the sun into empty space. In this image the sun stands for the One. The rays of the divine as they proceed outward become dimmer and dimmer till at last all light is lost in total darkness. This darkness is pure non-being.

Corresponding to the downward way from the One to the world is an upward way of return to the One. This is the ascent of the soul to mystical union with the One. This is the only part of Plotinus which directly concerns us here, and our selection is confined to Plotinus' account of this mystical union. He tells us that he himself experienced it several times.

The first two paragraphs of our selection are from A. H. Armstrong's translation.[1] The remainder of the selection is from the translation which is given by Dean William R. Inge in his Gifford lectures on Plotinus.[2] There have been later translations. Some of them may possess some advantages over Inge's rendering in respect of scholarly accuracy. But I have preferred to use Inge here because his version seemed to me to possess a greater degree of sympathy and insight into the spirit of mysticism than any other. The portions of Plotinus which are here strung together include Enneads 5.3.17 (in part), 6.7.34, 6.7.35, 6.9.7, 6.9.8, 6.9.9, 6.9.10, and 6.9.11.

The selection is on the whole straightforward and not difficult to understand provided one has grasped the central characteristics of mysticism as set forth in previous chapters. A point-by-point explanation is not necessary, and I will confine myself to emphasizing what seems to me to be most important. I reserve these points for the commentary at the end.

## The Ascent to Union with the One

Here the greatest, the ultimate contest is set before our souls; all our toil and trouble is for this, not to be left without a share in the best of visions. The man who attains this

---

[1] *Plotinus*, edited and translated by A. H. Armstrong. London: George Allen & Unwin, Ltd., 1953, pp. 136-37; New York: The Macmillan Company, 1953.

[2] W. R. Inge, *The Philosophy of Plotinus*. New York: Longmans, Green & Co., Inc., third edition, 1929, Vol. II, pp. 134-43.

is blessed in seeing that blessed sight, and he who fails to attain it has failed utterly. A man has not failed if he fails to win beauty of colours or bodies, or power or office or kingship even, but if he fails to win this and only this. For this he should give up the attainment of kingship and rule over all earth and sea and sky, if only by leaving and overlooking them he can turn to That and see.

But how shall we find the way? What method can we devise? How can one see the inconceivable Beauty Which stays within the holy sanctuary and does not come out where the profane may see It? Let him who can follow and come within, and leave outside the sight of his eyes and not turn back to the bodily splendours which he saw before. When he sees the beauty in bodies he must not run after them; we must know that they are images, traces, shadows, and hurry away to That which they image. For if a man runs to the image and wants to seize it as if it was the reality (like a beautiful reflection playing on the water, which some story somewhere, I think, said riddlingly a man wanted to catch and sank down into the stream and disappeared) then this man who clings to beautiful bodies and will not let them go, will, like the man in the story, but in soul, not in body, sink down into the dark depths where *Nous* has no delight, and stay blind in Hades, consorting with shadows there and here. This would be truer advice, "Let us fly to our dear country."

Where then is our way of escape? How shall we put out to sea? (Odysseus, I think, speaks symbolically when he says he must fly from the witch Circe, or Calypso, and is not content to stay though he has delights of the eyes and lives among much beauty of sense.) Our country from which we came is There, our Father is There. How shall we travel to it, where is our way of escape? We cannot get there on foot: for our feet only carry us everywhere in this world, from one country to another. You must not get ready a carriage, either, or a boat. Let all these things go, and do not look. Shut your eyes and change to and wake another way of seeing, which everyone has but few use.

The discursive reason, if it wishes to say anything, must seize first one element of the Truth and then another; such are the conditions of discursive thought. But how can discursive thought apprehend the absolutely simple? It is enough to apprehend it by a kind of spiritual intuition. But in this act of apprehension we have neither the power nor the time to say anything about it; afterwards we can reason about it. We may believe that we have really seen, when a sudden light illumines the Soul; for this light comes from the

One and is the One. And we may think that the One is present, when, like another god, he illumines the house of him who calls upon him; for there would be no light without his presence. Even so the Soul is dark that does not behold him; but when illumined by him, it has what it desired, and this is the true end and aim of the Soul, to apprehend that light, and to behold it by that light itself, which is no other than the light by which it sees. For that which we seek to behold is that which gives us light, even as we can only see the sun by the light of the sun. How then can this come to us? Strip thyself of everything.

We must not be surprised that that which excites the keenest of longings is without any form, even spiritual form, since the Soul itself, when inflamed with love for it, puts off all the form which it had, even that which belongs to the spiritual world. For it is not possible to see it, or to be in harmony with it, while one is occupied with anything else. The Soul must remove from itself good and evil and everything else, that it may receive the One alone, as the One is alone. When the Soul is so blessed, and is come to it, or rather when it manifests its presence, when the Soul turns away from visible things and makes itself as beautiful as possible and becomes like the One; (the manner of preparation and adornment is known to those who practise it;) and seeing the One suddenly appearing in itself, for there is nothing between, nor are they any longer two, but one; for you cannot distinguish between them, while the vision lasts; it is that union of which the union of earthly lovers, who wish to blend their being with each other, is a copy. The Soul is no longer conscious of the body, and cannot tell whether it is a man or a living being or anything real at all; for the contemplation of such things would seem unworthy, and it has no leisure for them; but when, after having sought the One, it finds itself in its presence, it goes to meet it and contemplates it instead of itself. What itself is when it gazes, it has no leisure to see. When in this state the Soul would exchange its present condition for nothing, no, not for the very heaven of heavens; for there is nothing better, nothing more blessed than this. For it can mount no higher; all other things are below it, however exalted they be. It is then that it judges rightly and knows that it has what it desired, and that there is nothing higher. For there is no deception there; where could one find anything truer than the True? What it says, that it is, and it speaks afterwards, and speaks in silence, and is happy, and is not deceived in its happiness. Its happiness is no titillation of the bodily senses; it is that the Soul has become again what it was formerly, when it was blessed. All the things which once pleased it, power, wealth, beauty, science, it declares that it despises; it could not say this if it had not met with something better than these. It fears no evil, while it is with the One, or even while it sees him; though all else perish around it, it is content, if it can only be with him; so happy is it.

The Soul is so exalted that it thinks lightly even of that spiritual intuition which it formerly treasured. For spiritual perception involves movement, and the Soul now does not wish to move. It does not call the object of its vision Spirit, although it has itself been transformed into Spirit before the vision and lifted up into the abode of Spirits. When the Soul arrives at the intuition of the One, it leaves the mode of spiritual perception. Even so a traveller, entering into a palace, admires at first the various beauties which adorn it; but when the Master appears, he alone is the object of attention. By continually contemplating the object before him, the spectator sees it no more. The vision is confounded with the object seen, and that which was before object becomes to him the state of seeing, and he forgets all else. The Spirit has two powers. By one of them it has a spiritual perception of what is within itself, the other is the receptive intuition by which it perceives what is above itself. The former is the vision of the thinking Spirit, the latter is the Spirit in love. For when the Spirit is inebriated with the nectar, it falls in love, in simple contentment and satisfaction; and it is better for it to be so intoxicated than to be too proud for such intoxication.

If you are perplexed because the One is none of those things which you know, apply yourself to them first, and look forth out of them; but so look, as not to direct your intellect to externals. For it does not lie in one place and not in another, but it is present everywhere to him who can touch it, and not to him who cannot. As in other matters one cannot think of two things at once, and must add nothing extraneous to the object of thought, if one wishes to identify oneself with it, so here we may be sure that it is impossible for one who has in his soul any extraneous image to conceive of the One while that image distracts his attention. Just as we said that Matter must be without qualities of its own, if it is to receive the forms of all things, so *a fortiori* must the Soul be formless if it is to receive the fullness and illumination of the First Principle. If so, the Soul must forsake all that is external, and turn itself wholly to that which is within; it will not allow itself to be distracted by anything external, but will ignore them all, as at first by not attending to them, so now last by not seeing them; it will not even know itself; and so it will come to the vision of the One and will be united with it; and then, after a sufficient converse with it, it will return and bring word, if it be possible, to others of its heavenly intercourse. Such probably was the converse which Minos was fabled to have had with Zeus, remembering which he made the laws which were the image of that converse, being inspired to be a lawgiver by the divine touch. Perhaps, however, a Soul which has seen much of the heavenly world may think politics unworthy of itself and may prefer to remain above. God, as Plato says, is not far from every one of us; he is present with all, though they know him not. Men flee away from him, or rather from themselves. They cannot grasp him from whom they have fled, nor when they have lost themselves can they find another, any more than a child who is mad and out of his mind can know his father. But he who has learnt to know himself will know also whence he is.

If a Soul has known itself throughout its course, it is aware that its natural motion has not been in a straight line (except during some deflection from the normal) but rather in a circle round a centre; and that this centre is itself in motion round that from which it proceeds. On this centre the Soul depends, and attaches itself thereto, as all Souls ought to do, but only the Souls of gods do so always. It is this that makes them gods. For a god is closely attached to this centre; those further from it are average men, and animals. Is then this centre of the Soul the object of our search? Or must we think of something else, some point at which all centres as it were coincide? We must remember that our "circles" and "centres" are only metaphors. The Soul is no "circle" like the geometrical figure; we call it a circle because the archetypal nature is in it and around it, and because it is derived from this first principle, and all the more because the Souls as wholes are separated from the body. But now, since part of us is held down by the body (as if a man were to have his feet under water), we touch the centre of all things with our own centre—that part which is not submerged—as the centres of the greatest circles coincide with the centre of the enveloping sphere, and then rest. If these circles were corporeal and not psychic, the coincidence of their centres would be spatial, and they would lie around a centre somewhere in space; but since the Souls belong to the spiritual world, and the One is above even

Spirit, we must consider that their contact is through other powers—those which connect subject and object in the world of Spirit, and further, that the perceiving Spirit is present in virtue of its likeness and identity, and unites with its like without hindrance. For bodies cannot have this close association with each other, but incorporeal things are not kept apart by bodies; they are separated from each other not by distance, but by unlikeness and difference. Where there is no unlikeness, they are united with each other. The One, which has no unlikeness, is always present; we are so only when we have no unlikeness. The One does not strive to encircle us, but we strive to encircle it. We always move round the One, but we do not always fix our gaze upon it: we are like a choir of singers who stand round the conductor, but do not always sing in time because their attention is diverted to some external object; when they look at the conductor they sing well and are really with him. So we always move round the One; if we did not, we should be dissolved and no longer exist; but we do not always look towards the One. When we do, we attain the end of our existence, and our repose, and we no longer sing out of tune, but form in very truth a divine chorus round the One.

In this choral dance the Soul sees the fountain of life and the fountain of Spirit, the source of Being, the cause of Good, the root of Soul. These do not flow out of the One in such a way as to diminish it; for we are not dealing with material quantities, else the products of the One would be perishable, whereas they are eternal, because their source remains not divided among them, but constant. Therefore the products too are permanent, as the light remains while the sun remains. For we are not cut off from our source nor separated from it, even though the bodily nature intervenes and draws us towards itself, but we breathe and maintain our being in our source, which does not first give itself and then withdraw, but is always supplying us, as long as it is what it is. But we are more truly alive when we turn towards it, and in this lies our well-being. To be far from it is isolation and diminution. In it our Soul rests, out of reach of evil; it has ascended to a region which is pure from all evil; there it has spiritual vision, and is exempt from passion and suffering; there it truly lives. For our present life, without God, is a mere shadow and mimicry of the true life. But life yonder is an activity of the Spirit, and by its peaceful activity it engenders gods also, through its contact with the One, and Beauty, and Righteousness, and Virtue. For these are the offspring of a Soul which is filled with God, and this is its beginning and end—its beginning because from this it had its origin, its end because the Good is there, and when it comes there it becomes what it was. For our life in this world is but a falling away, an exile, and a loss of the Soul's wings. The natural love which the Soul feels proves that the Good is there; this is why paintings and myths make Psyche the bride of Cupid. Because the Soul is different from God, and yet springs from him, she loves him of necessity; when she is yonder she has the heavenly love, when she is here below, the vulgar. For yonder dwells the heavenly Aphrodite, but here she is vulgarised and corrupted, and every Soul is Aphrodite. This is figured in the allegory of the birthday of Aphrodite, and Love who was born with her. Hence it is natural for the Soul to love God and to desire union with Him, as the daughter of a noble father feels a noble love. But when, descending to generation, the Soul, deceived by the false promises of a lover, exchanges its divine love for a mortal love, it is separated from its father and submits to indignities; but afterwards it is ashamed of these disorders and purifies itself and returns to its father and is happy. Let him who has not had this experience consider how blessed a thing it is in earthly love to obtain that which one most desires, although the objects of earthly loves are mortal and injurious and loves of shadows, which change and pass; since these are not the things which we truly love, nor are they our good, nor what we seek. But yonder is the true object of our love, which it is possible to grasp and to live with and truly to possess, since no envelope of flesh separates us from it. He who has seen it knows what I say, that the Soul then has another life, when it comes to God and having come possesses him, and knows, when in that state, that it is in the presence of the dispenser of the true life, and that it needs nothing further. On the contrary, it must put off all else, and stand in God alone, which can only be when we have pruned away all else that surrounds us. We must then hasten to depart hence, to detach ourselves as much as we can from the body to which we are unhappily bound, to endeavour to embrace God with all our being, and to leave no part of ourselves which is not in contact with Him. Then we can see Him and ourselves, as far as is permitted: we see ourselves glorified, full of spiritual light, or rather we see ourselves as pure, subtle, ethereal, light; we become divine, or rather we know ourselves to be divine. Then indeed is the flame of life kindled, that flame which, when we sink back to earth, sinks with us.

Why then does not the Soul abide yonder? Because it

has not yet wholly left its earthly abode. But the time will come when it will enjoy the vision without interruption, no longer troubled with the hindrances of the body. The part of the Soul which is troubled is not the part which sees, but the other part, when the part which sees is idle, though it ceases not from that knowledge which comes of demonstrations, conjectures, and the dialectic. But in the vision that which sees is not reason, but something greater than and prior to reason, something presupposed by reason, as is the object of vision. He who then sees himself, when he sees will see himself as a simple being, will be united to himself as such, will feel himself become such. We ought not even to say that he will *see,* but he will *be* that which he sees, if indeed it is possible any longer to distinguish seer and seen, and not boldly to affirm that the two are one. In this state the seer does not see or distinguish or imagine two things; he becomes another, he ceases to be himself and to belong to himself. He belongs to Him and is one with Him, like two concentric circles; they are one when they coincide, and two only when they are separated. It is only in this sense that the Soul is other [than God]. Therefore this vision is hard to describe. For how can one describe, as other than oneself, that which, when one saw it, seemed to be one with oneself?

This is no doubt why in the mysteries we are forbidden to reveal them to the uninitiated. That which is divine is ineffable, and cannot be shown to those who have not had the happiness to see it. Since in the vision there were not two things, but seer and seen were one (for the seeing was no seeing but a merging), if a man could preserve the memory of what he was when he was mingled with the Divine, he would have in himself an image of Him. For he was then one with Him, and retained no difference, either in relation to himself or to others. Nothing stirred within him, neither anger nor concupiscence nor even reason or spiritual perception or his own personality, if we may say so. Caught up in an ecstasy, tranquil and God-possessed, he enjoyed an imperturbable calm; shut up in his proper essence he inclined not to either side, he turned not even to himself; he was in a state of perfect stability; he had become stability itself. The Soul then occupies itself no more even with beautiful things; it is exalted above the Beautiful, it passes the choir of the virtues. Even as when a man who enters the sanctuary of a temple leaves behind him the statues in the temple, they are the objects which he will see first when he

leaves the sanctuary after he has seen what is within, and
entered there into communion, not with statues and images,
but with the Deity itself. Perhaps we ought not to speak of
*vision*; it is rather another mode of seeing, an ecstasy and
simplification, an abandonment of oneself, a desire for immediate contact, a stability, a deep intention to unite oneself
with what is to be seen in the sanctuary. He who seeks to see
[God] in any other manner, will find nothing. These are
but figures, by which the wise prophets indicate how we may
see this God. But the wise priest, understanding the symbol,
may enter the sanctuary and make the vision real. If he has
not yet got so far, he at least conceives that what is within
the sanctuary is something invisible to mortal eyes, that it is
the Source and Principle of all; he knows that it is by the
first Principle that we see the first Principle, and unites
himself with it and perceives like by like, leaving behind
nothing that is Divine, so far as the Soul can reach. And before the vision, the Soul desires that which remains for it to
see. But for him who has ascended above all things, that
which remains to see is that which is before all things. For
the nature of the Soul will never pass to absolute not-being:
when it falls, it will come to evil, and so to not-being, but not
to absolute not-being. But if it moves in the opposite direc-
tion, it will arrive not at something else, but at itself, and
so, being in nothing else, it is only in itself alone; but that
which is in itself alone and not in the world of Being
is in the Absolute. It ceases to be Being; it is above Being,
while in communion with the One. If then a man sees himself become one with the One, he has in himself a likeness
of the One, and if he passes out of himself, as an image to
its archetype, he has reached the end of his journey. And
when he comes down from his vision, he can again awaken
the virtue that is in him, and seeing himself fitly adorned in
every part he can again mount upward through virtue to
Spirit, and through wisdom to the One itself. Such is the life
of gods and of godlike and blessed men; a liberation from all
earthly bonds, a life that takes no pleasure in earthly things,
a flight of the alone to the Alone.

## Commentary

Although the entire selection has to do with the mystical
vision, the most important description of it comes in the last
two paragraphs. From these two paragraphs, therefore, I
will pick out a few sentences for special comment.

1. "But in the vision that which sees is not reason, but

something greater than and prior to reason, something presupposed by reason."

The discursive understanding, or reason, moves from point to point. But the mystical consciousness is one-pointed. Since it is the undivided unity, the pure oneness wherein there is no duality, it is impossible that discursive reason should operate here. We may call that part of us which sees the vision intuition if we like, and this is often done, although it really adds nothing to our knowledge except another word.

The sentence quoted tells us that this intuition is *prior* to reason and presupposed by it. Why is this? Because the unity of consciousness is presupposed by the multiplicity. The many would not be a many apart from its togetherness in the unity.

2. "We ought not even to say that he will *see*, but he will *be* that which he sees, if indeed it is possible any longer to distinguish seer and seen, and not boldly to affirm that the two are one."

In another translation the final clause "affirm that the two are one" is given as "affirm a simple unity." This brings out better one of the points involved. For the word "simple" means undivided and indivisible, so that the phrase becomes "an undivided unity" or an "undifferentiated unity." This rendering therefore emphasizes that the central characteristic of the experience in Plotinus is identical with the central characteristic of it everywhere else.

The passage in general says that words like "vision" and "seeing" are misleading because they imply a duality of subject and object which is transcended here in the simple unity. The same observation tends to apply to the phrase "mystical *experience*," although it is practically impossible to avoid it.

That in the mystical consciousness there is no duality of subject and object is often stated as a truth about all mysticism. Writers about Western theistic mysticism also say this. But here we have to pull them up sharp, and question their right to say this, for example, about Christian mysticism. For to say that there is no duality of subject and object in the mystical union with God is to say that there is, at the time of union, no distinction between the soul and God. This is true of the mysticism of the advaita Vedantism, and it is true of Plotinus. But by the orthodox Christian and Islamic theologians it is regarded as the heresy of pantheism.

It was of this, as we shall see, that Meister Eckhart was accused. We shall study this question in the next chapter. But in this chapter it is important to see on which side of the dividing line Plotinus stands. He stands here, as in so many other matters, with the dominant trend of Indian mysticism, and not with the West.

3. "Therefore this vision is hard to describe. For how can one describe, as other than oneself, that which, when one saw it, seemed to be one with oneself?"

This is an attempt not only to affirm but to give an explanation of the oft-asserted "ineffability" of the mystical consciousness. To "describe" something seems necessarily to involve a duality between one's self and what one describes. Whether this is the true solution of the problem of ineffability is another matter.

4. "Nothing stirred within him, neither anger nor concupiscence nor even reason or spiritual perception or his own personality. . . ."

In the undifferentiated unity nothing moves because there is nothing to move. Movement is only possible where there is a multiplicity, since movement or activity involves change of one item in relation to another. Hence the calmness and silence and peace of the vision. The sentence also notes the absence of "his own personality"—dissolution of individuality.

5. "Such is the life of gods and of godlike and blessed men; a liberation from all earthly bonds, a life that takes no pleasure in earthly things, a flight of the alone to the Alone."

The last phrase is famous. The passage stresses the blessedness which the mystical consciousness always brings, but Plotinus lays himself open to some criticism for speaking of it as "a liberation from all earthly bonds, a life that takes no pleasure in earthly things." This is in strong contrast both with Zen and with the best Christian mysticism. The highest development of the mystical consciousness will not represent it as a "flight," but rather as requiring further involvement in "earthly things." For the Zen Buddhist Nirvana is to be found *in* samsara, not apart from it. And the Christian mystic, at his best, feels powerfully the urge to pour out in love to mankind the riches which he has received in the divine union.

# -6-

# Christian Mysticism

(1) *Sources of Christian Mysticism.* At what point in history, and with whom, does Christian mysticism begin? Buddhist mysticism begins with the founder of the religion. The greatest of all Buddhist mystics was the Buddha himself. The Hindu religion cannot be traced back to any one founder, but Hindu mysticism goes back into the mists of past time. One might expect that in Christianity, too, mysticism would be an original element. One might expect that the founder of Christianity would stand to Christian mysticism in the same relation as the Buddha stood to Buddhist mysticism. But this would be a complete mistake.

We have now definitely crossed the line between East and West. We are in the area of the three great Western religions, Christianity, Judaism, and Islam. These three are Semitic in origin and "theistic" in character. They are not primarily mystical religions at all. Hinduism (at least in its higher developments) and Buddhism are essentially mystical. They are rooted in mysticism, have mysticism as their core, and would not be what they are without it. But mysticism is no part of the essence of the Western religions (unless in a peculiar sense in which it is sometimes said that all religion is mystical). It did not belong to them in their original forms but later became associated with them as a result of historical circumstances.

There is no good reason for supposing that Jesus was a mystic in the sense in which we are using the word in this book—i.e., in the sense of a person who possessed the mystical consciousness as we have described it. In the synoptic gospels there is no hint of it. When we come to the Gospel of St. John we find that certain mystical-sounding phrases are put into the mouth of the Johannine Jesus. He speaks of union with God. He says "I and my Father are one"; "He who has seen me has seen the Father"; "I am in the Father and the Father in me." But in view of the absence of any of these sayings in the synoptic gospels, we have good reason to believe that the historical Jesus did not utter them, and that they were the work of the author of the fourth gospel. Are we, then, to think that the author of that gospel was a mystic, so that we may think of Christian mysticism as originating with him? In my opinion we cannot make this inference. All we can say is that he was acquainted with some of the common phrases used by mystics and was sympathetic with mysticism. It is quite possible that he himself had mystical experience, but his use of these phrases does not constitute sufficient evidence of it. We do not have here, as we do in the Upanishads, in Plotinus, in Eckhart, in St. Teresa, any sort of specific and detailed descriptions of the mystical consciousness. Christian mysticism, then, does not begin either with Jesus or with the author of the fourth gospel.

Is there any better case for believing that it originates with St. Paul? The famous vision and voices on the road to Damascus do not constitute a mystical experience—though no doubt we should be right to classify them as being in some sense a religious experience—because, as we have seen, visions and voices involve sensuous imagery, whereas the mystical consciousness is non-sensuous. There are, however, one or two passages in St. Paul's writings which seem to have something of the genuine mystic ring and render it probable that he had some degree of mystical experience. Of these the most famous is the statement, "I live, yet not I but Christ liveth in me." To speak of the God, or the Christ, who is within my own mind or self might well be a phrase importing the introvertive mystical consciousness. On the other hand it might not. It is too brief and ambiguous and is left without further elaboration or explanation. One cannot say with any certainty what it means. And even if St. Paul was himself a mystic, there was a long gap between him and the later mystics that is not bridged by any continuity of mystical tradition.

It is easier to say who were not the originators of Christian mysticism than who were. The reader who wishes to pursue further the problem of historical origins as it presents itself in this field is advised to read the appendix to

Evelyn Underhill's *Mysticism*; but should bear in mind her strongly Christian bias. That bias causes her, for example, to underrate the greatness of Plotinus while admitting his enormous influence in Christianity. She thinks that "Neo-Platonism as a whole was a confused semireligious philosophy, containing many inconsistent elements." She also asserts that "St. Paul and the author of the fourth gospel are obvious [sic!] instances of mystics of the first rank." Her contributions to the whole subject are, however, immense.

(2) *The Great Divide: East and West.* If we take the five great world religions to be Hinduism, Buddhism, Judaism, Christianity, and Islam, it is important to realize that, as already briefly suggested, they fall into two groups with a well-marked division between them. One group consists of Hinduism and Buddhism, which are distinctively Eastern religions. The other group comprises Christianity, Islam, and Judaism, which are the three Western theistic religions. Hinduism is pantheistic. Buddhism can hardly be called pantheistic, but it sprang out of Hinduism and is in all respects a characteristically Indian religion. The contrast we have to emphasize is between the characteristic pantheism of India and the theism of the three Western religions.

We need not worry about the precise dictionary meanings of "pantheism" and "theism," or whether some philosophers or theologians will find fault with our usage of the words. I pre-empt the words here to stand for the two types of thought which I have to characterize and for which I require convenient labels. By pantheism I mean any theory—such as that of Plotinus or the Vedanta—in which God or the Absolute transforms himself or itself into the world, so that God and the world are of the same substance, though the form is different. By theism I mean any theory which regards God and the world as two distinct substances, each having its own independent existence, although the origin of the world may have been in an act of creation by God. In pantheism the world is a manifestation of God. In theism the world is the creation of God. Theism also believes in a personal God, whereas in pantheistic systems the idea of God tends more toward being an impersonal Absolute. The One of the Upanishads is indeed the Universal Self and is pure consciousness. But this is not an individual Self, and can hardly be called a person. The One of Plotinus is not even a Universal Self and is not conscious.

It is desirable to characterize in a profounder way the idea of a personal God as found in the theistic religions. It seems to me that it is a necessary part of the idea of a personal God that there exist, or logically could exist, other persons who are not God, and that God is therefore *one among other persons*. This means that he is an individual and that there exist other individuals alongside of him—for instance, human beings. These other persons, being parts of the world, were no doubt created by God as the world was. But they nevertheless have their separate and independent existence, as does the world in general. I do not know whether the description of God as one among other persons would be accepted by the theologians of any of the three Western religions. Perhaps it would be distasteful to them. But I nevertheless think it is a correct description. This difference between the Eastern and the Western religions also means that for the religions of the West a human self can never be or become God, cannot be transformed into God, and that on the other hand God cannot be or become a human being —with the exception, in the case of Christianity, of the one unique person of Jesus Christ. With the other two theistic religions there is no exception. God never becomes, or is, man; and man never becomes, or is, God.

According to the theistic religions, there is a "great gulf" between God and man, Creator and creature. Nothing can ever abolish or pass over this gulf.

It follows that according to any form of orthodox Christianity—and the same will be true of Judaism and Islam —the soul which is in mystical union with God never is or becomes *identical* with God. The great gulf still remains even in the mystical consciousness. For any man to claim identity with the Divine Being—this is, according to the orthodox theologies of the Western religions, heresy or perhaps even blasphemy. This is why, when Meister Eckhart used such expressions as "my eye and God's eye are one and the same" and "God and I, we are one" he found himself accused of heresy by the church.

Thus the declaration of the Upanishads, "That art thou" —the assertion of the Vedantist that the individual Self is identical with Brahman and realizes this identity in the mystical consciousness—is entirely ruled out of court by the theistic religions. But the stock phrase of the Christian mystics is "union with God." This is what the Christian mystic aspires to and believes that he attains. But how can union with God be possible if the soul does not in that union become identical with God? What effect will this problem have on the development of Christian mysticism? It has had, in fact, two results.

First, it created a state of tension between the mystics and the ecclesiastical authorities of the Roman church. By its very nature mysticism seeks to go beyond all dualism and to rest only in an absolute unity. To the mystic it appears that there is within his mystical consciousness no division whatsoever. We can see this plainly enough in Hindu mysticism and in Plotinus. In the unitary consciousness, says the Mandukya Upanishad, all multiplicity has been completely obliterated. But a duality between the individual self and the One is a multiplicity. According to Plotinus, "seer and seen are one," and there is no division between the One and the soul of the mystic. There is no doubt that this is the essential declaration of the developed mystical consciousness as such everywhere, whether in the East or the West. It is part of the experience of the Christian mystic just as it is part of the experience of the Hindu mystic or of Plotinus. But the ecclesiastical authorities think of this as the heresy of pantheism and condemn it accordingly. Hence you find in Western mysticism in general, both in Christianity and in Islam, this tension between the mystics and the orthodox.

In Christianity the Roman church was so powerful that in general it succeeded in enforcing its will upon the mystics. An Eckhart may tend toward heretical language and get himself into trouble. But the vast majority of the great Catholic mystics were submissive and managed to give an interpretation of "union with God" which could be accommodated to strict orthodoxy. And even Eckhart in his defense defers to the Church and attempts to explain away his pantheism. These remarks are not intended to impute any dishonesty or insincerity to the Christian mystics. They were no doubt perfectly sincere in their submission to the Church and at all times wished to be faithful to it. They no doubt truly believed that union with God could be thought of as compatible with Church doctrine, and what we now have to see is how they sought to solve this problem.

This brings us to the second effect of the conception of the impassable gulf between Creator and creature on Christian mysticism. Those Christian mystics who were not by nature intellectuals, such as St. Teresa, simply by-passed the problem and gave it no attention. They could, no doubt, speak in one breath of union with God, and of the gulf between God and man, without perceiving any inconsistency or being aware of any problem. But there were others, more philosophically minded, who sought a solution.

One may perhaps approach their attempts at solution by pointing out that the word "union," as used in ordinary English, is highly ambiguous. This linguistic approach is not, of course, that of the mystics themselves. But a present-day philosopher may be pardoned if he finds it useful as a means of exposition. We speak of the "union" of two rivers, for instance of the Mississippi and the Missouri. After the union there are not two rivers but only one. And I think if we were to say that the two rivers become one identical river the expression would be allowed. Here then we interpret union as implying *identity*. But now consider what we mean when we speak of a trade union or a student union. The separate members of these unions do not, of course, become identical with one another. They remain separate individuals. Their union means that they are associated with one another for the carrying out of some common purpose or set of purposes, improving the pay and working conditions of the members of the trade union, or organizing sports, entertainments, and recreation in the student union. Union is here interpreted not in terms of *identity* but in terms of *similarity of purpose*. This gives us the clue to at least one Christian theory of the nature of mystical union, namely that put forward by St. John of the Cross. He writes of "that union and transformation of the soul in God which is only then accomplished when there subsists the *likeness* which only love begets. For this reason shall this union be called the *union of likeness* . . . which takes place when the two wills, the will of God and the will of the soul are conformed together neither desiring aught repugnant to the other." [1] In other words, mystical union means only total and perfect agreement between the will of man and the will of God. There can be no doubt that this dualism is not compatible with the essence of mysticism. But there can also be no doubt that St. John of the Cross sincerely believed that it is.

A slightly different interpretation of union with God was given by Jan van Ruysbroeck, the great Flemish mystic. He

[1] St. John of the Cross, *The Ascent of Mount Carmel*, translated by David Lewis. New York: Benziger Brothers, 1906, Book I, Chapter I.

insists, of course, on the duality of God and the soul. They always remain separate existences. But their union, he suggests, is like that of sunlight and air, or heat and the red-hot iron. The sunlight completely permeates and interpenetrates the air, yet air remains air and sunlight remains sunlight. Likewise in the red-hot iron the heat interpenetrates the iron. But heat does not become iron, nor iron heat.

(3) *The Affective Tone of Christian Mysticism.* Although the cognitive core of mystical experience, the undifferentiated unity, is basically the same all over the world, there are two factors which vary from culture to culture and give rise to the different cultural types of mysticism. These two variable factors are (a) the intellectual interpretation of the experience, and (b) the emotional tone with which it is accompanied. Of the former, which is the most striking and important, we have already seen examples. It accounts for the fundamental differences between Buddhist mysticism, Christian mysticism, and so on. It now becomes important to mention the second variable factor. As illustrating it we may quote some apt words which will be found in our selection from Suzuki's Zen Buddhism.[2] He there wrote of Buddhist satori: "It has no personal note in it as is observable in Christian mystic experiences. There is no reference whatever in Buddhist satori to such personal and frequently sexual feelings and relationships as are to be gleaned from these terms: flame of love, a wonderful love shed in the heart, embrace, the beloved, bride, bridegroom, Father, God, the Son of God, God's child, etc. We may say that all these terms are interpretations . . . and really have nothing to do with the experience itself." This is admirable, and only needs, in my opinion, to be modified in one way. Suzuki does not distinguish between intellectual interpretations in terms of a set of theological beliefs, such as God, Son of God, and emotional reactions such as those expressed in such expressions as "flaming love" and the like. No doubt the two are closely connected. The belief influences the emotion, and the emotion influences the belief. The *belief* that Christ died for us may doubtless induce the *emotion* of love in the breasts of Christians. But although the belief and the emotion may be causally connected, they should be distinguished. Although the experience of the Christian mystic and the Buddhist,

2 See p. 93, above.

Hindu, or Moslem mystic may be the same, variations of type are caused by both of these factors, the intellectual and the emotional.

The emotional reaction is different not only with different cultures but with different individuals in the same culture —a fact which Suzuki does not mention. For instance, although St. Teresa of Avila talks in extravagant terms about "burning love," "being drunken with love," and the like, we find nothing at all of all this in Meister Eckhart. The emotional tone of the mystic varies all the way from the calm serenity of Buddha or Eckhart to the hyperemotionalism of St. Teresa. Eckhart expressly rejects hyperemotionalism as a part of the mystical experience. He refers to "storms of emotion," and asserts that they belong to the physical part of our nature, and that the "summit of the soul," wherein the mystic union takes place, "towers high above them."

But though we may, with Eckhart and Suzuki, discount the references to love of the hysterically emotional or passionate kind, we must insist that the emphasis on love—in the sense of both a mutual love between God and man and of man's love toward his fellow man—is especially characteristic of Christian mysticism to such an extent that this alone is sufficient to distinguish it from all other mysticism. That which comes nearest to it, however, is the Buddhist. In both cases, at their best the love which they emphasize is of the serene kind, calm, without gush, without violence. In Buddhism the love of all beings is definitely considered a part of the enlightenment experience. Says the author of *The Awakening of Faith*: "The fourth significance [of Mind-Essence or Enlightenment] is an affirmation of compassionate helpfulness, for . . . it draws all alike into its all-embracing purity and unity and peacefulness, illuminating their minds with equal brightness so that all sentient beings have an equal right to Enlightenment, an equal chance to practice the ultimate principle of kindness." [3]

Buddhist love, it will be noticed, extends to all "sentient beings," which will include all animals. In one place the obligation to exercise love toward snakes is mentioned! There is no recognition of the extension of love and compassion to animals in the Christian gospel.

Buddhism lays especial emphasis on pity or compassion,

[3] Dwight Goddard, ed., *A Buddhist Bible*. New York: E. P. Dutton & Co., Inc., revised and enlarged edition, 1952, p. 368.

which is not quite the same as love, but is included in it. When an opponent of the Buddha abuses him because he enjoined the duty of returning good for evil, the Buddha is represented as "pitying his folly," not as being indignant at his wickedness.

It is, however, very noticeable that love toward God, and God's love for man, and the good man's love for his fellows, is emphasized in Christian mysticism as being an essential part of the experience of mystical union, in a way and to a degree which is beyond anything found in the mysticisms of other cultures. Christian mysticism is not the equal of either Hindu or Buddhist mysticism in the power of its speculative interpretation (except in the case of Eckhart), but is superior to all other mysticism in its moral earnestness and its insistence on the practical application of the principle of love on the plane of daily existence. And this is no doubt a result of the strong emotional reaction of love in the experience itself.

We now proceed to our selections.

## Dionysius the Areopagite

This name is a pseudonym. Some purists therefore insist on calling the bearer of it Dionysius the pseudo-Areopagite. In the Acts of the Apostles one Dionysius the Areopagite is mentioned as having been converted to Christianity by St. Paul on his visit to Athens. Hence the pseudonym used by our author is apparently intended to identify him as an associate of St. Paul. We do not know who he actually was or anything about him. But it is clear from internal evidence that his date is not earlier than the fifth century. His work shows the influence of Plotinus, but he differs from Plotinus in being a Christian. He was the author of the books entitled *The Divine Names* and *The Mystical Theology*, from which our selections are taken. It is quite evident that these books were based upon his own mystical experience so that he himself was a mystic—not a mere theologian or philosopher.

Dionysius is especially noteworthy for having emphasized what is called the *via negativa*—which is in essence simply the negative side of the mystical consciousness. We have seen how the mystical consciousness is essentially paradoxical, being both negative and positive at the same time. On the negative side it is Emptiness, the Void, Nothingness. On the positive side it is union with the Absolute, the One, or God; and it is also pure consciousness and a state of peaceful bliss. For the negative side the metaphor of darkness is commonly used, for the positive side the metaphor of light. We read, both in Henry Suso and in Dionysius, that the mystical union is a "dazzling obscurity." If the negative is conceived as a "via" or road to union—i.e., as a means to an end—then in that aspect it may be identified with the essence of the technique of all mystics, namely the emptying oneself of the positive content of consciousness, first sensation, then imagery, then thought, desire, etc.

The *via negativa*, being in fact no more than the negative side of the paradox, is of course implicit in all mysticism. It is implied in the famous utterance of the Upanishad that the Self is incomprehensible—that it is *not this, not that*. God is unknowable or incomprehensible. On the subjective side of the human spirit this signifies that he cannot be comprehended by the intellect, but—and this is the positive side—he can be reached in the mystical consciousness.

Dionysius carried to its extreme limit the principle that no predicates attach to God and therefore no words can be used of him. He speaks of God as "the Super-essential Darkness" and writes: "It is not number, or order, or greatness, or littleness, or equality, or inequality. . . . It is not immovable nor in motion, or at rest, and has no power, and is not power or light, and does not live, and is not life; nor is it personal essence, or eternity, or time; . . . nor is it One . . . nor is It Godhead or Goodness; nor does It belong to the category of non-existence or to that of existence." [4]

But Dionysius, being a Christian, and believing in the Christian God with his positive characterizations of existence, love, justice, righteousness, power, wisdom, etc., has somehow to reconcile this with the passage just quoted. He must somehow explain how we use these positive words of God. This is the aim of his book *The Divine Names*. The essence of his theory is that although God in himself is unknowable so that everything we say of him is, strictly speaking, false, yet we apply terms importing empirical attributes to God because he is the cause of the existence of those empirical characteristics in the world. We say that God exists because he is the cause of all existence. We call him good because he is the cause or source of all good things; powerful because he is the cause of all power; loving because though

4 See p. 137, below.

in himself he is not love or loving, yet all love flows from him as its original source.

I think it is clear that this theory will not do. Apart from the fact that it conceives God as only the source of good things and not of bad things (the problem of evil), it also refutes itself by applying to God as he is in himself such positive concepts as "cause" and "source." If to call God love or power means only that he is the cause of the love and power which exist in the world, so likewise to call him cause can only mean that he is the cause of the causality which exists in the world. This leads to an infinite regress. For in the phrase "cause of causality" God is called the cause. But this can only mean on Dionysius' theory that he is the cause of the cause of causality, and so *ad infinitum*.

Nevertheless this theory of Dionysius is both interesting and important because it is a prominent source of the theory, which is still to be found among theologians such as Rudolph Otto and many others, that the words we use of God are always metaphorical or symbolic only, and never literal. That theory, even in its most modern forms, still leaves unexplained the problem how, if no words positive or negative apply literally to God, we ever can meaningfully use any words at all. Dionysius seems to waver between the view that both positive and negative words are inapplicable to God and the view that positive words are inapplicable but negative words can apply. Some passages seem to imply one view, some the other. Neither view is tenable. The objection to the view that negative words apply though not positive ones is that there is no absolute distinction between positive and negative. We may call motion positive and rest—because it is the absence of motion—negative. But motion after all is the absence of rest, and rest is just as positive an experience as motion. Likewise darkness and silence, although they may be defined as absence of light and sound respectively, are nevertheless positive experiences. The objection to the view that neither positive nor negative words apply to God is that in that case we have no right to call God "unknowable" or to call him "God." If God were really completely unknowable in this sense then we could never be aware of Him at all, and hence could not be aware of his unknowability. Thus Dionysius bequeathed to posterity this still unsolved problem of the nature and functioning of religious language.

### Chapter 1. What Is the Divine Gloom? [5]

Trinity, which exceedeth all Being, Deity, and Goodness! Thou that instructeth Christians in Thy heavenly wisdom! Guide us to that topmost height of mystic lore which exceedeth light and more than exceedeth knowledge, where the simple, absolute, and unchangeable mysteries of heavenly Truth lie hidden in the dazzling obscurity of the secret Silence, outshining all brilliance with the intensity of their darkness, and surcharging our blinded intellects with the utterly impalpable and invisible fairness of glories which exceed all beauty! Such be my prayer; and thee, dear Timothy, I counsel that, in the earnest exercise of mystic contemplation, thou leave the senses and the activities of the intellect and all things that the senses or the intellect can perceive, and all things in this world of nothingness, or in that world of being, and that, thine understanding being laid to rest, thou strain (so far as thou mayest) towards an union with Him whom neither being nor understanding can contain. For, by the unceasing and absolute renunciation of thyself and all things, thou shalt in pureness cast all things aside, and be released from all, and so shalt be led upwards to the Ray of that divine Darkness which exceedeth all existence.

These things thou must not disclose to any of the uninitiated, by whom I mean those who cling to the objects of human thought, and imagine there is no super-essential reality beyond, and fancy they know by human understanding Him that has made Darkness His secret place. And, if the Divine Initiation is beyond such men as these, what can be said of others yet more incapable thereof, who describe the Transcendent Cause of all things by qualities drawn from the lowest order of being, while they deny that it is in any way superior to the various ungodly delusions which they fondly invent in ignorance of this truth? That while it possesses all the positive attributes of the universe (being the universal Cause), yet in a stricter sense It does not

5 *Dionysius the Areopagite on the Divine Names and the Mystical Theology*, translated by C. E. Rolt. London: Society for Promoting Christian Knowledge, 1940; New York: The Macmillan Company, 1957, pp. 191-94.

possess them, since It transcends them all, wherefore there is no contradiction between affirming and denying that It has them inasmuch as It precedes and surpasses all deprivation, being beyond all positive and negative distinctions?

Such at least is the teaching of the blessed Bartholomew. For he says that the subject-matter of the Divine Science is vast and yet minute, and that the Gospel combines in itself both width and straitness. Methinks he has shown by these his words how marvellously he has understood that the Good Cause of all things is eloquent yet speaks few words, or rather none; possessing neither speech nor understanding because it exceedeth all things in a super-essential manner, and is revealed in Its naked truth to those alone who pass right through the opposition of fair and foul, and pass beyond the topmost altitudes of the holy ascent and leave behind them all divine enlightenment and voices and heavenly utterances and plunge into the Darkness where truly dwells, as saith the Scripture, that One Which is beyond all things. For not without reason is the blessed Moses bidden first to undergo purification himself and then to separate himself from those who have not undergone it; and after all purification hears the many-voiced trumpets and sees many lights flash forth with pure and diverse-streaming rays, and then stands separate from the multitudes and with the chosen priests presses forward to the topmost pinnacle of the Divine Ascent. Nevertheless he meets not with God Himself, yet he beholds—not Him indeed (for He is invisible)—but the place wherein He dwells. And this I take to signify that the divinest and the highest of the things perceived by the eyes of the body or the mind are but the symbolic language of things subordinate to Him who Himself transcendeth them all. Through these things His incomprehensible presence is shown walking upon those heights of His holy places which are perceived by the mind; and then It breaks forth, even from the things that are beheld and from those that behold them, and plunges the true initiate unto the Darkness of Unknowing wherein he renounces all the apprehensions of his understanding and is enwrapped in that which is wholly intangible and invisible, belonging wholly to Him that is beyond all things and to none else (whether himself or another), and being through the passive stillness of all his reasoning powers united by his highest faculty to Him that is wholly Unknowable, of whom thus by a rejection of all knowledge he possesses a knowledge that exceeds his understanding.

## FROM Chapter 2[6]

Unto this Darkness which is beyond Light we pray that we may come, and may attain unto vision through the loss of sight and knowledge, and that in ceasing thus to see or to know we may learn to know that which is beyond all perception and understanding (for this emptying of our faculties is true sight and knowledge), and that we may offer Him that transcends all things the praises of a transcendent hymnody, which we shall do by denying or removing all things that are. . . . Now we must wholly distinguish this negative method from that of positive statements. . . . We strip off all qualities in order that we may attain a naked knowledge of that Unknowing which in all existent things is enwrapped by all objects of knowledge, and that we may begin to see that super-essential Darkness which is hidden by all the light that is in existent things.

## FROM Chapter 5[7]

Once more, ascending yet higher we maintain that It is not soul, or mind, or endowed with the faculty of imagination, conjecture, reason, or understanding; nor is It any act of reason or understanding; nor can It be described by the reason or perceived by the understanding, since It is not number, or order, or greatness, or littleness, or equality, or inequality, and since It is not immovable nor in motion, or at rest, and has no power, and is not power or light, and does not live, and is not life; nor is It personal essence, or eternity, or time; nor can It be grasped by the understanding, since It is not knowledge or truth; nor is It kingship or wisdom; nor is It one, nor is It unity, nor is It Godhead or Goodness; nor is It a Spirit, as we understand the term, since It is not Sonship or Fatherhood; nor is It any other thing such as we or any other being can have knowledge of; nor does It belong to the category of non-existence or to that of existence; nor do existent beings know It as it actually is, nor does It know them as they actually are; nor can the reason attain to It to name It or to know It; nor is It darkness, nor is It light, or error; or truth; nor can any affirma-

6 *Ibid.*, pp. 194-96.
7 *Ibid.*, pp. 200-1.

tion or negation apply to It; for while applying affirmations or negations to those orders of being that come next to It, we apply not unto It either affirmation or negation, inasmuch as It transcends all affirmation by being the perfect and unique Cause of all things, and transcends all negation by the pre-eminence of Its simple and absolute nature—free from every limitation and beyond them all.

FROM *The Divine Names*

## Chapter 1[8]

These mysteries we learn from the Divine Scriptures, and thou wilt find that in well-nigh all the utterances of the Sacred Writers the Divine Names refer in a Symbolical Revelation to Its beneficent Emanations. Wherefore, in almost all consideration of Divine things we see the Supreme Godhead celebrated with holy praises as One and an Unity, through the simplicity and unity of Its supernatural indivisibility, from whence (as from an unifying power) we attain to unity, and through the supernal conjunction of our diverse and separate qualities are knit together each into a Godlike Oneness, and all together into a mutual Godly union. And It is called the Trinity because Its supernatural fecundity is revealed in a Threefold Personality, wherefrom all Fatherhood in heaven and on earth exists and draws Its name. And It is called the Universal Cause since all things came into being through Its bounty, whence all being springs; and It is called Wise and Fair because all things which keep their own nature uncorrupted are full of all Divine harmony and holy Beauty. . . . And in all the other Divine enlightenments which the occult Tradition of our inspired teachers hath, by mystic Interpretation, accordant with the Scriptures, bestowed upon us, we also have been initiated: apprehending these things in the present life (according to our powers), through the sacred veils of that loving kindness which in the Scriptures and the Hierarchical Traditions, enwrappeth spiritual truths in terms drawn from the world of sense, and superessential truths in terms drawn from Being, clothing with shapes and forms things which are shapeless and formless, and by a variety of separable symbols, fashioning manifold attributes of the imageless and supernatural Simplicity.

8 *Ibid.*, pp. 56-58.

# Meister Eckhart

To pass directly from Dionysius to Meister Eckhart is to skip over some eight centuries in order to come at once to the golden age of Christian mysticism in the thirteenth and fourteenth centuries. We do this not because in the intervening period there were no great mystics to quote, but on the contrary because the history of Christian mysticism is so full of famous names that we are compelled to leave vast areas of it untouched. The total count of only the well-known Christian mystics, none of whom can be called unimportant, lies in the neighborhood of one hundred. Hence we cannot do more in this book than select a few of the most famous or interesting and neglect all the others.

Meister Eckhart was born in Germany about the year 1260. Early in life he entered the Dominican Order. He received rapid preferment and in due course became head of that order for the areas of Saxony and Bohemia. He died in 1328. Even in his lifetime he was recognized as a remarkable, powerful, and controversial figure. He was the most profoundly philosophical, original, and independent of all Christian mystics. His originality and independence got him into trouble. He was accused of an heretical tendency to pantheistic conceptions and was summoned to defend himself before the ecclesiastical authorities. He wrote a long and elaborate defense insisting on his faithfulness to the Church and contending that he never went outside the limits of orthodox doctrine. There are countless passages in his writings which make this view of him difficult to accept. Nevertheless there is no reason to suspect his sincerity and honesty. But he died before the issues came to trial. The Pope condemned him posthumously, declaring that Eckhart had been "deceived by the father of lies" into "sowing thorns and thistles among the faithful and even the simple folk." [9]

It is a remarkable and significant fact that two very able books have been written in recent years, one of which likens Eckhart's thought to that of the great Hindu philosopher Sankara, while the other likens it to Buddhist mysticism. Both books attempt to show, not mere general resemblances, but point-by-point comparisons in matters of detail. The

[9] *Meister Eckhart: A Modern Translation*, translated by R. B. Blakney. New York and London: Harper & Brothers, 1941, p. xxiv.

first is Rudolph Otto's *Mysticism, East and West*. The second is D. T. Suzuki's *Mysticism: Christian and Buddhist*. Eckhart was of course ignorant of both Hindu and Buddhist mysticism. The fact of these remarkable resemblances is indicative of important conclusions. First, they bear witness to the greatness, depth, and width of Eckhart's spirit, showing that it could not be confined within any narrow limits but belongs to the world rather than to any compartmentalized religion—though this remark is not intended to throw doubt on his emphatically Christian outlook. Secondly, since his thought, like that of Plotinus, has strong affinities with Indian mysticism, both Hindu and Buddhist, it is not surprising that it produced the uneasy feeling of the Roman church that he tended to wander beyond the confines of what we have called the Great Divide.

Eckhart has his own remarkable vocabulary, some phrases at least of which have to be learned before we can understand him. He uses, with variations, the phrase "the birth of Christ in the soul" to mean the mystical consciousness. It is not meant that the phrase was for Eckhart a mere set of words or label meaning nothing more than the mystical consciousness. We cannot just substitute one phrase for the other. For Eckhart makes plain by the use of this language that his interpretation is in terms of Christian belief and that he stands where he believed that St. Paul stood when he wrote, "I live, yet not I but Christ liveth in me." It is, however, the case that what he *interprets* as the birth of Christ in the soul is in fact the introvertive mystical consciousness. And he tells us further that "this noble birth" takes place in what he calls by a great variety of names such as the "core of the soul," "the essence of the soul," "the apex or summit of the soul," etc. Sometimes he labels it "the aristocrat." In that core of the soul, he says in one place, "is the central silence, the pure peace, and abode of the heavenly birth." [10]

If we are to understand what he means by the apex of the soul, the best way is to see how, according to him, we can reach it by turning inward upon ourselves. We reach it, in fact, by the now familiar process of emptying consciousness of all its empirical contents—i.e., of all sensations, images, and thought processes. To prove that this is Eckhart's view we will consult his own words: "If you are to experience

[10] *Ibid.*, p. 97.

this noble birth," he writes in one of his sermons,[11] "you must depart from all crowds. . . . The crowds are the agents of the soul and their activities: memory, understanding, and will, in all their diversifications. You must leave them all: sense perception, imagination, and all that you discover in self or intend to do." "Crowds" is the picturesque word he uses for what the Mandukya Upanishad calls "multiplicity." The getting rid of the "crowds" of sensations, images, memories, etc., means the same as what the Upanishad calls the "obliteration of all multiplicity" in the "unitary consciousness."

Eckhart notes the extreme difficulty of carrying out these instructions. "This birth," he says, "is impossible without a complete withdrawal of the senses . . . and great force is required to repress all the agents of the soul and cause them to cease functioning. It takes much strength to gather them all in, and without that strength it cannot be done." [12]

If we empty the soul of all empirical contents, then, and only then, do we succeed in reaching inward in ourselves to the "apex of the soul" and to the "birth of Christ" which takes place in it. This makes it quite evident that what he means by the apex of the soul is nothing but what we have called the pure self, the pure unity of the ego when emptied of all multiplicity. It is identical with the self of the Upanishads and with the Mind-Essence of the Buddhist book *The Awakening of Faith*. In the Upanishads the individual pure self thus reached is identical with Brahman, or the Universal Self. In the same way, to reach back into the core of the soul means, for Eckhart, to attain union with God.

We have also in Eckhart the same recognition that the pure self, the core of the soul, is an empty unity, as we find everywhere else in the mystical tradition. This is the negative divine and the goal of the *via negativa*. God also, or rather the Godhead, is this Emptiness. As usual, Eckhart has his own vocabulary. As Buddhism speaks of the Emptiness, the Void (sūnyatā), Eckhart, with his liking for metaphors which are at once vivid and odd, uses of it such phrases as the "desert," the "barren wilderness," the "waste." He speaks also of the "barren Godhead" meaning that the Godhead is this Emptiness.

Since Eckhart, like Dionysius, thus emphasized the nega-

11 *Ibid.*, p. 118.
12 *Ibid.*, p. 109.

tive divine, he also, like Dionysius, has on his hands the problem of explaining the positive side of the paradox; in other words, he must show how we can speak of the Christian God as having personality, love, power, righteousness, creativity, and so on. He does not adopt the attempted solution of Dionysius but gives a most remarkable one of his own. He interprets the matter in terms of the Christian doctrine of the Trinity. Though there are three Persons, yet there is also an absolute unity. Eckhart separates the oneness from the threeness. He identifies the negative side of God with the unity, the positive side with the three persons. The unity he calls the Godhead and the three Persons God. The Godhead is the pure unity considered as not yet differentiated into the three Persons. The Godhead, being undifferentiated, is empty, void, dark, inert, and motionless. There is "nothing going on in it," to use his own language. It is the barren wilderness. And as in the Upanishads the pure unity of the self, being beyond all multiplicity, the Atman, is identical with Brahman, so for Eckhart the soul in the mystical consciousness ("this noble birth") is identical with the Godhead. "In this way," he says, "the soul enters into the Unity of the Holy Trinity, but it may become even more blessed by going further, to the barren Godhead, of which the Trinity is a revelation." [13]

In the whole of mystical literature this is perhaps the most remarkable example of how the pure experience of the undifferentiated unity, which is world-wide, can be locally interpreted in terms of a particular culture and the special doctrines of a particular religious creed.

Eckhart wrote a number of books, but his most pregnant work is to be found in his sermons, which were collected and edited and given titles after his death. All the following selections are from his sermons. I have used Dr. R. B. Blakney's translation, and the numbers given are the numbers of the sermons as printed in his version. I shall briefly introduce the three longer selections with a summary of their main points.

FROM *Sermon 1* [14]

[*Editor's introduction.* The question discussed in this selection is: Where, or in what part of the soul, does the mystical

---

[13] See p. 156, below.
[14] Blakney, *op. cit.*, pp. 95-98.

union with God or the Godhead take place? "This birth" takes place in the core or essence or apex of the soul, which is pure unity without multiplicity, the central silence "there where no creature may enter or any idea." "Idea" here presumably stands for "thought" or "image" or both; "creature" will cover all sensations and sensory existences. "There the soul neither thinks nor acts." For actions, thinking, remembering, understanding, willing, etc., are done by the soul's "agents" and not by the pure unity which is the soul itself. By "agents" Eckhart means what later came to be called "faculties," such as understanding, memory, imagination, etc. In Eckhart's psychology the soul itself, the pure unity, does not act. It acts by means of its "agents"—the imagination imagines, the understanding thinks, and so on. The soul itself, being the undifferentiated unity, from which the multiplicity of its ideas, thoughts, sensations, volitions, etc., have been excluded, is indistinguishable from the undifferentiated unity of the Godhead.]

"For while all things were wrapped in peaceful silence and night was in the midst of its swift course . . ."

Because the same One, who is begotten and born of God the Father, without ceasing in eternity, is born today, within time, in human nature, we make a holiday [15] to celebrate it. St. Augustine says that this birth is always happening. And yet, if it does not occur in me, how could it help me? Everything depends on that.

We intend to discuss, therefore, how it does occur in us, or how it is made perfect in a good soul, for it is in a good soul that God the Father is speaking his eternal word. What I shall say applies to that perfect person who has turned to the way of God and continues in it, and not to the natural undisciplined person who is far from this birth and ignorant of it. This, then, is the saying of the wise man: "While all things were wrapped in peaceful silence . . . a secret word leaped down from heaven, out of the royal throne, to me." This sermon is to be on that word.

Three points are, then, noteworthy. The first is: where does God the Father speak his word in the soul, or where does this birth take place—or what part of the soul is susceptible to this act? It must be in the purest, noblest, and subtlest element the soul can provide. Truly, if God could

[15] Christmas.

give the soul anything rarer out of his omnipotence, and if the soul could have received into its nature anything nobler from him, he must have awaited its coming to be born. Therefore the soul in which this birth is to happen must have purity and nobility of life, and be unitary and self-contained; it must not be dissipated in the multiplicity of things, through the five senses. What is more, it must continue to be self-contained and unitary and of the utmost purity, for that is its station and it disdains anything less.

The second part of this sermon will discuss what one should do about this act of God, this inward utterance, this birth: whether it is necessary to co-operate in some way to merit and obtain the birth. Should one construct an idea in his mind and thinking-process and discipline himself by meditating upon it, to the effect that God is wise, almighty, and eternal? Or should one withdraw from all thought and free his mind of words, acts, and ideas, doing nothing but being always receptive to God and allowing him to act? How shall one best serve the eternal birth?

The third part [of this sermon will discuss] the profitableness of this birth and how great it is.

In the first place, please note that I shall support what I have to say by citations from nature, which you may check for yourselves. Even though I believe more in the Scriptures than I do in myself, I shall follow [this policy] because you will get more out of arguments based on evidence.

Let us take first the text: "Out of the silence, a secret word was spoken to me." Ah, Sir!—what is this silence and where is that word to be spoken? We shall say, as I have heretofore, [it is spoken] in the purest element of the soul, in the soul's most exalted place, in the core, yes, in the essence of the soul. The central silence is there, where no creature may enter, nor any idea, and there the soul neither thinks nor acts, nor entertains any idea, either of itself or of anything else.

Whatever the soul does, it does through agents. It understands by means of intelligence. If it remembers, it does so by means of memory. If it is to love, the will must be used and thus it acts always through agents and not within its own essence. Its results are achieved through an intermediary. The power of sight can be effectuated only through the eyes, for otherwise the soul has no means of vision. It is the same with the other senses. They are effectuated through intermediaries.

In Being, however, there is no action and, therefore, there is none in the soul's essence. The soul's agents, by which it acts, are derived from the core of the soul. In that core is the central silence, the pure peace, and abode of the heavenly birth, the place for this event: this utterance of God's word. By nature the core of the soul is sensitive to nothing but the divine Being, unmediated. Here God enters the soul with all he has and not in part. He enters the soul through its core and nothing may touch that core except God himself. No creature enters it, for creatures must stay outside in the soul's agents, from whence the soul receives ideas, behind which it has withdrawn as if to take shelter.

When the agents of the soul contact creatures, they take and make ideas and likenesses of them and bear them back again into the self. It is by means of these ideas that the soul knows about external creatures. Creatures cannot approach the soul except in this way and the soul cannot get at creatures, except, on its own initiative, it first conceive ideas of them. Thus the soul gets at things by means of ideas and the idea is an entity created by the soul's agents. Be it a stone, or a rose, or a person, or whatever it is that is to be known, first an idea is taken and then absorbed, and in this way the soul connects with the phenomenal world.

But an idea, so received, necessarily comes in from outside, through the senses. Thus the soul knows about everything but itself. There is an authority who says that the soul can neither conceive nor admit any idea of itself. Thus it knows about everything else but has no self-knowledge, for ideas always enter through the senses and therefore the soul cannot get an idea of itself. Of nothing does the soul know so little as it knows of itself, for lack of means. And that indicates that within itself the soul is free, innocent of all instrumentalities and ideas, and that is why God can unite with it, he, too, being pure and without idea or likeness.

Whatever skill a master teacher may have, concede that skill to God, multiplied beyond measure. The wiser and more skillful a teacher is, the more simply, and with less artifice, he achieves his ends. Man requires many tools to do his visible work and, before he can finish it as he has conceived it, much preparation is required. It is the function and craft of the moon and sun to give light and they do it swiftly. When they emit their rays, all the ends of the world are filled with light in a moment. Higher than these are the angels who work with fewer instruments and also with fewer ideas. The highest seraph has only one. He comprehends as unity all that his inferiors see as manifold. But God needs no idea at all, nor has he any. He acts in the soul without instrument, idea or likeness. He acts in the core of the soul, which no idea ever penetrated—but he alone—his own essence. No creature can do this.

How does God beget his Son in the soul? As a creature might, with ideas and likenesses? Not at all! He begets him in the soul just as he does in eternity—and not otherwise. Well, then, how? Let us see.

God has perfect insight into himself and knows himself up and down, through and through, not by ideas, but of himself. God begets his Son through the true unity of the divine nature. See! This is the way: he begets his Son in the core of the soul and is made One with it. There is no other way. If an idea were interposed, there could be no true unity. Man's whole blessedness lies in that unity.

Now you might say: "Naturally! But there is nothing to the soul but ideas." No! Not at all! If that were so, the soul could never be blessed, for even God cannot make a creature in which a perfect blessing is found. Otherwise, God himself would not be the highest blessing, or the best of ends, as it is his nature and will to be—the beginning and the end of everything. A blessing is not a creature nor is it perfection, for perfection [that is, in all virtues] is the consequence of the perfecting of life, and for that you must get into the essence, the core of the soul, so that God's undifferentiated essence may reach you there, without the interposition of any idea. No idea represents or signifies itself. It always points to something else, of which it is the symbol. And since man has no ideas, except those abstracted from external things through the senses, he cannot be blessed by an idea. . . .

FROM *Sermon 4*[16]

[*Editor's introduction.* We cannot reach union with God by any intellectual process of thinking, for example by meditating on his wisdom, goodness, mercy, and so on. For thoughts, although they may be good and even divine, come *via* the senses from outside, whereas union comes from within, from the God within the soul. The mind must be empty and dark "in that darkness of unself-consciousness," or like a desert, alienated from self and all multiplicity, a "state of pure nothingness."]

WE READ in the gospel that when our Lord was twelve years old he went to the temple at Jerusalem with Mary and Joseph

[16] Blakney, *op. cit.,* pp. 118-21

and that, when they left, Jesus stayed behind in the temple without their knowledge. When they got home and missed him, they looked for him among acquaintances and strangers and relatives. They looked for him in the crowds and still they could not find him. Furthermore, they had lost him among the [temple] crowds and had to go back to where they came from. When they got back to their starting point, they found him.

Thus it is true that, if you are to experience this noble birth, you must depart from all crowds and go back to the starting point, the core [of the soul] out of which you came. The crowds are the agents of the soul and their activities: memory, understanding, and will, in all their diversifications. You must leave them all: sense perception, imagination, and all that you discover in self or intend to do. After that, you may experience this birth—but otherwise not—believe me! He was not found among friends, nor relatives, nor among acquaintances. No. He is lost among these altogether.

Thence we have a question to ask: Is it possible for man to experience this birth through certain things which, although they are divine, yet they come into the man through the senses from without? I refer to certain ideas of God, such as, for example, that God is good, wise, merciful, or whatever— ideas that are creatures of the reason, and yet divine. Can a man have the experience [of the divine birth] by means of these? No! Truly no. Even though [these ideas] are all good and divine, still he gets them all through his senses from without. If the divine birth is to shine with reality and purity, it must come flooding up and out of man from God within him, while all man's own efforts are suspended and all the soul's agents are at God's disposal.

This work [birth], when it is perfect, will be due solely to God's action while you have been passive. If you really forsake your own knowledge and will, then surely and gladly God will enter with his knowledge shining clearly. Where God achieves self-consciousness, your own knowledge is of no use, nor has it standing. Do not imagine that your own intelligence may rise to it, so that you may know God. Indeed, when God divinely enlightens you, no natural light is required to bring that about. This [natural light] must in fact be completely extinguished before God will shine in with his light, bringing back with him all that you have forsaken and a thousand times more, together with a new form to contain it all.

We have a parable for this in the gospel. When our Lord had held friendly conversation with the heathen woman at the well, she left her jug and ran to the city to tell the people that the true Messiah had come. The people, not believing her report, went out to see for themselves. Then they said to her: "Now we believe, not because of thy saying: for we have seen him ourselves." Thus it is true that you cannot know God by means of any creature science nor by means of your own wisdom. If you are to know God divinely, your own knowledge must become as pure ignorance, in which you forget yourself and every other creature.

But perhaps you will say: "Alas, sir, what is the point of my mind existing if it is to be quite empty and without function? Is it best for me to screw up my courage to this unknown knowledge which cannot really be anything at all? For if I know anything in any way, I shall not be ignorant, nor would I be either empty or innocent. Is it my place to be in darkness?"

Yes, truly. You could do not better than to go where it is dark, that is, unconsciousness.

"But, sir, must everything go and is there no turning back?"

Certainly not. By rights, there is no return.

"Then what is the darkness? What do you mean by it? What is its name?"

It has no name other than "potential sensitivity" and it neither lacks being nor does it want to be. It is that possible [degree of] sensitivity through which you may be made perfect. That is why there is no way back out of it. And yet, if you do return, it will not be for the sake of truth but rather on account of the world, the flesh, and the devil. If you persist in abandoning it, you necessarily fall [a victim to spiritual] malady and you may even persist so long that for you the fall will be eternal. Thus there can be no turning back but only pressing on to the attainment and achievement of this potentiality. There is no rest [in the process] short of complete fulfillment of Being. Just as matter can never rest until it is made complete by form, which represents its potential Being, so there is no rest for the mind until it has attained all that is possible to it.

On this point, a heathen master says: "Nature has nothing swifter than the heavens, which outrun everything else in their course." But surely the mind of man, in its course, outstrips them all. Provided it retains its active powers and keeps itself free from defilement and the disintegration of lesser and cruder things, it can outstrip high heaven and never slow down until it has reached the highest peak, and is fed and lodged by the highest good, which is God.

Therefore, how profitable it is to pursue this potentiality, until empty and innocent, a man is alone in that darkness of unself-consciousness, tracking and tracing [every clue] and never retracing his steps! Thus you may win that [something] which is everything, and the more you make yourself like a desert, unconscious of everything, the nearer you come to that estate. Of this desert, Hosea writes: "I will allure her, and bring her into the wilderness, and speak to her heart." The genuine word of eternity is spoken only in that eternity of the man who is himself a wilderness, alienated from self and all multiplicity. The prophet longed for this desolated alienation from self, for he said: "Oh that I had wings like a dove! for then would I fly away, and be at rest." Where may one find peace and rest? Really only where he rejects all creatures, being alienated from them and desolate. So David said: "I would choose rather to sit at the threshold of the house of my God than to dwell with great honor and wealth in the tents of wickedness."

But you may say: "Alas, sir, does a man have to be alienated from creatures and always desolate, inwardly as well as outwardly, the soul's agents together with their functions —must all be done away? That would put one in a hard position—if then God should leave him without his support, and add to his misery, taking away his light and neither speaking to him nor acting in him, as you now seem to mean. If a person is to be in such a state of pure nothingness, would it not be better for him to be doing something to make the darkness and alienation supportable? Should he not pray, or read, or hear a sermon or do something else that is good to help himself through it?"

No! You may be sure that perfect quiet and idleness is the best you can do. For, see, you cannot turn from this condition to do anything, without harming it. This is certain: you would like in part to prepare yourself and in part to be prepared by God, but it cannot be so, for however quickly you desire or think of preparing, God gets there first. But suppose that the preparation could be shared between you and God for the [divine] work of ingress—which is impossible —then you should know that God must act and pour in as soon as he finds that you are ready. Do not imagine that God is like a carpenter who works or not, just as he pleases, suiting his own convenience. It is not so with God, for when he finds you ready he must act, and pour into you, just as when the air is clear and pure the sun must pour into it and may not hold back. Surely, it would be a very great defect in God if he did not do a great work, and anoint you with great good, once he found you empty and innocent. . . .

FROM *Sermon 3*[17]

[*Editor's introduction.* To rid the mind of all sensations, images, thoughts, etc., requires great strength. Since the soul cannot thus put out its strength continuously, its union with God can only be intermittent. Moreover, if it were without interruption, practical action would be impossible. One would remain inactive in contemplation. But the active life of good deeds is better than the contemplative life, for in the active life one pours out the love he has received in contemplation. What we plant in the soil of contemplation we must reap in the harvest of action. The tree which does not bear fruit shall be hewn down.

It will be noticed that this sermon stresses the love and the strong sense of moral obligation which are the special notes of Christian mysticism. On the other hand, the emphasis on the intermittent character of the mystical consciousness seems to show that Eckhart, at any rate at the time he composed this sermon, was not acquainted with the unitive life or "deification" (see page 87) or the stage which in Buddhist mysticism insists that Nirvana is to be found in samsara and in the life of action (see page 87).]

"I MUST be about my Father's business!" This text is quite convenient to the discussion in which I shall now engage, dealing with the eternal birth, which occurred at one point of time, and which occurs every day in the innermost recess of the soul—a recess to which there is no avenue of approach. To know this birth at the core of the soul it is necessary above all that one should be about his Father's business.

What are the attributes of the Father? More power is attributed to him than to the other persons [of the Trinity]. Accordingly, no one can be sure of the experience of this birth, or even approach it, except by the expenditure of a great deal of energy. It is impossible without a complete withdrawal of the senses from the [world of] things and great force is required to repress all the agents of the soul and cause them to cease functioning. It takes much strength to gather them all in, and without that strength it cannot be done. So Christ said: "The kingdom of heaven suffereth violence and the violent take it by force."

Now it may be asked about this birth: does it occur con-

17 *Ibid.,* pp. 109-12.

stantly or intermittently—only when one applies himself with all his might to forgetting the [world of] things while yet knowing that he does so?

. . . when the mind goes to work in real earnest, then God is enlisted and he is both seen and felt. Still, the vision and experience of God is too much of a burden to the soul while it is in the body and so God withdraws intermittently, which is what [Christ] meant by saying: "A little while, and ye shall not see me: and again, a little while, and ye shall see me."

When our Lord took three disciples up the mountain and showed them the transfiguration of his body, made possible by his union with the Godhead—which shall come to us also in the resurrection of the body—St. Peter at once, when he saw it, wanted to stay there with it forever. In fact, to the extent that one finds anything good, he never wants to part with it. What one grows to know and comes to love and remember, his soul follows after. Knowing this, our Lord hides himself from time to time, for the soul is an elemental form of the body, so that what once gains its attention holds it. If the soul were to know the goodness of God, as it is and without interruption, it would never turn away and therefore would never direct the body.

Thus it was with Paul. If he had remained a hundred years at that point where he first knew God's goodness, even then he would not have wanted to return to his body and would have forgotten it altogether. Since, then, the divine goodness is alien to this life and incompatible with it, faithful God veils it or reveals it when he will, or when he knows it will be most useful and best for you that he do so. He is like a trustworthy physician. The withdrawal does not depend on you but upon him whose act it is. He reveals himself or not as he thinks best for you. It is up to him to show himself to you or not, according as he knows you are ready for him, for God is not a destroyer of nature but rather one who fulfills it, and he does this more and more as you are prepared.

You may, however, say: Alas, good man, if, to be prepared for God, one needs a heart freed from ideas and activities which are natural to the agents of the soul, how about those deeds of love which are wholly external, such as teaching and comforting those who are in need? Are these to be denied? Are we to forgo the deeds that occupied the disciples of our Lord so incessantly, the work that occupied St. Paul on behalf of the people, so much that he was like a father to them? Shall we be denied the [divine] goodness because we do virtuous deeds?

Let us see how this question is to be answered. The one [contemplation] is good. The other [deeds of virtue] is necessary. Mary was praised for having chosen the better part but Martha's life was useful, for she waited on Christ and his disciples. St. Thomas [Aquinas] says that the active life is better than the contemplative, for in it one pours out the love he has received in contemplation. Yet it is all one; for what we plant in the soil of contemplation we shall reap in the harvest of action and thus the purpose of contemplation is achieved. There is a transition from one to the other but it is all a single process with one end in view—that God is, after which it returns to what it was before. If I go from one end of this house to the other, it is true, I shall be moving and yet it will be all one motion. In all he does, man has only his one vision of God. One is based on the other and fiulfills it. In the unity [one beholds] in contemplation, God foreshadows [variety of] the harvest of action. In contemplation, you serve only yourself. In good works, you serve many people.

The whole life of Christ instructs us in this matter, and the lives of his saints as well, all of whom he sent out into the world to teach the Many the one truth. St. Paul said to Timothy: "Beloved, preach the word!" Did he mean the audible word that beats the air? Certainly not! He referred to the inborn, secret word that lies hidden in the soul. It was this that he preached, so that it might instruct the faculties of people and nourish them, and so that the behavior of men might proclaim it and so that one might be fully prepared to serve the need of his neighbor. It should be in the thoughts, the mind, and the will. It should shine through your deeds. As Christ said: "Let your light so shine before men!" He was thinking of people who care only for the contemplative life and not for the practice of virtue, who say that they have no need for this, for they have got beyond it. Christ did not include such people when he said: "Some seed fell in good ground and brought forth fruit an hundredfold." But he did refer to them when he spoke of "the tree that does not bear fruit and which shall be hewn down."

The above selections may be supplemented by a number of brief miscellaneous passages from other sermons to enable the reader to gain a fuller knowledge of the riches of Eckhart's mystical experience and thought.

### FROM *Sermon 6*[18]

Nothing hinders the soul's knowledge of God as much as time and space, for time and space are fragments, whereas God is one! And therefore, if the soul is to know God, it must know him above time and outside of space; for God is neither this nor that, as are these manifold things. God is One!

### Commentary

The mystical consciousness is timeless and spaceless, and therefore has penetrated beyond the space-time world.

### FROM *Sermon 12*[19]

These three dimensions represent three kinds of knowledge. The first is sensual: the eye sees things at a distance. The second is intellectual and is much higher in rank. The third represents [the function of] that aristocratic agent of the soul, which ranks so high that it communes with God, face to face, as he is. This agent has nothing in common with anything else. It is unconscious of yesterday or the day before, and of tomorrow and the day after, for in eternity there is no yesterday nor any tomorrow, but only Now, as it was a thousand years ago and as it will be a thousand years hence, and is at this moment, and as it will be after death. This agent reaches God in his closet, or as the Scripture says: in him, above him and through him. "In him"—that is, in the Father. "Above him"—that is, above the Son. "Through him"—that is, through the Holy Spirit.

### Commentary

The mystical consciousness, being beyond time, is in the eternal Now—where there is no past or future.

### FROM *Sermon 18*[20]

In eternity, the Father begets the Son in his own likeness. "The Word was with God and the Word was God." Like

[18] *Ibid.,* p. 131.
[19] *Ibid.,* p. 153.
[20] *Ibid.,* p. 181.

God, it had his nature. Furthermore, I say that God has begotten him in my soul. Not only is the soul like him and he like it, but he is in it, for the Father begets his Son in the soul exactly as he does in eternity and not otherwise. He must do so whether he will or not. The Father ceaselessly begets his Son and, what is more, he begets me as his Son—the self-same Son! Indeed, I assert that he begets me not only as his Son but as himself and himself as myself, begetting me in his own nature, his own being. At that inmost Source, I spring from the Holy Spirit and there is one life, one being, one action. All God's works are one and therefore He begets me as he does his Son and without distinction. My physical father is not my real Father, except for some small bit of his nature. For I am cut off from him. He may be dead and yet I alive. Therefore the heavenly Father is my true Father and I am his Son and have all that I have from him. I am identically his Son and no other, because the Father does only one kind of thing, making no distinctions. Thus it is that I am his only begotten Son.

St. Paul says: "We are always being transformed into God and changed." . . . If, therefore, I am changed into God and he makes me one with himself, then, by the living God, there is no distinction between us.

## Commentary

The mystical consciousness is described, in the language peculiar to Eckhart, as the Son being begotten by the Father in the soul. This begetting, of course, is timeless. The reader will easily see how such language as Eckhart uses in this extract gave offense to the orthodox and produced accusations of heresy. "I am identically his Son and no other. . . . I am his only begotten Son." "If . . . I am changed into God—then, by the living God, there is no distinction between us."

### FROM *Sermon 21*[21]

. . . we, too, should be baptized by the Holy Spirit and thus experience what it is to live beyond time in eternity. We do not get the Holy Spirit in temporal things. When a person turns from temporal things inwards, into himself, he becomes aware of a heavenly light. . . . The human spirit

[21] *Ibid.*, pp. 192-3.

can never be satisfied with what light it has but storms the firmament and scales the heavens to discover the spirit by which the heavens are driven in revolutions and by which everything on the earth grows and flourishes.

Even then, the human spirit takes no rest. It presses on further into the vortex, the source in which the spirit originates. There, the spirit, in knowing, has no use for number, for numbers are of use only within time, in this defective world. No one can strike his roots into eternity without being rid [of the concept] of number. The human spirit must go beyond all number-ideas, must break past and away from ideas of quantity and then he will be broken into by God. As God penetrates me I penetrate God in return. God leads the human spirit into the desert, into his own unity, in which he is pure One and self-creating.

### Commentary

There is no particular difficulty in this extract. We note that there can be no numbers in the pure One because there is no multiplicity. If the future life to which Christians look forward is to be an eternity of the mystical consciousness, mathematicians, apparently, will not be as happy in heaven as they deserve to be.

### FROM *Sermon 22*[22]

. . . we are not wholly blessed, even though we are looking at divine truth; for while we are still looking at it, we are not in it. As long as a man has an object under consideration, he is not one with it. Where there is nothing but One, nothing but One is to be seen. Therefore, no man can see God except he be blind, nor know him except through ignorance, nor understand him except through folly.

### Commentary

There is no distinction between subject and object in the experience. This alone really implies the denial of the dualistic theories of mystical union put forward by St. John of the Cross, Ruysbroeck, and others, and insisted on by the Church.

The last sentence reveals Eckhart's love of striking paradoxes.

[22] *Ibid.*, p. 200.

### FROM *Sermon 22*[23]

In this way the soul enters the unity of the Holy Trinity, but it may become even more blessed by going further, to the barren Godhead, of which the Trinity is a revelation. In this barren Godhead, activity has ceased and therefore the soul will be most perfect when it is thrown into the desert of the Godhead, where both activity and forms are no more, so that it is sunk and lost in this desert where its identity is destroyed. . . .

#### Commentary

This is a statement of Eckhart's interpretation of the un-differentiated unity in terms of the doctrine of the Trinity which was explained on page 142.

The last sentence also speaks of the dissolution of individuality, the soul's identity being "lost" in the desert, which is one of the universal characteristics of introvertive mystical experience. But in the next extract Eckhart uses language which modifies this and is more in line with orthodoxy.

### FROM *Another Sermon* [24]

In this exalted state she [the soul] has lost her proper self and is flowing full-flood into the unity of the divine nature. But what, you may ask, is the fate of this lost soul: does she find herself or not? . . . It seems to me that . . . though she sink all sinking in the oneness of divinity she never touches bottom. Wherefore God has left her one little point from which to get back to herself . . . and know herself as creature.

#### Commentary

In the previous extract Eckhart wrote as if the soul became wholly identical with God and its own identity were destroyed. But in the present extract he may be said to correct this by asserting that there remains "one little point" of creatureliness, i.e., of personal identity.

[23] *Ibid.*, pp. 200-1.
[24] Franz Pfeiffer, *Meister Eckhart*, translated by C. de B. Evans. London: J. M. Watkins, 1924, Vol. I, p. 282.

FROM *Sermon 23*[25]

The eye by which I see God is the same as the eye by which God sees me. My eye and God's eye are one and the same—one in seeing, one in knowing, and one in loving.

### Commentary

This is one of Eckhart's most famous paradoxical sayings. The actual meaning, if we are to take it as it stands, is the identity of God and the soul in the experience. But we may interpret it more interestingly in terms of Eckhart's special psychology. The apex of the soul is like an eye from which one may look in two directions, upward into the Godhead, and downward into the world. Compare with Eckhart's passage the following from the Buddhist treatise *The Awakening of Faith:* "The mind has two doors from which issue its activities. One leads to a realization of the mind's Pure Essence, the other leads to the differentiations of appearing and disappearing, of life and death" (see page 79).

FROM *Sermon 27*[26]

Thus creatures speak of God—but why do they not mention the Godhead? Because there is only unity in the Godhead and there is nothing to talk about. God acts. The Godhead does not. It has nothing to do and there is nothing going on in it. It never is on the lookout for something to do. The difference between God and the Godhead is the difference between action and nonaction.

### Commentary

From the point of view of the pulpit style of the present day this would be extremely unconventional language! But it is only a way of saying that the Godhead is emptiness. The last sentence draws attention to the point that the Godhead is the Divine in its aspect of the unchangeable, whereas the personal God is the aspect of creativity. Even in common religious conceptions there is the concealed paradox that God is said to be both "unchangeable" and yet the creator of

[25] Blakney, *op. cit.,* p. 206.
[26] *Ibid.,* p. 226.

the world. The unchangeable cannot act or create, since action and creation imply change. Eckhart implicitly separates the two contradictory aspects, putting one in the Godhead, the other in God.

# Jan van Ruysbroeck

Ruysbroeck, the great Flemish mystic, was born in 1293 at the village of Ruysbroeck not far from Brussels. In 1317 he took orders and was for many years a cathedral chaplain in Brussels. At the age of fifty, becoming dissatisfied with the formalism and externalism of cathedral worship, he left Brussels with two religious friends and sought refuge in the peaceful atmosphere of a hermitage situated in forest country near Brussels. There he was able to devote himself wholly to the inner life of the spirit. Gradually disciples gathered around him. He remained thirty-eight years in this place, living a life of worship and contemplation. But he held that the inner mystical life must be balanced by an outward life of charitable and helpful action to his fellow beings. This expressed itself in a search within the priory for "opportunities of service, especially those of the most menial kind," to use Miss Underhill's words, and in the work of initiating his many disciples into the life of the mystic. He died in 1381 at the age of eighty-eight.

In many respects Ruysbroeck duplicates both the thought and the language of Eckhart. But there are also great differences. It will help us in our study of Ruysbroeck if we begin by noting some of the main resemblances and differences. He speaks of the man who possesses the highest degree of the mystical consciousness sometimes as the "God-seeing man," sometimes as the "enlightened man." These are his own phrases. But he also makes use of Eckhart's metaphor of the birth of Christ in the soul. "For in this darkness," he says, "is born an incomprehensible light which is the Son of God." [27] On almost every other page he uses the almost universal metaphor of "darkness" for the unity in which all distinctions have disappeared. Another of his metaphors for the same concept is "nudity." He calls the timelessness of the mystical experience, as does Eckhart, "the eternal Now." As will be obvious from the title of his book *The Adornment*

---

[27] All the quotations in this introductory section will be found in the selections that follow, except where otherwise stated.

*of the Spiritual Marriage,* he uses the metaphor of human marital union for mystical union. And in the same strain the experience is spoken of as "the coming of our Bridegroom." However, he does not indulge, as some Christian and Islamic mystics have done, in passionate sex-language. It is true that he uses such phrases as "the fire of love." Yet their context is quiet and calm. And on the whole he belongs to the calm and serene type of mystic, and not to the wildly emotional kind. But his writing shows deep artistic and poetical feeling.

Ruysbroeck's style is far more polished than that of Eckhart. The latter's language is rough and angular and full of jolts and surprises, whereas Ruysbroeck's prose is smooth and beautiful. Part of the reason for this difference is that Ruysbroeck, great mystic as he undoubtedly was, had little of the originality and daring of Eckhart.

Sentences descriptive of his mystical experience are scattered throughout the pages of our selections. They leave no doubt that, as always with the introvertive mystic, the core of the experience is the undifferentiated unity. As already noted, the metaphor of darkness carries this meaning. So does the word "silence." "This is the dark silence in which all lovers lose themselves," he says, combining the two metaphors. The sentence means, of course, that the lovers of God who attain to divine union lose their individual identity in the undifferentiated unity. In line with the testimony of other introvertive mystics, Ruysbroeck teaches that to attain to mystical union it is necessary to empty the mind of sensations, images, and thoughts. It is especially characteristic of him to emphasize the absence of images in the mystical vision. He writes, "Such enlightened men are, with a free spirit, lifted above reason into a *bare and imageless vision* wherein lies the eternal indrawing summons of the Divine Unity; and with an *imageless and bare understanding* they . . . reach the summit of their spirits. There, their bare understanding is drenched through by the Eternal Brightness" (italics mine). The "bare understanding" means the understanding bared of all thoughts—that is, empty. Consequently he speaks of it as "the idle emptiness," and again as "the imageless void." We have become accustomed in these selections to the characterization of the experience as "void" and "empty." The adjective "idle" by which Ruysbroeck characterizes the emptiness refers, of course, to the absence of change, motion, activity, and means the same as Eckhart's statement that in the Godhead "there is nothing going on."

In another phrase which refers to the undifferentiated unity, but which clothes it in more poetic language, Ruysbroeck calls it the "wayless abyss." And he speaks of it as "onefold." "Onefold" means, of course, that there is no multiplicity in it. "Abyss" and "abysmal" for Ruysbroeck mean "infinite." Why is it called "wayless"? Because a way or a path is a track which divides a terrain in two parts. "Wayless" therefore means undivided, undifferentiated. Elsewhere he writes: "The God-seeing man . . . can always enter, naked and unencumbered with images, into the inmost part of his spirit . . . . If it [the spirit] observes itself, it finds a distinction and otherness between itself and God; but where it is burnt up [in the fire of love] it is undifferentiated and without distinction, and therefore it feels nothing but unity." [28]

There are two points to note about this remarkable passage. First, it is a direct statement that the experience is an undifferentiated unity. Thus Ruysbroeck makes it clear that his experience is aligned with that of Plotinus, the Mandukya Upanishad, the Buddhist enlightenment, etc. But the second point is that an element of doubt is injected into the matter by the somewhat ambiguous attitude of the passage on the question whether there is a duality between God and the soul or not. The question raised is that between orthodox Christian dualism and the pantheistic interpretations of Plotinus and the mystics of India and shared in part by Eckhart. Ruysbroeck was, during his life, criticized as teaching the heretical pantheistic view of union. There was, in fact, very little ground for this criticism, although passages can be found here and there which, seized upon by unfriendly readers and taken out of their context, could be made a basis for it. There is no doubt where, in the matter of *doctrine*, he stands. He takes the orthodox Christian view and makes this very clear by his likening of mystical union to the interpenetration of air by sunlight or of iron by heat. The air remains always a different existence from the sunlight, and the iron from the heat. But doctrine is a matter of the intellect; and even if Ruysbroeck's doctrine is based

---

[28] Jan van Ruysbroeck, *The Adornment of the Spiritual Marriage,* translated by C. A. Wynschenck Dom. London: J. M. Dent & Sons, Ltd., 1916; New York: E. P. Dutton & Co., Inc., 1916, pp. 185-86.

upon his experience, it still remains an intellectual interpretation to be distinguished from the experience itself. That Ruysbroeck should hold the dualistic doctrine is nothing to be wondered at. The overwhelming pressure of the Church and the theologians, most of whom, of course, have no mystical experience, is enough to account for this. What is of interest here, and may be thought to present a difficulty, is what he says about the experience itself.

If we were to accept Ruysbroeck's statement at its face value, we should have to hold that sometimes he experienced ("felt" is his own word) a duality between the soul and God and sometimes a pantheistic unity. The spirit feels the former "when it observes itself" and the latter when it is "burnt up in the fire of love." Ruysbroeck's interpretation of this curious situation seems to be that the dualism is the truth but that the spirit becomes deluded by love into not noticing the difference between itself and God. This is very difficult to swallow. It seems to depend on the metaphor of being burned up. It seems much more likely that Ruysbroeck is reading the doctrine of the Church into his experience. The true explanation would seem to be that when the experience is complete and perfect there is no distinction between subject and object, but that it is possible to stop at a stage at which the experiencer still takes notice of *himself* as an individual and has not achieved complete union. This is the only hypothesis which, accepting Ruysbroeck's introspective account of what he felt as truthful, is still consistent with the hypothesis that the introspective experience is basically the same in different cultures though it is interpreted differently. We can, of course, insist, as Professor R. C. Zaehner does,[29] that the actual experience of the Christian mystic is fundamentally different from and superior to that described in the Upanishads and elsewhere all over the world. But it seems to me that this is contrary to the whole spirit of mysticism and contrary to the weight of world-wide evidence. It is I think, nothing but an *ad hoc* hypothesis designed by Professor Zaehner to uphold the view that Christianity, and Roman Catholic Christianity at that, is the only one absolutely true and revealed religion, and that Christian mystical experience is superior to all others.

Ruysbroeck adopts the same interpretation of the undi-

[29] In *Mysticism Sacred and Profane.* Oxford: Clarendon Press, 1957.

vided unity in terms of the doctrine of the Trinity as Eckhart did. The mystical consciousness penetrates beyond the three persons of the Trinity and achieves union with the undifferentiated Unity beyond or behind the differentiation of the three persons. Enlightened men, he says in the last paragraph of our selections, "immerse themselves in a wayless abyss of fathomless beatitude, where the Trinity of the Divine Persons possess Their Nature in the essential Unity. . . . There all light is turned to darkness; there the three Persons give place to the Essential Unity, and abide without distinction in fruition of essential blessedness." He also uses Eckhart's term "Godhead" of this ultimate Unity.

Ruysbroeck makes a distinction between union "with means" and union "without means" which may tend to puzzle the reader. This might be of importance to a disciple of Ruysbroeck attempting to lead the life of the mystic. But from our point of view in this study—which is chiefly concerned with the nature of the highest degree of the mystical consciousness—it is of little or no importance, and the reader might well be advised to ignore it. But it may be said briefly that "means" refers to virtuous activity. One may attain a certain stage of the devotional life by means of active works of duty. But the final stage, which is what we are trying to study here, is "without means"—i.e., all activity has ceased. "Every creaturely work, and every exercise of virtue, must here cease," says Ruysbroeck.

FROM *The Adornment of the Spiritual Marriage*

### Chapter 1. *Showing the three ways by which one enters into the God-seeing life*[30]

THE inward lover of God, who possesses God in fruitive love, and himself in adhering and active love, and his whole life in virtues according to righteousness; through these three things, and by the mysterious revelation of God, such an inward man enters into the God-seeing life. Yea, the lover who is inward and righteous, him will it please God in His freedom to choose and to lift up into a superessential contemplation, in the Divine Light and according to the Divine Way. This contemplation sets us in purity and clearness above all

---

[30] Ruysbroeck, *op. cit.*, pp. 167-70.

our understanding, for it is a singular adornment and a heavenly crown, and besides the eternal reward of all virtues and of our whole life. And to it none can attain through knowledge and subtlety, neither through any exercise whatsoever. Only he with whom it pleases God to be united in His Spirit, and whom it pleases Him to enlighten by Himself, can see God, and no one else. The mysterious Divine Nature is eternally and actively beholding and loving according to the Persons, and has everlasting fruition in a mutual embrace of the Persons in the unity of the Essence. In this embrace, in the essential Unity of God, all inward spirits are one with God in the immersion of love; and are that same one which the Essence is in Itself, according to the mode of Eternal Bliss. And in this most high unity of the Divine Nature, the heavenly Father is origin and beginning of every work which is worked in heaven and on earth. And He says in the deep-sunken hiddenness of the spirit: BEHOLD, THE BRIDEGROOM COMETH; GO YE OUT TO MEET HIM.

These words we will now explain and set forth in their relation to that superessential contemplation which is the source of all holiness, and of all perfection of life to which one may attain. Few men can attain to this Divine seeing, because of their own incapacity and the mysteriousness of the light in which one sees. And therefore no one will thoroughly understand the meaning of it by any learning or subtle consideration of his own; for all words, and all that may be learnt and understood in a creaturely way, are foreign to, and far below, the truth which I mean. But he who is united with God, and is enlightened in this truth, he is able to understand the truth by itself. For to comprehend and to understand God above all similitudes, such as He is in Himself, is to be God with God, without intermediary, and without any otherness that can become a hindrance or an intermediary. And therefore I beg every one who cannot understand this, or feel it in the fruitive unity of his spirit, that he be not offended at it, and leave it for that which it is: for that which I am going to say is true, and Christ, the Eternal Truth, has said it Himself in His teaching in many places, if we could but show and explain it rightly. And therefore, whosoever wishes to understand this must have died to himself, and must live in God, and must turn his gaze to the eternal light in the ground of his spirit, where the Hidden Truth reveals Itself without means. For our Heavenly Father wills that we should see; for He is the Father of Light, and this is why He utters eternally, without intermediary and without interruption, in the hiddenness of our spirit, one unique and abysmal word, and no other. And in this word, He utters Himself and all things. And this word is none other than: BEHOLD. And this is the coming forth and the birth of the Son of Eternal Light, in Whom all blessedness is known and seen.

Now if the spirit would see God with God in this Divine Light without means, there needs must be on the part of man three things.

The first is that he must be perfectly ordered from without in all the virtues, and within must be unencumbered, and as empty of every outward work as if he did not work at all: for if his emptiness is troubled within by some work of virtue, he has an image; and as long as this endures within him, he cannot contemplate.

Secondly, he must inwardly cleave to God, with adhering intention and love, even as a burning and glowing fire which can never more be quenched. As long as he feels himself to be in this state, he is able to contemplate.

Thirdly, he must have lost himself in a Waylessness and in a Darkness, in which all contemplative men wander in fruition and wherein they never again can find themselves in a creaturely way. In the abyss of this darkness, in which the loving spirit has died to itself, there begin the manifestation of God and eternal life. For in this darkness there shines and is born an incomprehensible Light, which is the Son of God, in Whom we behold eternal life. And in this Light one becomes seeing; and this Divine Light is given to the simple sight of the spirit, where the spirit receives the brightness which is God Himself, above all gifts and every creaturely activity, in the idle emptiness in which the spirit has lost itself through fruitive love, and where it receives without means the brightness of God, and is changed without interruption into that brightness which it receives. Behold, this mysterious brightness, in which one sees everything that one can desire according to the emptiness of the spirit: this brightness is so great that the loving contemplative, in his ground wherein he rests, sees and feels nothing but an incomprehensible Light; and through that Simple Nudity which enfolds all things, he finds himself, and feels himself, to be that same Light by which he sees, and nothing else. And this is the first condition by which one becomes seeing in the Divine Light. Blessed are the eyes which are thus seeing, for they possess eternal life.

## Chapter 2. How the eternal birth of God is renewed without interruption in the nobility of the spirit[31]

WHEN we have thus become seeing, we can behold in joy the eternal coming of our Bridegroom; and that is the second point of which we would speak. What is this coming of our Bridegroom which is eternal? It is the new birth and a new enlightenment without interruption; for the ground from which the Light shines forth, and which is the Light itself, is life-giving and fruitful, and therefore the manifestation of the Eternal Light is renewed without ceasing in the hiddenness of the spirit. Behold, every creaturely work, and every exercise of virtue, must here cease; for here God works alone in the high nobility of the spirit. And here there is nothing but an eternal seeing and staring at that Light, by that Light, and in that Light. And the coming of the Bridegroom is so swift that He is perpetually coming, and yet dwelling within with unfathomable riches; and ever coming anew, in His Person, without interruption, with such new brightness that it seems as though he had never come before. For His coming consists, beyond time, in an eternal Now, which is ever received with new longings and new joy. Behold, the delight and the joy which this Bridegroom brings with Him in His coming are boundless and without measure, for they are Himself. And this is why the eyes with which the spirit sees and gazes at its Bridegroom, have opened so wide that they can never close again. For the spirit continues for ever to see and to stare at the secret manifestation of God. And the grasp of the spirit is opened so wide for the coming in of the Bridegroom, that the spirit itself becomes that Breadth Which it grasps. And so God is grasped and beheld through God; wherein rests all our blessedness. This is the second point: in which we receive, without interruption, the eternal coming of our Bridegroom in our spirit.

## Chapter 3. How our spirit is called to go out in contemplation and fruition[32]

Now the Spirit of God says in the secret outpouring of our spirit: GO YE OUT, in an eternal contemplation and fruition, according to the way of God. All the riches which are in

31 *Ibid.*, pp. 170-71
32 *Ibid.*, pp. 172-75.

God by nature we possess by way of love in God, and God in us, through the unmeasured love which is the Holy Ghost; for in this love one tastes of all that one can desire. And therefore through this love we are dead to ourselves, and have gone forth in loving immersion into Waylessness and Darkness. There the spirit is embraced by the Holy Trinity, and dwells for ever within the superessential Unity, in rest and fruition. And in that same Unity, according to Its fruitfulness, the Father dwells in the Son, and the Son in the Father, and all creatures dwell in Both. And this is above the distinction of the Persons; for here by means of the reason we understand Fatherhood and Sonhood as the life-giving fruitfulness of the Divine Nature.

Here there arise and begin an eternal going out and an eternal work which is without beginning; for here there is a beginning with beginning. For, after the Almighty Father had perfectly comprehended Himself in the ground of His fruitfulness, so the Son, the Eternal Word of the Father, came forth as the second Person in the Godhead. And, through the Eternal Birth, all creatures have come forth in eternity, before they were created in time. So God has seen and known them in Himself, according to distinction, in living ideas, and in an otherness from Himself; but not as something other in all ways, for all that is in God is God. This eternal going out and this eternal life, which we have and are in God eternally, without ourselves, is the cause of our created being in time. And our created being abides in the Eternal Essence, and is one with it in its essential existence. And this eternal life and being, which we have and are in the eternal Wisdom of God, is like unto God. For it has an eternal immanence in the Divine Essence, without distinction; and through the birth of the Son it has an eternal outflowing in a distinction and otherness, according to the Eternal Idea. And through these two points it is so like unto God that He knows and reflects Himself in this likeness without cessation, according to the Essence and according to the Persons. For, though even here there are distinction and otherness according to intellectual perception, yet this likeness is one with that same Image of the Holy Trinity, which is the wisdom of God and in which God beholds Himself and all things in an eternal Now, without before and after. In a single seeing He beholds Himself and all things. And this is the Image and the Likeness of God, and our Image and our Likeness; for in it God reflects Himself and all things. In this Divine Image all creatures have an eternal life, outside themselves, as in their eternal Archetype; and after this eternal Image, and in this Likeness, we have been made by the Holy Trinity. And therefore God wills that we shall go forth from ourselves in this Divine Light, and shall reunite ourselves in a supernatural way with this Image, which is our proper life, and shall possess it with Him, in action and in fruition, in eternal bliss.

For we know well that the bosom of the Father is our ground and origin, in which we begin our being and our life. And from our proper ground, that is from the Father and from all that lives in Him, there shines forth an eternal brightness, which is the birth of the Son. And in this brightness, that is, in the Son, the Father knows Himself and all that lives in Him; for all that He has, and all that He is, He gives to the Son, save only the property of Fatherhood, which abides in Himself. And this is why all that lives in the Father, unmanifested in the Unity, is also in the Son actively poured forth into manifestation: and the simple ground of our Eternal Image ever remains in darkness and in waylessness, but the brightness without limit which streams forth from it, this reveals and brings forth within the Conditioned the hiddenness of God. And all those men who are raised up above their created being into a God-seeing life are one with this Divine brightness. And they are that brightness itself, and they see, feel, and find, even by means of this Divine Light, that, as regards their uncreated essence, they are that same onefold ground from which the brightness without limit shines forth in the Divine way, and which, according to the simplicity of the Essence, abides eternally onefold and wayless within. And this is why inward and God-seeing men will go out in the way of contemplation, above reason and above distinction and above their created being, through an eternal intuitive gazing. By means of this inborn light they are transfigured, and made one with that same light through which they see and which they see. And thus the God-seeing men follow after their Eternal Image, after which they have been made; and they behold God and all things, without distinction, in a simple seeing, in the Divine brightness. And this is the most noble and the most profitable contemplation to which one can attain in this life; for in this contemplation, a man best remains master of himself and free. And at each loving introversion he may grow in nobility of life beyond anything that we are able to understand; for he remains free and master of himself in inwardness and virtue. And this gazing at the Divine Light holds him up above all inwardness and all virtue and all merit, for it is the crown and the reward after which we strive, and which we have and possess now in this wise; for a God-seeing life is a heavenly life. But were we set free from this misery and this exile, so we should have, as regards our created being, a greater capacity to receive this brightness; and so the glory of God would shine through us in every way better and more nobly. This is the way above all ways, in which one goes out through Divine contemplation and an eternal intuitive gazing, and in which one is transfigured and transmuted in the Divine brightness. This going out of the God-seeing man is also in love; for through the fruition of love he rises above his created being, and finds and tastes the riches and the delights which are God Himself, and which He causes to pour forth without interruption in the hiddenness of the spirit, where the spirit is like unto the nobility of God.

### Chapter 4. Of a divine meeting which takes place in the hiddenness of our spirit[33]

WHEN the inward and God-seeing man has thus attained to his Eternal Image, and in this clearness, through the Son, has entered into the bosom of the Father: then he is enlightened by Divine truth, and he receives anew, every moment, the Eternal Birth, and he goes forth according to the way of the light, in a Divine contemplation. And here there begins the fourth and last point; namely, a loving meeting, in which, above all else, our highest blessedness consists.

You should know that the heavenly Father, as a living ground, with all that lives in Him, is actively turned towards His Son, as to His own Eternal Wisdom. And that same Wisdom, with all that lives in It, is actively turned back towards the Father, that is, towards that very ground from which It comes forth. And in this meeting, there comes forth the third Person, between the Father and the Son; that is the Holy Ghost, Their mutual Love, who is one with them Both in the same nature. And He enfolds and drenches through both in action and fruition the Father and the Son, and all that lives in Both, with such great riches and such joy that as to this all creatures must eternally be silent; for

[33] *Ibid.*, pp. 176-78.

the incomprehensible wonder of this love, eternally transcends the understanding of all creatures. But where this wonder is understood and tasted without amazement, there the spirit dwells above itself, and is one with the Spirit of God; and tastes and sees without measure, even as God, the riches which are the spirit itself in the unity of the living ground, where it possesses itself according to the way of its uncreated essence.

Now this rapturous meeting is incessantly and actively renewed in us, according to the way of God; for the Father gives Himself in the Son, and the Son gives Himself in the Father, in an eternal content and a loving embrace; and this renews itself every moment within the bonds of love. For like as the Father incessantly beholds all things in the birth of His Son, so all things are loved anew by the Father and the Son in the outpouring of the Holy Ghost. And this is the active meeting of the Father and of the Son, in which we are lovingly embraced by the Holy Ghost in eternal love.

Now this active meeting and this loving embrace are in their ground fruitive and wayless; for the abysmal Waylessness of God is so dark and so unconditioned that it swallows up in itself every Divine way and activity, and all the attributes of the Persons, within the rich compass of the essential Unity; and it brings about a Divine fruition in the abyss of the Ineffable. And here there is a death in fruition, and a melting and dying into the Essential Nudity, where all the Divine names, and all conditions, and all the living images which are reflected in the mirror of Divine Truth, lapse in the Onefold and Ineffable, in waylessness and without reason. For in this unfathomable abyss of the Simplicity, all things are wrapped in fruitive bliss; and the abyss itself may not be comprehended, unless by the Essential Unity. To this the Persons, and all that lives in God, must give place; for here there is nought else but an eternal rest in the fruitive embrace of an outpouring Love. And this is that wayless being which all interior spirits have chosen above all other things. This is the dark silence in which all lovers lose themselves. But if we would prepare ourselves for it by means of the virtues, we should strip ourselves of all but our very bodies, and should flee forth into the wild Sea, whence no created thing can draw us back again.

May we possess in fruition the essential Unity, and clearly behold unity in the Trinity; this may Divine love, which turns no beggar away, bestow upon us. AMEN.

FROM *The book of Supreme Truth*

*Chapter 8. Showing how the inward man should exercise himself, that he may be united with God without means*[34]

BUT now I will tell you how the inward man, who has health amidst all miseries, should feel himself to be one with God without means. When such a quickened man rises up, with his whole being and all his powers, and joins himself to God with life-giving and active love, then he feels that his love is, in its ground, where it begins and ends, fruitive and without ground. If he then wishes to penetrate further, with his active love, into that fruitive love: then, all the powers of his soul must give way, and they must suffer and patiently endure that piercing Truth and Goodness which is God's self. For, as the air is penetrated by the brightness and heat of the sun, and iron is penetrated by fire; so that it works through fire the works of fire, since it burns and shines like the fire; and so likewise it can be said of the air—for, if the air had understanding, it could say: "I enlighten and brighten the whole world"—yet each of these keeps its own nature. For the fire does not become iron, and the iron does not become fire, though their union is without means; for the iron is within the fire and the fire within the iron; and so also the air is in the sunshine and the sunshine in the air. So likewise is God in the being of the soul; and whenever the soul's highest powers are turned inward with active love, they are united with God without means, in a simple knowledge of all truth, and in an essential feeling and tasting of all good. This simple knowing and feeling of God is possessed in essential love, and is practised and preserved through active love. And therefore it is accidental to our powers through the dying introversion in love; but it is essential to our being, and always abides within it. And therefore we must perpetually turn inwards and be renewed in love, if we would seek out love through love. And this is taught us by St. John, where he says: HE THAT DWELLETH IN LOVE DWELLETH IN GOD AND GOD IN HIM. And though this union of the loving spirit with God is without means, yet there is here a great distinction, for the creature never becomes God, nor does God ever become the creature; as I explained to you heretofore in the example of the iron and the fire. And if

[34] *Ibid.*, pp. 236-38.

material things, which have been made by God, may thus be united without means; so much the more may He, whenever such is His pleasure, unite Himself with His beloved, if they, through His grace, submit to it and make themselves ready for it. And so in such an inward man, whom God has adorned with virtues, and, above that, has lifted up into a contemplative life, there is no intermediary between himself and God in his highest introversion but his enlightened reason and his active love. And through these two things, he has an adherence to God; and this is "becoming one with God," says St. Bernard. But above reason, and above active love, he is lifted up into a naked contemplation, and dwells without activity in essential love. And there he is one love and one spirit with God, as I said heretofore. In this essential love, through the unity which he has essentially with God, he infinitely transcends his understanding; and this is a life common to all God-seeing men. For in this transcendence such a man is able to see in one sight—if it be God's pleasure to show it to him—all the creatures in heaven and on earth, with the distinction of their lives and their rewards. But before the Infinity of God, he must yield, and must follow after It essentially and without end; for This no creature, not even the soul of our Lord Jesus Christ, which yet received the highest union above all other creatures, can either comprehend or overtake.

### Chapter 11. *How good men in their contemplation have the love of God before them, and how they are lifted up into God*[35]

THEY have the Love of God before them in their inward seeing, as a common good pouring forth through heaven and earth; and they feel the Holy Trinity inclined towards them, and within them, with fulness of grace. And therefore they are adorned without and within with all the virtues, with holy practices and with good works. And thus they are united with God through Divine grace and their own holy lives. And because they have abandoned themselves to God in doing, in leaving undone, and in suffering, they have steadfast peace and inward joy, consolation and savour, of which the world cannot partake; neither any dissembler, nor the man who seeks and means himself more than the glory of God. Moreover, those same inward and enlightened men have

[35] *Ibid.*, pp. 242-44.

before them in their inward seeing whenever they will, the Love of God as something drawing or urging them into the Unity; for they see and feel that the Father with the Son through the Holy Ghost, embrace Each Other and all the chosen, and draw themselves back with eternal love into the unity of Their Nature. Thus the Unity is ever drawing to itself and inviting to itself everything that has been born of It, either by nature or by grace. And therefore, too, such enlightened men are, with a free spirit, lifted up above reason into a bare and imageless vision, wherein lives the eternal indrawing summons of the Divine Unity; and, with an imageless and bare understanding, they pass through all works, and all exercises, and all things, until they reach the summit of their spirits. There, their bare understanding is drenched through by the Eternal Brightness, even as the air is drenched through by the sunshine. And the bare, uplifted will is transformed and drenched through by abysmal love, even as iron is by fire. And the bare, uplifted memory feels itself enwrapped and established in an abysmal Absence of Image. And thereby the created image is united above reason in a threefold way with its Eternal Image, which is the origin of its being and its life; and this origin is preserved and possessed, essentially and eternally, through a simple seeing in an imageless void: and so a man is lifted up above reason in a threefold manner into the Unity, and in a onefold manner into the Trinity. Yet the creature does not become God, for the union takes place in God through grace and our homeward-turning love: and therefore the creature in its inward contemplation feels a distinction and an otherness between itself and God. And though the union is without means, yet the manifold works which God works in heaven and on earth are nevertheless hidden from the spirit. For though God gives Himself as He is, with clear discernment, He gives Himself in the essence of the soul, where the powers of the soul are simplified above reason, and where, in simplicity, they suffer the transformation of God. There all is full and overflowing, for the spirit feels itself to be one truth and one richness and one unity with God. Yet even here there is an essential tending forward, and therein is an essential distinction between the being of the soul and the Being of God; and this is the highest and finest distinction which we are able to feel.

## Chapter 12. Of the highest union, without difference or distinction[36]

AND after this there follows the union without distinction. For you must apprehend the Love of God not only as an out-pouring with all good, and as drawing back again into the Unity; but it is also, above all distinction, an essential fruition in the bare Essence of the Godhead. And in conse-quence of this enlightened men have found within themselves an essential contemplation which is above reason and with-out reason, and a fruitive tendency which pierces through every condition and all being, and through which they im-merse themselves in a wayless abyss of fathomless beatitude, where the Trinity of the Divine Persons possess Their Na-ture in the essential Unity. Behold, this beatitude is so one-fold and so wayless that in it every essential gazing, ten-dency, and creaturely distinction cease and pass away. For by this fruition, all uplifted spirits are melted and noughted in the Essence of God, Which is the superessence of all es-sence. There they fall from themselves into a solitude and an ignorance which are fathomless; there all light is turned to darkness; there the three Persons give place to the Es-sential Unity, and abide without distinction in fruition of essential blessedness. This blessedness is essential to God, and superessential to all creatures; for no created essence can become one with God's Essence and pass away from its own substance. For so the creature would become God, which is impossible; for the Divine Essence can neither wax nor wane, nor can anything be added to It or taken from It. Yet all loving spirits are one fruition and one blessedness with God without distinction; for that beatific state, which is the fruition of God and of all His beloved, is so simple and onefold that therein neither Father, nor Son, nor Holy Ghost, is distinct according to the Persons, neither is any creature. But all enlightened spirits are here lifted up above them-selves into a wayless fruition, which is an abundance be-yond all the fulness that any creature has ever received or shall ever receive. For there all uplifted spirits are, in their superessence, one fruition and one beatitude with God with-out distinction; and there this beatitude is so onefold that no distinction can enter into it. And this was prayed for by Christ when He besought His Father in heaven that all His beloved might be made perfect in one, even as He is one

36 *Ibid.*, pp. 244-46.

with the Father through the Holy Ghost: even so He prayed and besought that He in us and we in Him and His heavenly Father might be one in fruition through the Holy Ghost. And this I think the most loving prayer which Christ ever made for our blessedness.

## St. Teresa of Avila

Eckhart the German and Ruysbroeck the Fleming flourished in the thirteenth and fourteenth centuries. In passing now to St. Teresa and St. John of the Cross we move to Spain in the sixteenth century. We should expect the mysticism of Spain in the sixteenth century to exhibit considerable differences from the Germanic mysticism of the thirteenth century, and this is in fact the case. The writings of the Spanish mystics have, as it were, a flavor and an atmosphere of their own, while still exhibiting the universal characteristics of all mysticism. It is natural to take St. Teresa and St. John of the Cross together. They lived and worked in close co-operation with each other. Both belonged to the Carmelite Order. Although St. John was twenty-seven years younger than St. Teresa, she took him as her spiritual director.

In those days the monasteries of the Carmelites had grown lax in observing the spiritual disciplines originally laid down for the government of their order. St. Teresa and St. John took it as their mission in life to reform the existing monasteries, to found new ones, and to reintroduce the full rigor of the religious life which they considered proper for the cloister. To this end they worked in collaboration against the most determined opposition. The unreformed Carmelites even went so far as to kidnap and imprison St. John in a dungeon at Toledo. After a period of great suffering, he made a dramatic escape by climbing down from a window on a rope made of strips of old blankets and clothing. The two saints lived to see the subsidence of the opposition to their work and to bring it to a successful conclusion.

St. Teresa was born in 1515 and died in 1582. There is little to tell of her life apart from her work with St. John. She has become famous for the intimate account she has given of her own mystical experiences in her autobiographical writings. To quote one of the commentators,[37] "The

[37] Kurt F. Reinhardt, in the introduction to St. John of the Cross, *The Dark Night of the Soul* (Milestones of Thought Series), translated by Kurt F. Reinhardt. New York: Frederick Ungar Publishing Company, 1957, p. xii.

German mystics of the fourteenth century (notably Master Eckhardt, Suso, and Tauler) as well as the great Spanish mystics of the 'Golden Age' (especially St. Theresa of Avila and St. John of the Cross) offer in their works a minute psychological description of these highest stages of the mystical life." That this is true of the German mystics mentioned there is no doubt. It is also true of St. John of the Cross, who exhibits a remarkable gift of psychological introspection and analysis. But there is grave doubt whether the same can properly be said of St. Teresa. She writes with much vivid detail of the physical or bodily accompaniments of union and rapture. This information is interesting and valuable. But of the inward spiritual life she actually tells us very little, in spite of making great preparatory gestures for doing so. Nor has she any power of psychological analysis— or, indeed, of analysis of any kind. While St. John shows a surprisingly analytic mind, any such gift is conspicuously absent in St. Teresa. She writes of herself, "The way in which this that we call union comes, and the nature of it, I do not know how to explain. It is described in mystical theology, but I am unable to use the proper terms, and I cannot understand what is meant by 'mind' or how this differs from 'soul' or 'spirit.' They all seem the same to me." [38] Very likely they "all seem the same" to many modern readers. But the point is that these were evidently familiar distinctions in her time (and maybe in certain circles today), and she admits her incapacity to handle them. Nor can this mental inability have been confined to distinguishing between these three particular terms. It is evident that what she says about herself in connection with them is characteristic of her mentality generally. She was unable to cope with any sort of subtle distinctions. She was, in fact, a wholly unintellectual person. This, of course, involves no derogation of her saintliness and of the depth and importance of her mystical consciousness. It is certain that she reached up to the supreme enlightenment of the unitive life. But her lack of intellectual power renders it unlikely that we shall get from her writings any very valuable insights

[38] All quotations in this introduction are from St. Teresa of Avila, "The Life of the Holy Mother Saint Teresa of Jesus," *The Complete Works of Saint Teresa,* translated and edited by E. Allison Peers from the critical edition of P. Silverio de Santa Teresa, C. D. London: Sheed & Ward, Ltd., 1946; New York: Sheed & Ward, Inc., 1946, Vol. I, Chapter 18.

into the inner nature of the mystical consciousness. She experienced it to the full but was too mentally untrained to impart any very valuable information about it. We have her own word for it that she does "not know how to explain" it.

In spite of this, she does very often tell us that she is going to describe the mystical union. Only a few lines after her statement that she cannot explain it she proceeds, "What I do seek to explain is the feelings of the soul when it is in this Divine Union." The sentences which follow read, "It is quite clear what union is—two different things becoming one. O my Lord, how good Thou art! Blessed be Thou for ever!" The last words led the saint into several pages of devout and pious ejaculations in the writing of which she apparently forgot that she had set out with the intention of explaining "the feelings of the soul when it is in this Divine Union." It is true that she speaks a great deal of the bliss and rejoicing which accompany union, and perhaps this is all she means when she promises to tell us of the "feelings" of the soul.

Since she thinks that "it is quite clear what union is—two different things becoming one," and since she thinks that statement clear enough, it is evident that we cannot expect her to notice the ambiguity of the word "union" which we discussed on an earlier page. Nor can we hope that she will throw any light on the difference between the dualistic and pantheistic interpretations of mystical experience. Nor again should we look in her writings for any understanding of the distinction between the mystical experience itself and its interpretation. The experience for her is simply "union with God," and that is enough. Naturally, therefore, she cannot be quoted as a witness that the cognitive core of the experience is the undifferentiated unity. The absence of any such testimony might perhaps be made the basis of a charge that her experience cannot have been the same in kind as that of the other great mystics whose work we have been examining. Her experience, it might be alleged, was not an undifferentiated unity like that of Eckhart, Ruysbroeck, Plotinus, and the mystics of the East. This would be, I believe, a very shallow inference. It is common to all Christian mystics that they believe themselves to experience "union with God." This is the traditional Christian interpretation of the experience. Because St. Teresa fails to make any distinction between experience and interpretation, and makes no attempt to isolate and analyze its essential core—as the more philosophic Christian mystics Eckhart and Ruysbroeck do—are we to conclude that the union with God which she tells us about was of a wholly different kind from theirs? It is in the highest degree unlikely that there should be two different kinds of Christian union and that the Christian mystics, in their communications with one another, never discovered this fact. Especially is this true of her communications with her collaborator and spiritual director, St. John of the Cross. There is excellent evidence, as we shall see, that St. John's experience was of the same kind as that of the introvertive mystics already discussed—although it is true that his linguistic idiom, because it belongs to the Spanish culture of the sixteenth century, was somewhat different from theirs. It is quite incredible that St. Teresa and St. John should have meant by union with God two quite different kinds of experience and never have discovered this in all their long years of collaboration with each other.

Among the pious utterances with which St. Teresa's writing abounds may be found many expressions of her sense of sin—as is, of course, proper in a Christian saint. She speaks of herself as "this miserable woman" and gently reproaches the Lord for bestowing the favor of union "upon a creature so wretched, so base, so weak, so miserable and so worthless" as herself. She adds "I am in short a woman, and not even a good one, but wicked."

Occasionally we find approaches to introspective psychological description of some value as corroborating what we have learned from our study of other mystics. Mystics usually insist on the sense of certainty they feel that their experience has objective reference and brings them in contact with a reality outside themselves. St. Teresa confirms this: "The soul feels close to God and . . . there abides within it such a certainty that it cannot possibly do other than believe." The "faculties" of the soul, she tells us, are "in suspension" during union—including the will and the imagination—and in this state they are "completely lost." She writes that at the "highest point" of union all the faculties are lost and the subject "will neither see, nor hear, nor perceive." Possibly this refers to the emptying of the self of its empirical contents. But it is somewhat doubtful that this is what she means. The emptying oneself of sensations, thoughts, etc., is usually a deliberate process which the subject undertakes and in which he succeeds, as Eckhart says, only with the greatest difficulty.

But St. Teresa writes very much as if the loss of the faculties of which she speaks were something which just happened to her as she fainted off in a trance.

As the reader will discover, the word "rapture" which St. Teresa uses is a sort of technical term. It does not merely mean, as in ordinary English, a state of extreme joy, although that is included in it. As used by St. Teresa and other Christian mystics it means much the same as "trance," and it manifests itself in the strange bodily changes which St. Teresa describes.

The first part of the following selection is from Chapter 18 of the autobiography of St. Teresa. But I have, with some hesitation, added a part of Chapter 2 of *The Interior Castle*. The reason for hesitation is that this passage, although clearly of great importance, is extremely obscure, especially in what it says about visions. The following facts, however, seem clear. The difference between Spiritual Betrothal and Spiritual Marriage is the difference between occasional union and permanent union. I understand permanent union to be such that the mystical consciousness and the sensory-intellectual consciousness are integrated. The subject, while all the time enjoying the mystical consciousness, continues to be active in the world and to carry out his ordinary tasks. We have discussed this in connection with Zen. It is clear that St. Teresa had attained this final stage of the mystical life by the time she wrote *The Interior Castle*, but apparently not when she wrote her autobiography.

### FROM *The Life of St. Teresa*

#### Mystical Union[39]

While seeking God in this way, the soul becomes conscious that it is fainting almost completely away, in a kind of swoon, with an exceeding great and sweet delight. It gradually ceases to breathe and all its bodily strength begins to fail it: it cannot even move its hands without great pain; its eyes involuntarily close, or, if they remain open, they can hardly see. If a person in this state attempts to read, he is unable to spell out a single letter: it is as much as he can do to recognize one. He sees that letters are there, but, as the understanding gives him no help, he cannot read them even if he so wishes. He can hear, but he cannot understand what he

[39] St. Teresa of Avila, *op. cit.*, Vol. I, Chapter 18, pp. 108-10.

hears. He can apprehend nothing with the senses, which only hinder his soul's joy and thus harm rather than help him. It is futile for him to attempt to speak: his mind cannot manage to form a single word, nor, if it could, would he have the strength to pronounce it. For in this condition all outward strength vanishes, while the strength of the soul increases so that it may the better have fruition of its bliss. The outward joy experienced is great and most clearly recognized.

This prayer, for however long it may last, does no harm; at least, it has never done any to me, nor do I ever remember feeling any ill effects after the Lord has granted me this favour, however unwell I may have been: indeed, I am generally much the better for it. What harm can possibly be done by so great a blessing? The outward effects are so noteworthy that there can be no doubt some great thing has taken place: we experience a loss of strength but the experience is one of such delight that afterwards our strength grows greater.

It is true that at first this happens in such a short space of time—so, at least, it was with me—that because of its rapidity it can be detected neither by these outward signs nor by the failure of the senses. But the exceeding abundance of the favours granted to the soul clearly indicates how bright has been the sun that has shone upon it and has thus caused the soul to melt away. And let it be observed that, in my opinion, whatever may be the length of the period during which all the faculties of the soul are in this state of suspension, it is a very short one: if it were to last for half an hour, that would be a long time—I do not think it has ever lasted so long as that with me. As the soul is not conscious of it, its duration is really very difficult to estimate, so I will merely say that it is never very long before one of the faculties becomes active again. It is the will that maintains the contact with God but the other two faculties soon begin to importune it once more. The will, however, is calm, so they become suspended once again; but eventually, after another short period of suspension, they come back to life.

With all this happening, the time spent in prayer may last, and does last, for some hours; for, once the two faculties have begun to grow inebriated with the taste of this Divine wine, they are very ready to lose themselves in order to gain the more, and so they keep company with the will and all three rejoice together. But this state in which they are completely lost, and have no power of imagining anything—for the imagination, I believe, is also completely lost—is, as I say, of brief duration, although the faculties do not recover to such an extent as not to be for some hours, as it were, in disorder, God, from time to time, gathering them once more to Himself.

Let us now come to the most intimate part of what the soul experiences in this condition. The persons who must speak of it are those who know it, for it cannot be understood, still less described. As I was about to write of this (I had just communicated and had been experiencing this very prayer of which I am writing), I was wondering what it is the soul does during that time, when the Lord said these words to me: "It dies to itself wholly, daughter, in order that it may fix itself more and more upon Me; it is no longer itself that lives, but I. As it cannot comprehend what it understands, it is an understanding which understands not." One who has experienced this will understand something of it; it cannot be more clearly expressed, since all that comes to pass in this state is so obscure. I can only say that the soul feels close to God and that there abides within it such a certainty that it cannot possibly do other than believe. All the faculties now fail and are suspended in such a way that, as I have said, it is impossible to believe they are active. If the soul has been meditating upon any subject, this vanishes from its memory as if it had never thought of it. If it had been reading, it is unable to concentrate upon what it was reading or to remember it; and the same is true if it has been praying. So it is that this importunate little butterfly—the memory—is now burning its wings and can no longer fly. The will must be fully occupied in loving, but it cannot understand how it loves; the understanding, if it understands, does not understand how it understands, or at least can comprehend nothing of what it understands. It does not seem to me to be understanding, because, as I say, it does not understand itself. Nor can I myself understand this.

### Rapture[40]

I should like, with the help of God, to be able to describe the difference between union and rapture, or elevation, or what they call flight of the spirit, or transport—it is all one. I mean that these different names all refer to the same thing, which is also called ecstasy. It is much more beneficial than union: the effects it produces are far more important and it has a great many more operations, for union gives the impression of being just the same at the beginning,

40 Ibid. Chapter 20, pp. 119-20, 125-26.

in the middle and at the end, and it all happens interiorly. But the ends of these raptures are of a higher degree, and the effects they produce are both interior and exterior. May the Lord explain this, as He has explained everything else, for I should certainly know nothing of it if His Majesty had not shown me the ways and manners in which it can to some extent be described.

Let us now reflect that this last water which we have described is so abundant that, were it not that the ground is incapable of receiving it, we might believe this cloud of great Majesty to be with us here on this earth. But as we are giving Him thanks for this great blessing, and doing our utmost to draw near to Him in a practical way, the Lord gathers up the soul, just (we might say) as the clouds gather up the vapours from the earth, and raises it up till it is right out of itself (I have heard that it is in this way that the clouds or the sun gather up the vapours) and the cloud rises to Heaven and takes the soul with it, and begins to reveal to it things concerning the Kingdom that He has prepared for it. I do not know if the comparison is an exact one, but that is the way it actually happens.

In these raptures the soul seems no longer to animate the body, and thus the natural heat of the body is felt to be very sensibly diminished: it gradually becomes colder, though conscious of the greatest sweetness and delight. No means of resistance is possible, whereas in union, where we are on our own ground, such a means exists: resistance may be painful and violent but it can almost always be effected. But with rapture, as a rule, there is no such possibility: often it comes like a strong, swift impulse, before your thought can forewarn you of it or you can do anything to help yourself; you see and feel this cloud, or this powerful eagle, rising and bearing you up with it on its wings.

You realize, I repeat, and indeed see, that you are being carried away, you know not whither. For, though rapture brings us delight, the weakness of our nature at first makes us afraid of it, and we need to be resolute and courageous in soul, much more so than for what has been described. For, happen what may, we must risk everything, and resign ourselves into the hands of God and go willingly wherever we are carried away, for we are in fact being carried away, whether we like it or no. In such straits do I find myself at such a time that very often I should be glad to resist, and I exert all my strength to do so, in particular at times when it happens in public and at many other times in private, when I am afraid that I may be suffering deception. Occasionally I have been able to make some resistance, but at the cost of great exhaustion, for I would feel as weary afterwards as though I had been fighting with a powerful giant. At other times, resistance has been impossible: my soul has been borne away, and indeed as a rule my head also, without my being able to prevent it: sometimes my whole body has been affected, to the point of being raised up from the ground.

This has happened only rarely; but once, when we were together in choir, and I was on my knees and about to communicate, it caused me the greatest distress. It seemed to me a most extraordinary thing and I thought there would be a great deal of talk about it; so I ordered the nuns (for it happened after I was appointed Prioress) not to speak of it. On other occasions, when I have felt that the Lord was going to enrapture me (once it happened during a sermon, on our patronal festival, when some great ladies were present), I have lain on the ground and the sisters have come and held me down, but none the less the rapture has been observed. I besought the Lord earnestly not to grant me any more favours which had visible and exterior signs; for I was exhausted by having to endure such worries and after all (I said) His Majesty could grant me that favour without its becoming known. He seems to have been pleased of His goodness to hear me, for since making that prayer I have never again received any such favours: it is true, however, that this happened not long since. . . .

Let us now return to raptures, and to their most usual characteristics. I can testify that after a rapture my body often seemed as light as if all weight had left it: sometimes this was so noticeable that I could hardly tell when my feet were touching the ground. For, while the rapture lasts, the body often remains as if dead and unable of itself to do anything: it continues all the time as it was when the rapture came upon it—in a sitting position, for example, or with the hands open or shut. The subject rarely loses consciousness: I have sometimes lost it altogether, but only seldom and for but a short time. As a rule the consciousness is disturbed; and though incapable of action with respect to outward things, the subject can still hear and understand, but only dimly, as though from a long way off. I do not say that he can hear and understand when the rapture is at its highest point—by "highest point" I mean when the faculties are lost through being closely united with God. At that point, in my opinion, he will neither see, nor hear, nor perceive; but, as I said in describing the preceding prayer of union, this complete transformation of the soul in God lasts but a short time, and it is only while it lasts that none of the soul's faculties is able to perceive or know what is taking place. We cannot be meant to understand it while we are on earth— God, in fact, does not wish us to understand it because we have not the capacity for doing so. I have observed this myself.

FROM *The Interior Castle*

### Spiritual Marriage[41]

Let us now come to treat of the Divine and Spiritual Marriage, although this great favour cannot be fulfilled perfectly in us during our lifetime, for if we were to withdraw ourselves from God this great blessing would be lost. When granting this favour for the first time, His Majesty is pleased to reveal Himself to the soul through an imaginary vision of His most sacred Humanity, so that it may clearly understand what is taking place and not be ignorant of the fact that it is receiving so sovereign a gift. To other people the experience will come in a different way. To the person of whom we have been speaking the Lord revealed Himself one day, when she had just received Communion, in great splendour and beauty and majesty, as He did after His resurrection, and told her that it was time she took upon her His affairs as if they were her own and that He would take her affairs upon Himself; and He added other words which are easier to understand than to repeat.

This, you will think, was nothing new, since on other occasions the Lord had revealed Himself to that soul in this way. But it was so different that it left her quite confused and dismayed: for one reason, because this vision came with great force; for another, because of the words which He spoke to her; and also because, in the interior of her soul, where He revealed Himself to her, she had never seen any visions but this. For you must understand that there is the greatest difference between all the other visions we have mentioned and those belonging to this Mansion, and there is the same difference between the Spiritual Betrothal and the Spiritual Marriage as there is between two betrothed persons and two who are united so that they cannot be separated any more.

As I have already said, one makes these comparisons be-

41 St. Teresa of Avila, *The Interior Castle, loc. cit.*, Vol. II, Seventh Mansions, Chapter II, pp. 333-35.

cause there are no other appropriate ones, yet it must be
realized that the Betrothal has no more to do with the body
than if the soul were not in the body, and were nothing but
spirit. Between the Spiritual Marriage and the body there is
even less connection, for this secret union takes place in the
deepest centre of the soul, which must be where God Himself
dwells, and I do not think there is any need of a door because all that has so far been described seems to have come
through the medium of the senses and faculties and this appearance of the Humanity of the Lord must do so too. But
what passes in the union of the Spiritual Marriage is very
different. The Lord appears in the centre of the soul, not
through an imaginary, but through an intellectual vision
(although this is a subtler one than that already mentioned),
just as He appeared to the Apostles, without entering
through the door, when He said to them: "Pax vobis." This
instantaneous communication of God to the soul is so great
a secret and so sublime a favour, and such delight is felt by
the soul, that I do not know with what to compare it, beyond
saying that the Lord is pleased to manifest to the soul at
that moment the glory that is in Heaven, in a sublimer
manner than is possible through any vision or spiritual
consolation. It is impossible to say more than that, as far as
one can understand, the soul (I mean the spirit of this soul)
is made one with God, Who, being likewise a Spirit, has
been pleased to reveal the love that He has for us by showing
to certain persons the extent of that love, so that we may
praise His greatness. For He has been pleased to unite
Himself with His creature in such a way that they have become like two who cannot be separated from one another:
even so He will not separate Himself from her.

The Spiritual Betrothal is different: here the two persons
are frequently separated, as is the case with union, for, although by union is meant the joining of two things into one,
each of the two, as is a matter of common observation, can
be separated and remain a thing by itself. This favour of
the Lord passes quickly and afterwards the soul is deprived
of that companionship—I mean so far as it can understand.
In this other favour of the Lord it is not so: the soul remains
all the time in that centre with its God. We might say that
union is as if the ends of two wax candles were joined so
that the light they give is one: the wicks and the wax and
the light are all one; yet afterwards the one candle can be
perfectly well separated from the other and the candles become two again, or the wick may be withdrawn from the
wax. But here it is like rain falling from the heavens into a

river or a spring; there is nothing but water there and it is impossible to divide or separate the water belonging to the river from that which fell from the heavens. Or it is as if a tiny streamlet enters the sea, from which it will find no way of separating itself, or as if in a room there were two large windows through which the light streamed in: it enters in different places but it all becomes one.

## St. John of the Cross

St. John was born in 1542 and died in 1591. Something of his life and work has been included in the previous section on St. Teresa.

His style of writing presents a great contrast with that of St. Teresa. Though he is not intellectually comparable with the great Germanic mystics, Eckhart and Ruysbroeck, he is nevertheless clearheaded and orderly in his expositions. He proceeds methodically from point to point according to what is evidently a well-thought-out plan. He never rambles as St. Teresa does. Though properly reverential, he does not, like St. Teresa, lard his work with conventional pious verbiage. He shows considerable analytic ability and great psychological insight. The result is that his pages are, by contrast with those of St. Teresa, pleasant to read. It is not necessary to provide a long introduction nor any running commentary. For the reader will find no difficulty in following him. In this introductory note I shall refer briefly to two aspects of his work, first what he says of the nature of union, and secondly, a part of his account of the "dark night of the soul."

He strongly emphasizes the absence of imagery in the mystical consciousness and the necessity of getting rid of images—as do Ruysbroeck and introvertive mystics in general. What he calls "meditation"—to be carefully distinguished from the use of the word in the Indian mystical tradition—is, as stated in the following selection, "a discursive mental activity by means of images, forms, and figures that are produced imaginatively . . . as happens, for example, when we picture in our imagination Christ crucified. . . ." He continues: "The soul must be emptied of all these imagined forms, figures, and images, and it must remain in darkness in respect to these internal senses if it is to attain Divine union." That the mind must be emptied of actual physical sensations is also made clear. Moreover, the soul must "halt the operation of its faculties in particular acts." For instance, "the memory has lost its strength; the understanding is in darkness, unable to comprehend anything, and hence the will too." The "inward wisdom cannot enter into the understanding in any conceptual form or sensory image." All these quotations, which the reader will meet in their proper context in the selections which follow, make it clear that St. John's experience of union is brought about by the same emptying of the self of all its empirical contents which we have found to be the universal precondition of the introvertive mystical experience.

Furthermore, the spirit which has attained this consciousness "feels as though it had been placed in a vast and profound solitude, in an immense and boundless desert." This is plainly the same as Eckhart's "barren desert" which is a metaphor for the negative side of the experience, its emptiness or nothingness, the "void" of the Buddhists.

St. John is, of course, famous for the phrase "the dark night of the soul"; and this is a conception which we have not yet encountered in this book, and which is not to be found in Hindu, Buddhist, Taoist, or Plotinian mysticism. It is in fact entirely peculiar to Christian mysticism. The experience of the dark night is well known not only to St. John, but to other Christian mystics such as Madame Guyon, Ruysbroeck and Tauler. The manifestations of the "dark night" are somewhat different in different individuals, but in large measure it is an emotional reaction. We have seen that although the cognitive core of the mystical experience, the undifferentiated unity, is found everywhere, there are cultural and individual variations in respect of (1) intellectual interpretation (2) affective tone. Hence the fact that the "dark night" is found only in Christian mysticism does not invalidate the hypothesis of the fundamental sameness of the experience everywhere.

In St. John's account "the dark night" appears to have two different meanings; or perhaps we should say that we have two different aspects of one thing. The phrase already quoted that the soul "must remain in darkness in respect of sensations, images, and understanding" gives us one meaning. The self which has got rid of sensations, images, and concepts is blind to these things, and so St. John speaks of it as being in darkness "in respect of them." This, of course, is a metaphorical way of describing the undifferentiated unity and has in itself nothing to do with the emotions. It is, however, the emotional aspect of the dark night which is usually stressed. The mystic suffers from periods of despair in which he feels that God has forsaken him and left him to struggle in the darkness alone. "But what the sorrowing soul feels most painfully in this condition is the dreadful thought that God has abandoned it and has flung it into utter darkness. . . . it feels most vividly the shadows and laments of death and the torments of hell which consist in the conviction that God in His anger has chastized and forsaken it for ever." [42] The self passes through long periods of such despair but ultimately emerges from them into the supreme bliss of union. And St. John insists that the dark night is sent by God as part of the mystic's spiritual education, as part of the necessary purgation and purification from selfhood and as producing that utter humbling and "noughting" of the spirit which is necessary to its perfect union.

### FROM *The Dark Night of the Soul*

*The union of the soul with God is a union of love and of likeness, not division of substance* [43]

To understand, then, the nature of this union, it must be known that God dwells or is present substantially [*per essentiam*] in every soul, even in the soul of the greatest sinner. This kind of union between God and all His creatures is never lacking, since it is in and by this union that He sustains their being; and if it were ever lacking, these creatures would immediately cease to be and would fall back into nothingness. Thus, if we here speak of the union of the soul with God, we do not have in mind this ever-present substantial union, but we do mean that union of the soul with God which is consummated in the soul's transformation in God—a union which can come about only when the soul attains to a likeness with God by virtue of love. We shall therefore call this the union of likeness, to distinguish it from the union of substance or essence. The former is supernatural, the latter natural. And the supernatural union comes about when the two wills—that of the soul and that of God —are conformed in one, so that there is nothing in the one that is repugnant to the other. Thus, when the soul rids itself totally of that which is repugnant to and not in conformity with the Divine will, it is transformed in God through love.

This applies not only to whatever is repugnant to God in

42 St. John of the Cross, *op. cit.*, p. 91.
43 *Ibid.*, Part I, Book II, Chapter V, pp. 34-37.

human action, but also in habit, so that the soul must not only desist from all voluntary acts of imperfection but must also completely overcome the acquired habits of these imperfections. And since no creature nor the actions or capabilities of any creature can ever measure up or attain to that which is God, the soul must be stripped of all creaturely attachments as well as of its own activities and capabilities —that is to say, of its understanding, its likings, and its feelings—so that, when all that which is unlike God and unconformed to Him is cast out, the soul may then receive the likeness of God.

Supernatural being is communicated only by love and grace. Not all souls, however, abide in God's love and grace, and those who do abide in them do not possess them in the same degree; for some attain higher degrees of love than others. And thus, God communicates Himself most to that soul which has progressed farthest in love and has most conformed its will to God's will. And that soul which has attained to a total conformity and likeness of its will and God's will is totally united with him and supernaturally transformed in him.

Let me clarify [the nature of this union] by a simile. Picture a ray of sunlight that is striking a window. Now if the window is coated with stains or vapors, the ray will be unable to illumine it and transform it into its own light; this it could do only if the window were stainless and pure. And the greater or lesser degree of illumination will be strictly in proportion to the window's greater or lesser purity; and this will be so, not because of the ray of sunlight but because of the condition of the window. Thus, if the window were entirely clean and pure, the ray would transform and illumine it in such a way that it would become almost undistinguishable from the brightness of the ray and would diffuse the same light as the ray. And yet, however much the window may resemble the ray of sunlight, it actually retains its own distinct nature. But this does not prevent us from saying that this window is luminous as a ray of the sun or is sunlight by participation. Now the soul is like this window: the Divine light of the Being of God is unceasingly beating upon it, or, to use a better expression, the Divine light is ever dwelling in it.

When the soul thus allows God to work in it, it will soon be transformed and transfigured in God, and God will communicate to it His supernatural Being in such a way that the soul appears to be God Himself, and it will indeed be God by participation. Yet it remains true nevertheless that the soul's natural being—notwithstanding the soul's supernatural transformation—remains as distinct from the Being of God as it was before, even as the window has and retains a nature of its own, distinct from the nature of the ray, although it owes its luminosity to the light of the sun.

This consideration should make it clearer why a soul can not dispose itself for this union by either understanding, or sensory apperception, or inner feelings and imaginings, or by any other experiences relating either to God or to anything else, but only by purity and love, that is, by perfect resignation and total detachment from all things for the sake of God alone. And as there can be no perfect transformation unless there be perfect purity, the soul will not be perfect unless it be totally cleansed and wholly pure.

Those souls [who attain to Divine union] do so according to their greater or smaller capacity and thus not in the same degree; and the degree of union depends also on what the Lord wishes to grant to each soul. And it is similar in the beatific vision: though some souls will have a more perfect vision of God in Heaven than others, they all see God, and all are content, since their capacity is satisfied. And in this life, too, all souls [who have attained to the state of perfection] will be equally satisfied, each one according to its knowledge of God and thus according to its capacity. A soul, on the other hand, that does not attain to a degree of purity corresponding to its capacity, will never find true peace and contentment.

> *Natural imaginary apprehensions cannot be a proportionate means to attain to union with God*[44]

What must first be discussed now is that internal bodily sense known as imagination and fancy. This internal sense must likewise be emptied of all those imaginative forms and apprehensions with which it may be naturally occupied; and we must show here how impossible it is for the soul to attain to union with God until it ceases to be actively preoccupied with them.

It must be known, then, that the sense of which we are here speaking in particular consists really of two internal bodily senses—imagination and fancy—which are subservient one to the other in due order. For the one thinks, as it were, by imagining, while the other uses the power of fancy

44 *Ibid.*, Part I, Book II, Chapter XII, pp. 50-53.

to give form to the imagination (or to that which is imagined). All the things, then, which these senses can receive and construe are called imaginations and fantasies [or phantasms], that is, forms which are represented in these senses by means of corporeal images and figures. These can be of two kinds: they are supernatural if they can be and are represented in these senses *passively;* and these we call supernaturally induced imaginary visions. Others are natural, which means that the soul can produce them within itself *actively,* by its own operative ability, in the shape of forms, figures, and images. And thus to these two faculties pertains *meditation,* which is a discursive mental activity by means of images, forms, and figures that are produced imaginatively by these two senses; as happens, for example, when we picture in our imagination Christ crucified, or bound to the pillar, or at one of the other stations [of the Cross]. Or our imagination may envision God seated upon a throne with great majesty; or we may meditate imaginatively on the radiant beauty of the light of Glory, and so on. Now the soul must be emptied of all these imagined forms, figures, and images, and it must remain in darkness with respect to these [internal] senses if it is to attain to Divine union; for these [contents of the imagination] cannot serve as proportionate means of union with God any more than can the corporeal objects of the five external senses.

The reason of this is that the imagination cannot fashion or imagine anything beyond that which it has experienced by means of the external senses—that is, beyond that which it has seen with the eyes, heard with the ears, and so on. The most it can do is to compound likenesses of the things which it has seen, or heard, or felt; and these composites do not even possess as much substantial reality as the apprehensions that have been received by the external senses. For, though one may envision with the imagination palaces made of pearls and mountains of gold—because the sight of pearls and of gold is familiar to sense experience—all this is actually less than the essence of one small piece of gold or one single pearl, although to the imagination the composite appears greater in quantity and ideal splendor.

Those, therefore, who imagine they can find God beneath any of these figures, are very far indeed from approaching Him. For, though these forms and modes of meditation are necessary for beginners, so that by means of sensory perceptions they may feed and enkindle their souls with love—thus using them as remote means to union with God and spiritual repose—yet they must merely pass through them and never allow themselves to be detained by them. Just so the stairs of a staircase are merely the means to reach the top of the staircase and the room to which it leads. And if the person who climbs the stairs would want to stay on any one of them, he would never arrive at the top. Similarly, the soul which is to attain in this life to the union of that supreme repose and bliss must pass through and leave behind all the steps of these meditations, forms, and apprehensions; for they bear no resemblance or proportion to the goal to which they lead, which is God.

Many spiritual persons commit this grave error: they have started out—as it befits beginners—by trying to approach God by means of certain images, forms, and meditations; but now God wishes to use their collected spiritual strength to lead them further on to more spiritual—internal and invisible—treasures, by depriving them of all taste for the delights of discursive meditation; and they do not possess the required ability, courage, and knowledge that would enable them to detach themselves from those more tangible methods to which they have grown accustomed. And so they continually labor to retain them, finding, however, little or no sweetness in their efforts but rather experience an increasing aridity and weariness of soul. For, as we have pointed out, the soul enjoys no longer that food of sense but needs another kind of food, more delicate, more internal and less of the nature of sense, a food which imparts to the soul deep spiritual quietude and repose. And the more the soul learns to abide in the spiritual, the more comes to a halt the operation of its faculties in particular acts, since the soul becomes more and more collected in one undivided and pure act. And thus the faculties cease to work, even as the feet cease to move and come to a halt when the journey is ended. For if the movement of going were forever to continue, one would never arrive; and if there were nothing but end-less means, it is hard to see when and where there could ever be a fruition of the end and the goal.

As these souls, however, are unfamiliar with the mystery of this novel experience, they are apt to believe that they are idle and are doing nothing at all [in this state]; and they allow themselves no rest, but endeavor to continue their meditating and reasoning. The result is that they are filled with desolation and aridity, since they are trying to find sweetness where none can any longer be found. We may even say that the greater their endeavor, the smaller their progress, for the more they persist in the pursuit [of this method], the worse becomes their state of mind, because their soul is drawn farther and farther away from spiritual peace. By trying to retrace their steps and to do all over again what has already been done, they give up the greater for the less. To such persons, therefore, we must give the advice to learn how to abide in the quietude of the presence of God, attentively, patiently, and lovingly, paying no heed to the work of the imagination. For, as we have previously stated, here the faculties [of the soul] are at rest, or rather, they are working not actively, but passively, by receiving that which God works in them.

> *The signs whereby the spiritual person may know when to pass to the state of contemplation are (1) inability to meditate discursively; (2) inability to fix the imagination on particular objects; (3) concentration of attention on God.*[45]

Although it is quite proper for a spiritual person to lay aside [discursive imaginative meditation] in due time, it is nonetheless mandatory that he not give up this kind of meditation prematurely, lest he should turn backward. We shall therefore here set down certain signs and indications which the spiritual person will find in himself, whereby he may know whether or not the time has come [to pass from the state of meditation to the state of contemplation].

The first sign is an inner awareness that he is no longer able to meditate discursively and with the accustomed spiritual gain by way of the imagination; he rather finds now aridity in that which formerly used to attract his senses and bring him sweet delight. But as long as he finds delight in meditation and discursive reasoning, he should not abandon them, unless his soul has entered into that peace and quiet which are described below as the third sign.

The second sign is a realization that he has no longer any desire to fix his imagination or his senses on particular objects, whether they be external or internal.

The third and surest sign is that the soul delights in being alone, its loving attention being fixed upon God in inward peace, quietude, and rest, without engaging in any particular meditation and without positing acts and exercising the faculties of memory, understanding, and will—at least, without any discursive acts, that is, without passing from one thing to another.

These three signs at least the spiritual person must recog-

45 *Ibid.*, Part I, Book II, Chapter XIII, pp. 53-54.

nize in himself, and *in conjunction*, before he can safely venture to leave behind the state of meditation and sense, and enter the state of contemplation and spirit.

And it is not sufficient if the first sign is present without the second, for it may well be that the reason for a person's inability to use the imagination in meditating on the things of God is his distraction and indolence. Nor does it suffice that he observe in himself the first and second sign, if he does not observe, conjoined with these, the third also; for, though he may find himself unable to reason and meditate on the things of God, this inability may be caused by melancholy or by some other kind of indisposition having its seat in the brain or in the heart.

> *Even those already advanced in the spiritual life may at times derive benefit from natural meditation. The nature of infused contemplation.*[46]

It should not be assumed that those who are beginning to experience this loving knowledge must, generally speaking, never try to return to meditation; for, at the time they are first beginning to make progress, the habit of contemplation is not yet so perfect that they can posit in themselves this act whenever they desire; nor have they progressed as yet so far beyond meditation that they cannot occasionally meditate and reason in the natural and accustomed way and discover something new in those diverse figures and steps of which they had made use before. Rather, until they reach a more advanced stage of the contemplative life, they do well to use sometimes the one and sometimes the other [kind of prayer].

The soul, then, will frequently find itself in this loving and peaceful attentiveness without in any way making use of its faculties and without working actively, but only by way of passive receptivity. But in order to reach this state, the soul will frequently have to make discreet and moderate use of discursive meditation. Once, however, the soul is placed in the state of contemplation, it acts no longer with its faculties; and so it would be more correct to say that the insight of the intellect and the sweetness of the will are at work within it rather than that the soul works anything at all; for its only remaining activity is its love of God, but without a desire to feel or see anything. And in this state

[46] *Ibid.*, Part I, Book II, Chapter XV, pp. 59-61.

[of contemplative love] God communicates Himself to the soul passively, in the manner in which light is communicated passively to a person who has his eyes open, without his doing more than merely to keep them open. Thus, what is meant by *passive understanding* is this reception of a light that is infused supernaturally. And when we say that the soul does not work, we do not mean that it has no understanding but that what it understands are not things which it has discovered by its own exertion; for in these illuminations, enlightenments or inspirations of God the soul receives only that which is given to it. Wherefore if at this time the will desires to understand and consider particular things, however spiritual they may be, it will thereby obstruct the pure and simple light of the spirit. Hence it is evident that when the soul has purified and emptied itself of all forms and images that can be apprehended, it will remain in that pure and simple light and will be transformed therein into a state of perfection.

When, therefore, the spiritual person is no longer able to meditate, let him learn to rest calmly in loving attention upon God, in the tranquillity of his understanding, even though it may seem to him that he is doing nothing. For thus, little by little, and indeed very soon, Divine calm and peace will be infused into his soul, together with a wondrous and sublime knowledge of God, enclothed in Divine love.

*Though in darkness, the soul walks securely.*[47]

The sensual and the spiritual desires are now put to sleep and mortified so that they can no longer enjoy the taste of any Divine or human thing; the affections of the soul are restrained and subdued so that they can neither move nor find support in anything; the imagination is bound and can no longer reflect in a rational manner; the memory has lost its strength; the understanding is in darkness, unable to comprehend anything; and hence the will, too, is in aridity and constraint. In short, all the faculties are void and useless; and, in addition to all this, a thick and heavy cloud oppresses the soul and keeps it, as it were, away from God. It is in this kind of darkness that the soul, according to its own words, travels securely. For, when all these operations and movements are arrested, it is evident that the soul is safe from going astray. And the deeper the darkness is in which the

47 *Ibid.*, Part II, Book II, Chapter XVI, pp. 207-9.

soul travels and the more the soul is voided of its natural operations, the greater is its security.

Now if the soul observes itself at the time of this darkness, it will soon notice how safe it is from vainglory, pride, and presumption, from vain and false joy and many other things. And so we see clearly that, by walking in dark faith, the soul by no means runs the risk of being lost, but, on the contrary, is gaining much, since in this state it is perfecting itself in all the virtues.

Therefore, oh spiritual soul, when you find your desire obscured, your affections in aridity and constraint, and your faculties deprived of their capacities for any internal exercise: be not saddened by this, but rather consider it a blessed lot, since God is now about to liberate you from yourself and to take the labor from your hands. For with your own powers, no matter how well you might have used them, you would never have been able to work so efficiently, perfectly, and securely as now, when God takes your hand and guides you in darkness to a goal and by a way which you would never have found with the aid of your own eyes and feet, no matter how sturdy a traveller you may be.

When an explorer wants to travel into new and unknown lands, he must seek new roads of which he does not know anything either by his own past experience or by the reports of others. Similarly, when the soul is making most progress, it is travelling in darkness and unknowing. And since, as we have said, God is the teacher and guide of such a blind soul, it may—once it has learned to understand this—truly and wholeheartedly rejoice and say: I travelled "securely and protected by darkness."

There is yet another reason why the soul has walked securely in this darkness, and this is because its way has been a way of suffering. For the road of suffering is far more secure and profitable than that of rejoicing and of action: first, because in suffering man receives added strength from God, while in action and in any kind of fruition the soul is indulging its own weaknesses and imperfections; and second, because in suffering the soul activates the virtues and thus becomes purer, wiser, and more cautious.

But there is another and even more potent cause of the soul's security on this dark road, and this cause is the dark light or wisdom of God. For this dark night of contemplation so strongly attracts and envelops the soul, and brings it so near to God, that He Himself now protects it and detaches it from all that is not God. And since the soul is now, as it were, undergoing a cure, so that it may regain its health (that is, God, Who is the health of the soul), His Majesty restricts it to a diet and an abstinence from all things, so that it may lose its appetite for all of them. The soul is like a sick man who is carefully nursed in his house; he is being protected from the wind, from the rays of the sun, and from noise; and he is given only small portions of delicate food—food that is more nourishing than pleasing to the palate.

Finally, there is one more reason, no less weighty than those mentioned, which makes it clear to our understanding why the soul walks securely in this darkness. We are referring to the fortitude which is transmitted to the soul by the influx of these dark and turbulent waters of God. For the soul forthwith perceives in itself a firm determination and resolve to do nothing that it knows will offend God, and to omit nothing that it knows will serve and please Him. All the desires, energies, and faculties of the soul are now detached from all other things, and all its powers are recollected and employed in the effort to please Him. In this manner the soul goes forth from itself and from all created things and travels "securely and protected by darkness" toward the sweet and blissful union of love with God.

*This dark contemplation is a secret, nameless, purely spiritual wisdom.*[48]

"I climbed the secret ladder, in disguise."

In order to understand the three specific terms which occur in this line, it is necessary to explain three things. Two of these terms—namely, "secret" and "ladder"—are used with reference to the dark night of contemplation, while the third expression—namely, "in disguise"—refers to the way the soul conducts itself in this night.

First of all, the soul calls this dark contemplation "secret," because, as we have indicated above, it is that mystical theology which the theologians describe as secret or hidden wisdom, and which, according to St. Thomas [Aquinas], is communicated and infused into the soul through love (cf. *Summa Theologica*, 2a, 2ae, q. 45, a.2). This is being done secretly, while the natural activity of the understanding and of the other faculties is in darkness. And, inasmuch as this contemplation is not brought about by any of these faculties, but is infused by the Holy Spirit, without the soul's knowledge or understanding, it is called secret.

48 *Ibid.*, Part II, Book II, Chapter XVII, pp. 209-11.

It is not, however, for this reason alone that this contemplation may be called secret, but also because of the effects which it produces in the soul. For this contemplation is secret or hidden not only in the darknesses and afflictions of purgation, but likewise afterwards in illumination, when this wisdom is communicated to the soul with much greater clarity. Even then, however, it is still so secret that the soul is unable to name it or to speak of it. Not only has the soul no desire to speak of it or to name it, but it is unable to find any suitable similitude by which it might describe such a sublime knowledge and such a delicate spiritual experience. For this inward wisdom is so simple, general, and spiritual that it cannot enter into the understanding in any conceptual form or sensory image, notwithstanding the fact that the soul is clearly aware that it is partaking of that wondrous and blissful wisdom. For it is a characteristic of the language of God that, on account of its being so intimate and spiritual, it wholly transcends the sphere of sense and at once nullifies and voids all the harmony and capacity of the internal and external senses. And, inasmuch as the wisdom of this contemplation is the language of God addressed to the soul, and spoken by pure spirit to pure spirit, nothing that is less than spirit can comprehend it, and it therefore remains hidden to the senses.

This mystical wisdom is called "secret" also on account of the fact that it has the property of hiding the soul within itself. For it sometimes takes possession of the soul and draws it into its secret abyss, in such a way that the soul clearly sees what a distance there is between it and every creature and how far it has been carried away. It feels as though it had been placed into a profound and vast solitude, into an immense and boundless desert, inaccessible to any human being. And the deeper, vaster, and more hidden the solitude, the more it delights and pleases the soul. This abyss of wisdom greatly exalts and enriches the soul and places it at the very source of the science of love.

This property of secrecy or concealment and of transcendence with respect to the natural capacity pertains to this Divine contemplation not only because it is supernatural, but also because it acts as a guide in leading the soul to the perfections of the union with God. And inasmuch as these perfections cannot be known in the human manner, they must be approached by human unknowing and by supernatural ignorance. For, speaking mystically (as we are doing here), these Divine things and perfections are not known and understood in their true being when they are merely sought or theoretically explored, but only when they have been found and practically experienced.

> *This secret wisdom is a ladder on which the soul climbs upward and downward, until it attains to mystical union.*[49]

It remains now to consider the second point, namely, to explain in what sense this secret wisdom is also a "ladder." This name applies, first of all, because, just as soldiers climb up on ladders and enter fortified places in order to gain possession of provisions, material treasures, and other objects, so the soul, by means of this secret contemplation, mounts (without knowing how) to gain knowledge and possession of the goods and treasures of Heaven.

Furthermore, we may call this secret contemplation a ladder because, even as the steps of a ladder serve men to ascend and descend, so this secret contemplation—by means of the identical supernatural communications—alternately raises the soul up to God and humbles it with respect to its own self. For it is the common property of all truly Divine communications that they both humble and exalt the soul. For on this road every descent is an ascent, and every ascent is a descent, because "everyone who humbles himself shall be exalted, and he who exalts himself shall be humbled" (Luke 14:11). And it is the ordinary way and rule of the state of contemplation that one never remains for long at the same place, but is continually ascending and descending, until the soul arrives at the state of quiet. For, since the state of perfection consists in the perfect love of God and the contempt of oneself, the soul cannot be without this dichotomy, namely, the knowledge of God and the knowledge of its own self —that is, without ever recurring exaltations and humiliations —until it has acquired the habits of perfection. Only then will this ascending and descending cease, because the soul will then have reached its goal and will have become united with Him Who stands at the summit of this ladder and upon Whom the ladder leans and rests.

This ladder of contemplation is prefigured in that ladder which Jacob saw in his dream, on which angels were ascending from man to God and descending from God to man (cf. Gen. 28:12). And all this, according to Holy Scripture, took place by night, when Jacob was asleep, which indicates how secret and how different from the human mode of knowing is this road and this ascent to God.

[49] *Ibid.*, Part II, Book II, Chapter XVIII, pp. 211-13.

But the principal characteristic and the main reason why this contemplation is here called a "ladder" is that it is a *science of love*, that is, an infused and loving knowledge of God, which at one and the same time illumines the soul and enkindles it with love, to the end that it may be raised step by step to God its Creator. For it is love alone that unites and joins the soul with God. And in order that this may be seen more clearly, we shall here indicate the several steps of this Divine ladder and point out briefly the marks and effects of each, so that the soul may be able to observe on which of them it is standing. We shall therefore now proceed to distinguish these steps by their effects, as do St. Bernard [of Clairvaux] and St. Thomas [Aquinas].

### The dark night of the spirit [50]

This dark night is an inflowing of God into the soul, which purges it from its ignorance and its habitual—natural and spiritual—imperfections. The theologians call it *infused contemplation* and treat of it in *mystical theology*. In this state God mysteriously teaches the soul the perfection of love, without its doing anything and without its understanding the nature of this infused contemplation. For what produces such striking effects in the soul is the loving wisdom of God, which by its purifying and illuminating action prepares the soul for the union of love with God. And this loving wisdom is the same which also purifies and illumines the blessed spirits.

But now the question arises: Why does the soul call this Divine light a dark night? The answer is that for two reasons this Divine wisdom is for the soul not only night and darkness, but also affliction and torment. The first reason is the sublime grandeur of Divine Wisdom, which transcends the capacity of the soul and is therefore darkness to it. The second reason is the lowliness and impurity of the soul, and in this respect Divine Wisdom is for the soul painful, bitter, and dark.

In order to prove the first point, we must refer to a doctrine of the Philosopher [i.e., Aristotle], which says that, the clearer and more manifest Divine things are in themselves, the darker and more hidden they are to the soul; just as, the brighter the light is, the more it blinds and darkens the eye of the night-owl. When, therefore, this Divine light of contemplation invades a soul which is not yet wholly illumined,

50 *Ibid.*, Part II, Book I, Chapter V, pp. 188-90.

it causes spiritual darkness in it; for it not only transcends the soul's natural intellectual capacity, but it also drowns out and darkens the act of intellection. This is why Dionysius [the Areopagite] and other mystical theologians call this infused contemplation a ray of darkness for the soul that is not yet wholly purified and illumined.

And [with respect to the second point] it is clear that this dark contemplation is in its early stages very painful to the soul; for, as this Divine infused contemplation comprises in itself a plentitude of the highest perfections, and since the soul which receives them is not yet wholly purified and thus still engulfed in a sea of miseries, it follows that—because two contraries cannot coexist in one subject—the soul must of necessity endure much pain and suffering. Thus, when this pure light invades the soul, in order to expel its impurity, the soul feels its own impurity so intensely that it believes God to be its enemy and comes to think of itself as an enemy of God. This causes it so much grief and sadness that it feels actually rejected and forsaken by God. And what gives it the greatest pain is the fear that it will never be worthy of God and that therefore all its blessings are lost for ever. For this Divine and dark light now reveals to the soul's sight all its faults and miseries, so that it may see clearly how by its own powers it can never have anything else.

The second kind of torment which the soul suffers is caused by its natural, moral, and spiritual weakness; for, when this Divine contemplation takes hold of the soul with some degree of violence, in order to strengthen it and make it obedient, it suffers so much pain in its weakness that it almost faints. Both sense and spirit suffer such pain and agony as if they were weighed down by some immense load, so that even death would appear as a release and relief. And it is indeed very strange and very sad that the soul is so weak and impure that the light and gentle hand of God appears to it as such a prodigious weight and such a hostile force, since this hand does not really weigh the soul down, but only touches it mercifully, in order to bestow favors and graces upon it.

# -7-

# Islamic Mysticism

Islamic mysticism is more familiarly known as Sufism. The word Sufi appears to have originated as a nickname which was connected with the wool clothing worn by some of the earlier mystics. Sufism flourished chiefly in Arab countries and in Persia. No precise date can be given for its origin, but it may be thought of as beginning to be important in the ninth century A.D. and as reaching its golden age in the tenth century. It continued at a high level for some centuries and entered on its decline from about the fifteenth century. We may briefly sketch some of its main characteristics.

The natural drift toward pantheism which is a general feature of mysticism in the West—where the theologians and ecclesiastical authorities try to suppress it and brand it as heresy—is even more pronounced in Sufism than in Christianity, although Muslim orthodoxy disapproves of it quite as emphatically as Christian orthodoxy does. Indeed, the Islamic disapproval may be stronger than the Christian, owing to its more rigid monotheism. After all, no Christian mystic was ever martyred for his pantheistic utterances, whereas this did happen in Baghdad. The language used by some of the Sufis was very much wilder and more "rash" than anything ever said by Meister Eckhart. Abu Yazid al Bistami (died 875), having declared that God was in his soul, horrified the orthodox by exclaiming "Glory to Me! How great is my Majesty." He was amongst the earliest of the so-called "intoxicated" Sufis. Al Hallaj was accused of using language which, taken with other tendencies of his teaching, was thought to imply a claim to being an incarnation of

201

God. The words that formed the basis of this charge were, "I am the Truth." Whatever he may have meant by this, he was found guilty of blasphemy and was crucified in Baghdad in 922. Another Sufi is stated to have pointed to his own clothing and to have said, "There is nothing inside this coat except Allah."

Undoubtedly this kind of language is preposterous—ridiculous, however, rather than wicked. But we must try to penetrate more deeply into the problem than this. The fact that in Islam the pantheistic tendency of mysticism resulted in wild extremes of language which were never heard from the more sober Christian mystics may perhaps be due to the fact that there is in Islam no strong central religious authority corresponding to the Roman church in Christianity. According to the opinion of the present writer, the pantheistic interpretation of mystical experience which is found in the major Vedantist tradition and in Plotinus is not only natural but constitutes the more perfect type of mysticism, while its dualistic interpretation—as expressed, for example, by Ruysbroeck and St. John of the Cross—is relatively undeveloped. The essence of the mystical experience, since it transcends all multiplicity, must transcend the dualism of subject and object. Dualistic interpretations, consequently, do violence to the experience. It is therefore amusing to see with what horror the conventional orthodoxies of the West speak of the deadly sin of pantheism. If it is correct that in the developed mystical consciousness there is no division of subject and object, and if one interprets the experience in theistic terms as is done in Western religions, it of course follows that there is no distinction between the self of the mystic and God. This is the basis of the pantheistic claim, and it is the excuse which must be made for the wilder utterances of the intoxicated Sufis. Nevertheless there must be something wrong with a statement which simply says, "I am God," and leaves it at that. There must be some qualifying consideration. It is natural to ask what it is. This is not the place for the prolonged philosophical discussion which would be necessary to answer this question fully. I shall here simply say that "I am God" is only half of the truth, the other half being "I am not God." As usual, the mystical consciousness is paradoxical. The truth, if expressed in theistic language, is not simple identity with God but rather identity in difference.

It is impossible to write of Sufism without some mention of the great al-Ghazzali (died 1111). I have not included anything by him in my selections. The reason is that although he was the great philosopher of Sufism, it is doubtful whether he was himself a mystic in the sense of having personally attained to the mystical consciousness, although we cannot be certain that he did not at least glimpse it. He states himself that theory came easier to him than practice. His writing is definitely logical, analytic, and philosophical both in substance and style. It cannot be called mystical writing although it is about mysticism. He became professor of divinity in Baghdad in 1091, but after four years of teaching he resigned his professorship in order to follow the mystic path himself. He had, he says, learned everything about Sufism which it is possible to acquire by learning and hearing, and had perceived that he could get no further by the use of the intellect. Only by immediate experience and ecstasy could the goal be reached. Seeking that goal, he lived the rest of his life in retirement. There is no question of the greatness of his philosophical ability. Even in translation his writing is a delight to read because of its clarity and because of his rare gift for elucidating abstract discussion by happy examples. In regard to the great question of pantheism versus orthodoxy, he took the orthodox view, condemning the extravagances of the wilder Sufi brethren. Yet his position is wholly sympathetic to the mystic claim to immediate experience of God, and one of his central aims was to reconcile Sufism and Islamic orthodoxy. His position in Islam has been compared both to that of St. Augustine and that of St. Thomas Aquinas in Christian history.

Persian Sufism is notable for the fact that it tended to express itself in poetry and produced a number of great mystical poets. Of these Farid al-Din Attar (died 1229) and Jalal al-Din Rumi (died 1273) are represented in our selections. Many of the poets were notable for their use of erotic imagery and for imagery drawn from phenomena of alcoholic intoxication.

If the reader keeps in mind the general character of mysticism and mystical experience as it has appeared in previous chapters, he will have no difficulty in understanding any of the following selections. I therefore refrain from further commentary or explanation except a few words of introduction to the selection from Attar.

# Ziyad B. al-Arabi (9th Century)

*Ecstasy*[1]

The beginning of ecstasy is the lifting of the veil and the vision of the Divine Guardian, and the presence of understanding, and the contemplation of the invisible, and the discoursing on secret things and perceiving the non-existent, and it means that you pass away from where you are. Ecstasy is the first of the stations of the elect and it is the inheritance of assurance of the thing desired, and for those who have experienced it, when its light has been shed abroad in their hearts, all doubt and suspicion have passed from them. He who is veiled from ecstasy and dominated by the claims of the self, is hampered by making a living and by worldly motives, for the self is veiled by such motives. But if these are banished and devotion to God is made pure from self-interest and the heart comes to itself again and is made refined and pure and gains benefit from exhortation, when it worships God and utters prayers in intimate converse with Him, drawing near to Him, and He addresses it and it hears with attention Him Who speaks, and is contemplating Him and its conscience is pure, then it beholds from what it was freed and there is ecstasy, because it has found what was lost.

Ecstasy in this world comes not from revelation, but consists in the vision of the heart and realisation of the truth and gaining assurance, and he who has attained to it beholds with the joy of certainty and with a devotion free of self-interest, for he is all-attentive. When he awakes from the vision, he loses what he has found, but his knowledge remains with him, and for a long time his spirit enjoys that, with the increase of certainty, which he has gained through the vision. This depends upon the servant's proximity to his Lord, or his distance from Him, and upon the vision given to him by his Creator.

But if anyone asks for a further description of ecstasy, let him cease to do that, for how can a thing be described which has no description but itself, and no witness to it but itself, and its reality is known from itself, to him who has it: he knows of its existence from his ecstasy. He who does not know it, denies its existence and both he who knows it and he who does not know it are altogether unable to deal with

[1] Margaret Smith, *Readings from the Mystics of Islam*. London: Luzac & Company, Ltd., 1950, pp. 20-22.

the matter. For it is felt by experience only, and he who has it can contemplate the vision and he is one of the chosen, truly existent, but inaccessible and lost, for he is veiled by his own light from its light, and by his own attributes from its apprehension and by the names by which he calls it, from its essence, I mean the essence of ecstasy, for certainty and faith and truth and likewise love and longing, and proximity—all that is but a poor description of it. He who asks about its flavour and experience asks about the impossible, for flavour and experience are not known by description, without tasting and experience.

# Abu Yazid al-Bistami (Died A.D. 875)

### The Great Silence [2]

Be in a domain where neither good nor evil exists: both of them belong to the world of created things; in the presence of Unity there is neither command nor prohibition.

All this talk and turmoil and noise and movement is outside of the veil; within the veil is silence and calm and rest.

Dost thou hear how there comes a voice from the brooks of running water? But when they reach the sea they are quiet, and the sea is neither augmented by their incoming nor diminished by their outgoing.

### Dissolution of Individuality [3]

Creatures are subject to "states," but the gnostic has no "state," because his vestiges are effaced and his essence is annihilated by the essence of another and his traces are lost in another's traces.

I went from God to God, until they cried from me in me, "O Thou I!"—i.e. I attained the stage of annihilation in God.

Nothing is better for Man than to be without aught, having no asceticism, no theory, no practice. When he is without all he is with all. . . . They asked (Bistami), "When does a man know that he has attained real gnosis?" He said: "At the time when he becomes annihilated under the knowledge of God, and is made everlasting on the carpet of God, without self and without creature."

2 R. A. Nicholson, *Eastern Poetry and Prose.* London: Cambridge University Press, 1922.
3 Journal of the Royal Asiatic Society. London, 1906.

# Ibn Sina (Avicenna) (Died A.D. 1037)

### Stages of the Mystical Life[4]

Every created thing, by its nature, longs for the perfection which means its well-being, and the perfection of the created being is brought about by the grace of that One Who is essentially perfect. The most perfect object of love is the First Cause of all things: for His Glory is revealed, except to those who are not able to receive the revelation. . He is hidden only from those who are veiled by shortcoming and weakness and defect.

But the gnostics have stripped off the veils of their bodies and have devoted themselves to concern with God. . the soul then has reached the light of the Sun and is able to receive the Divine Illumination when it wills, free from all worldly distractions, until it is wholly sanctified. The gnostic desires God only, none other and adores Him as the only Object worthy of adoration and he is moved not by hope of recompense nor by fear of punishment nor anything else, for his eyes are fixed upon his Lord alone.

There are stages and degrees in the contemplative life, to which the gnostic alone in this world attains. The first step for the gnostic is called Will, which means certainty as to the Way. Through this the gnostic will discipline his soul, through his faith, and will direct it towards God, so that he may attain the joy of union. The second stage is that of self-discipline, which is directed towards three things, removing all save God from the gnostic's choice, subduing his carnal soul to his rational soul, so that the imagination and intellect shall be attracted to the higher things, not the lower, and making the conscience mindful of admonition. The third stage means that the soul, now free from sensual desires, is filled with good thoughts and gives itself up to the spiritual love which seeks to be ruled by the qualities of the Beloved.

Now appear to the gnostic flashes of the Divine Light, like fleeting gleams of lightning, which pass away. By those who experience them, these are called "mystic states" and every state brings joy and becomes more frequent, as the gnostic is more able to receive them. In the fourth stage the mystic sees God in all things and then in the fifth stage he becomes accustomed to God's Presence, the brief flashes of lightning

4 Smith, *op. cit.*, pp. 47-49.

become a shining flame, and he attains to direct knowledge of God and is continually in fellowship with Him.

Then the gnostic passes on to the stage of contemplating God in Himself: he is absent, yet present, he is departing yet abiding. Then he turns to the world of Reality and his contemplation of God is stable and continuous, and when he passes from striving to attainment, his inmost soul becomes a polished mirror reflecting the Face of God. Then he passes away from himself and contemplates only the Divine Glory and if he looks upon himself, it is only as the one contemplating, and when he has come to this, he has attained complete union with God.

# Farid al-Din Attar (Died A.D. 1229)

## *The Conference of the Birds* [5]

[Attar's poem is an elaborate allegory. All the birds of the world have assembled and asked the Hoopoe to lead them to the abode of the Simurgh, the King of all birds and the sovereign lord of creation. The Hoopoe describes at length to them the terrors and sufferings of the journey they will have to make. They must pass through seven valleys, to wit, the Valley of the Quest, the Valley of Love, the Valley of Understanding, the Valley of Independence and Detachment, the Valley of Pure Unity, the Valley of Astonishment, the Valley of Poverty and Nothingness. This description—interlarded with a variety of stories, anecdotes, parables, and reflections—occupies the greater part of the poem which concludes with the following words:]

When the birds had listened to this discourse of the Hoopoe their heads drooped down, and sorrow pierced their hearts. Now they understood how difficult it would be for a handful of dust like themselves to bend such a bow. So great was their agitation that numbers of them died then and there. But others, in spite of their distress, decided to set out on the long road. For years they travelled over mountains and valleys, and a great part of their life flowed past on this journey. But how is it possible to relate all that happened to them? It would be necessary to go with them and see their difficulties for oneself, and to follow the wanderings of this long road. Only then could one realize what the birds suffered.

[5] Farid al-Din Attar, *The Conference of the Birds*, translated by S. C. Nott. London: The Janus Press.

In the end, only a small number of all this great company arrived at that sublime place to which the Hoopoe had led them. Of the thousands of birds almost all had disappeared. Many had been lost in the ocean, others had perished on the summits of the high mountains, tortured by thirst; others had had their wings burnt and their hearts dried up by the fire of the sun; others were devoured by tigers and panthers; others died of fatigue in the deserts and in the wilderness, some went mad and killed each other for a grain of barley; others, enfeebled by suffering and weariness, dropped on the road unable to go further; others, bewildered by the things they saw, stopped where they were, stupefied; and many, who had started out from curiosity or pleasure, perished without an idea of what they had set out to find.

So then, out of all those thousands of birds, only thirty reached the end of the journey. And even these were bewildered, weary and dejected, with neither feathers nor wings. But now they were at the door of this Majesty that cannot be described, whose essence is incomprehensible—that Being who is beyond human reason and knowledge. Then flashed the lightning of fulfilment, and a hundred worlds were consumed in a moment. They saw thousands of suns each more resplendent than the other, thousands of moons and stars all equally beautiful, and seeing all this they were amazed and agitated like a dancing atom of dust, and they cried out: "O Thou who art more radiant than the sun! Thou, who hast reduced the sun to an atom, how can we appear before Thee? Ah, why have we so uselessly endured all this suffering on the Way? Having renounced ourselves and all things, we now cannot obtain that for which we have striven. Here, it little matters whether we exist or not."

Then the birds, who were so disheartened that they resembled a cock half-killed, sank into despair. A long time passed. When, at a propitious moment, the door suddenly opened, there stepped out a noble chamberlain, one of the courtiers of the Supreme Majesty. He looked them over and saw that out of thousands only these thirty birds were left.

He said: "Now then, O Birds, where have you come from, and what are you doing here? What is your name? O you who are destitute of everything, where is your home? What do they call you in the world? What can be done with a feeble handful of dust like you?"

"We have come," they said, "to acknowledge the Simurgh as our king. Through love and desire for him we have lost our reason and our peace of mind. Very long ago, when we started on this journey, we were thousands, and now only thirty of us have arrived at this sublime court. We cannot believe that the King will scorn us after all the sufferings we have gone through. Ah, no! He cannot but look on us with the eye of benevolence!"

The Chamberlain replied: "O you whose minds and hearts are troubled, whether you exist or do not exist in the universe, the King has his being always and eternally. Thousands of worlds of creatures are no more than an ant at his gate. You bring nothing but moans and lamentations. Return then to whence you came, O vile handful of earth!"

At this, the birds were petrified with astonishment. Nevertheless, when they came to themselves a little, they said: "Will this great king reject us so ignominiously? And if he really has this attitude to us may he not change it to one of honour? Remember Majnūn who said, 'If all the people who dwell on earth wished to sing my praises, I would not accept them; I would rather have the insults of Laīla. One of her insults is more to me than a hundred compliments from another woman!' "

"The lightning of his glory manifests itself," said the Chamberlain, "and it lifts up the reason of all souls. What benefit is there if the soul be consumed by a hundred sorrows? What benefit is there at this moment in either greatness or littleness?"

The birds, on fire with love, said: "How can the moth save itself from the flame when it wishes to be one with the flame? The friend we seek will content us by allowing us to be united to him. If now we are refused, what is there left for us to do? We are like the moth who wished for union with the flame of the candle. They begged him not to sacrifice himself so foolishly and for such an impossible aim, but he thanked them for their advice and told them that since his heart was given to the flame for ever, nothing else mattered."

Then the Chamberlain, having tested them, opened the door; and as he drew aside a hundred curtains, one after the other, a new world beyond the veil was revealed. Now was the light of lights manifested, and all of them sat down on the masnad, the seat of the Majesty and Glory. They were given a writing which they were told to read through; and reading this, and pondering, they were able to understand their state. When they were completely at peace and detached from all things they became aware that the Simurgh was there with them, and a new life began for them in the Simurgh. All that they had done previously was washed away. The sun of majesty sent forth his rays, and in the reflection of each other's faces these thirty birds of the outer world contemplated the face of the Simurgh of the inner world. This so astonished them that they did not know if they were still themselves or if they had become the Simurgh. At last, in a state of contemplation, they realized that they were the Simurgh and that the Simurgh was the thirty birds. When they gazed at the Simurgh they saw that it was truly the Simurgh who was there, and when they turned their eyes towards themselves they saw that they themselves were the Simurgh. And perceiving both at once, themselves and Him, they realized that they and the Simurgh were one and the same being. No one in the world has ever heard of anything to equal it.

Then they gave themselves up to meditation, and after a little they asked the Simurgh, without the use of tongues, to reveal to them the secret of the mystery of the unity and plurality of beings. The Simurgh, also without speaking, made this reply: "The sun of my majesty is a mirror. He who sees himself therein sees his soul and his body, and sees them completely. Since you have come as thirty birds, si-murgh, you will see thirty birds in this mirror. If forty or fifty were to come, it would be the same. Although you are now completely changed you see yourselves as you were before.

"Can the sight of an ant reach to the far-off Pleiades? And can this insect lift an anvil? Have you ever seen a gnat seize an elephant in its teeth? All that you have known, all that you have seen, all that you have said or heard—all this is no longer that. When you crossed the valleys of the Spiritual Way and when you performed good tasks, you did all this by my action; and you were able to see the valleys of my essence and my perfections. You, who are only thirty birds, did well to be astonished, impatient and wondering. But I am more than thirty birds. I am the very essence of the true Simurgh. Annihilate then yourselves gloriously and joyfully in me, and in me you shall find yourselves."

Thereupon, the birds at last lost themselves for ever in the Simurgh—the shadow was lost in the sun, and that is all.

All that you have heard or seen or known is not even the beginning of what you must know, and since the ruined habitation of this world is not your place you must renounce it. Seek the trunk of the tree, and do not worry about whether the branches do or do not exist.

# Ibn al-Arabi (Died A.D. 1240)

## *There Is No Existence Except God* [6]

He is and there is with Him no before or after, nor above nor below, nor far nor near, nor union nor division, nor how nor where nor place. He is now as He was, He is the One without oneness and the Single without singleness. He is the very existence of the First and the very existence of the Last, and the very existence of the Outward and the very existence of the Inward. So that there is no first nor last nor outward nor inward except Him, without those becoming Him or His becoming them. He is not in a thing nor a thing in Him, whether entering in or proceeding forth. It is necessary that you know Him, after this fashion, not by learning nor by intellect, nor by understanding, nor by imagination, nor by sense, nor by the outward eye nor by the inward eye, nor by perception. By Himself He sees Himself and by Himself He knows Himself. . His veil, that is, phenomenal existence, is but the concealment of His existence in His oneness, without any attribute. . There is no other and there is no existence for any other than He. He whom you think to be other than God, he is not other than God, but you do not know Him and do not understand that you are seeing Him. He is still Ruler as well as ruled, and Creator as well as created. He is now as He was, as to His creative power and as to His sovereignty, not requiring a creature nor a subject. . When He called into being the things that are, He was already endowed with all His attributes and He is as He was then. In His oneness there is no difference between what is recent and what is original: the recent is the result of His manifestation of Himself and the original is the result of His remaining within Himself.

There is no existence save His existence. To this the Prophet pointed when he said: "Revile not the world, for God is the world," pointing to the fact that the existence of the world is God's existence without partner or like or equal. It is related that the Prophet declared that God said to Moses: "O My servant, I was sick and thou didst not visit Me: I asked help of thee and thou didst not give it to Me," and other like expressions. This means that the existence of the beggar is His existence and the existence of the sick is His existence. Now when this is admitted, it is acknowledged

6 Smith, *op. cit.*, pp. 98-101.

that this existence is His existence and that the existence of all created things, both accidents and substances, is His existence, and when the secret of one atom of the atoms is clear, the secret of all created things, both outward and inward, is clear, and you do not see in this world or the next, anything except God, for the existence of these two Abodes and their name, and what they name, all of them are assuredly He.

When the mystery—of realising that the mystic is one with the Divine—is revealed to you, you will understand that you are no other than God and that you have continued and will continue . . without when and without times Then you will see all your actions to be His actions and all your attributes to be His attributes and your essence to be His essence, though you do not thereby become He or He you, in either the greatest or the least degree. "Everything is perishing save His Face," that is, there is nothing except His Face, "then, whithersoever you turn, there is the Face of God."

Just as he who dies the death of the body, loses all his attributes, both those worthy of praise and those worthy of condemnation alike, so in the spiritual death all attributes, both those worthy of praise and those to be condemned, come to an end, and in all the man's states what is Divine comes to take the place of what was mortal. Thus, instead of his own essence, there is the essence of God and in place of his own qualities, there are the attributes of God. He who knows himself sees his whole existence to be the Divine existence, but does not realise that any change has taken place in his own nature or qualities. For when you know yourself, your "I-ness" vanishes and you know that you and God are one and the same.

### Effects of the Beatific Vision [7]

In the Beatific Vision God manifests Himself to the elect in a general epiphany which, nevertheless, assumes various forms corresponding to the mental conceptions of God formed by the faithful on earth. There is, then, one single epiphany, which is multiple only by reason of the difference of forms by which it is received. The Vision impregnates the elect with Divine light, each experiencing the Vision ac-

[7] Miguel Asin Palacio, *Islam and the Divine Comedy*. London: John Murray (Publishers) Ltd., 1926.

cording to the knowledge of the Divine dogma or dogmas gained by him on earth.

The Divine light pervades the beings of the elect and radiates from them, reflected as if by mirrors, on everything around them. The spiritual enjoyment produced by the contemplation of this reflection is even greater than that of the Vision itself. For, at the moment when they experience the Beatific Vision, the elect are transported and losing all consciousness, cannot appreciate the joy of the Vision. Delight they feel, but the very intensity of the vision makes it impossible for them to realise it. The reflected light, on the other hand, does not overpower them, and they are thus able to participate in all its joys.

# Jalal al-Din Rumi (Died A.D. 1273)

Most of the following selections are from Rumi's most famous poem, the Mathnawi, but a few are from other books.

## UNITY OF SPIRIT[8]

WHEN the rose is dead and the garden ravaged, where shall we find the perfume of the rose? In rose-water.

Inasmuch as God comes not into sight, the prophets are His vicars.

Do not mistake me! 'Tis wrong to think that the vicar and He Whom the vicar represents are two.

To the form-worshipper they are two; when you have escaped from consciousness of form, they are One.

Whilst you regard the form, you are seeing double: look, not at the eyes, but at the light which flows from them.

You cannot distinguish the lights of ten lamps burning together, so long as your face is set towards this light alone.

In things spiritual there is no partition, no number, no individuals.

How sweet is the oneness of the Friend with His friends! Catch the spirit and clasp it to your bosom.

Mortify rebellious form till it wastes away: unearth the treasure of Unity!

Simple were we and all one essence: we were knotless and pure as water.

[8] *Rumi: Poet and Mystic*, translated by R. A. Nicholson. London: George Allen & Unwin, Ltd., 1950; New York: The Macmillan Company, 1950, p. 134.

When that goodly Light took shape, it became many, like shadows cast by a battlement.

Demolish the dark battlement, and all difference will vanish from amidst this multitude.

## DEIFICATION [9]

WHEN a fly is plunged in honey, all the members of its body are reduced to the same condition, and it does not move. Similarly the term *istighrāq* (absorption in God) is applied to one who has no conscious existence or initiative or movement. Any action that proceeds from him is not his own. If he is still struggling in the water, or if he cries out, "Oh, I am drowning," he is not said to be in the state of absorption. This is what is signified by the words *Ana 'l-Haqq* "I am God." People imagine that it is a presumptuous claim, whereas it is really a presumptuous claim to say *Ana 'l-'abd* "I am the slave of God"; and *Ana 'l-Haqq* "I am God" is an expression of great humility. The man who says *Ana 'l-'abd* "I am the slave of God" affirms two existences, his own and God's, but he that says *Ana 'l-Haqq* "I am God" has made himself non-existent and has given himself up and says "I am God," *i.e.* "I am naught, He is all: there is no being but God's." This is the extreme of humility and self-abasement.

## THE SHEPHERD'S PRAYER [10]

MOSES saw a shepherd on the way, crying, "O Lord Who choosest as Thou wilt,

Where art Thou, that I may serve Thee and sew Thy shoon and comb Thy hair?

That I may wash Thy clothes and kill Thy lice and bring milk to Thee, O worshipful One;

That I may kiss Thy little hand and rub Thy little feet and sweep Thy little room at bed-time."

On hearing these foolish words, Moses said, "Man, to whom are you speaking?

What babble! What blasphemy and raving! Stuff some cotton into your mouth!

Truly the friendship of a fool is enmity: the High God is not in want of suchlike service."

The shepherd rent his garment, heaved a sigh, and took his way to the wilderness.

9 *Ibid.*, p. 184.
10 *Ibid.*, p. 170.

Then came to Moses a Revelation: "Thou hast parted My
   servant from Me.
Wert thou sent as a prophet to unite, or wert thou sent to
   sever?
I have bestowed on every one a particular mode of worship,
   I have given every one a peculiar form of expression.
The idiom of Hindustān is excellent for Hindūs; the idiom
   of Sind is excellent for the people of Sind.
I look not at tongue and speech, I look at the spirit and
   the inward feeling.
I look into the heart to see whether it be lowly, though the
   words uttered be not lowly.
Enough of phrases and conceits and metaphors! I want
   burning, burning: become familiar with that burning!
Light up a fire of love in thy soul, burn all thought and
   expression away!
O Moses, they that know the conventions are of one sort,
   they whose souls burn are of another."

The religion of love is apart from all religions. The lovers
of God have no religion but God alone.

## THE ONE TRUE LIGHT[11]

THE lamps are different, but the Light is the same: it comes
   from Beyond.
If thou keep looking at the lamp, thou art lost: for thence
   arises the appearance of number and plurality.
Fix thy gaze upon the Light, and thou art delivered from
   the dualism inherent in the finite body.
O thou who art the kernel of Existence, the disagreement
   between Moslem, Zoroastrian and Jew depends on the
   standpoint.

Some Hindūs brought an elephant, which they exhibited in a
   dark shed.
As seeing it with the eye was impossible, every one felt it
   with the palm of his hand.
The hand of one fell on its trunk: he said, "This animal is
   like a water-pipe."
Another touched its ear: to him the creature seemed like a
   fan.
Another handled its leg and described the elephant as having the shape of a pillar.

[11] Ibid., p. 166.

Another stroked its back. "Truly," said he, "this elephant resembles a throne."

Had each of them held a lighted candle, there would have been no contradiction in their words.

## THE SONG OF THE REED[12]

> HEARKEN to this Reed forlorn,
> Breathing, even since 'twas torn
> From its rushy bed, a strain
> Of impassioned love and pain.
>
> "The secret of my song, though near,
> None can see and none can hear.
> Oh, for a friend to know the sign
> And mingle all his soul with mine!
>
> 'Tis the flame of Love that fired me,
> 'Tis the wine of Love inspired me.
> Wouldst thou learn how lovers bleed,
> Hearken, hearken to the Reed!"

## "THE MARRIAGE OF TRUE MINDS"[13]

HAPPY the moment when we are seated in the palace, thou and I,

With two forms and with two figures but with one soul, thou and I.

The colours of the grove and the voices of the birds will bestow immortality

At the time when we shall come into the garden, thou and I.

The stars of Heaven will come to gaze upon us:

We shall show them the moon herself, thou and I.

Thou and I, individuals no more, shall be mingled in ecstasy,

Joyful and secure from foolish babble, thou and I.

All the bright-plumed birds of Heaven will devour their hearts with envy

In the place where we shall laugh in such a fashion, thou and I.

[12] Ibid., p. 31.
[13] Ibid., p. 35.

This is the greatest wonder, that thou and I, sitting here
   in the same nook,
Are at this moment both in 'Irāq and Khorāsān, thou
   and I.

## PHENOMENA THE BRIDGE TO REALITY[14]

IN the hour of absence Love fashions many a form of
   phantasy; in the hour of presence the Formless One reveals Himself,
Saying, "I am the ultimate origin of sobriety and intoxication: the beauty in all forms is reflected from Me.
Now, because thou hast often gazed on My reflexion, thou
   art able to contemplate My Pure Essence."

## LOVE IN ABSENCE[15]

How should not I mourn, like night, without His day and
   the favour of His day-illuming countenance?
His unsweetness is sweet to my soul: may my soul be sacri-
   ficed to the Beloved who grieves my heart!
I am in love with grief and pain for the sake of pleasing
   my peerless King.
Tears shed for His sake are pearls, though people think
   they are tears.
I complain of the Soul of my soul, but in truth I am not
   complaining: I am only telling.
My heart says it is tormented by Him, and I have long
   been laughing at its poor pretence.
Do me right, O Glory of the righteous, O Thou Who art
   the dais, and I the threshold of Thy door!
Where are threshold and dais in reality? Where the Beloved
   is, where are "we" and "I"?
O Thou Whose soul is free from "we" and "I," O Thou
   Who art the essence of the spirit in men and women,
When men and women become one, Thou art that One;
   when the units are wiped out, lo, Thou art that Unity.
Thou didst contrive this "I" and "we" in order to play
   the game of worship with Thyself,
That all "I"s and "thou"s might become one soul and at
   last be submerged in the Beloved.

[14] *Ibid.*, p. 139.
[15] *Ibid.*, p. 33.

## THE FAITHFUL ARE ONE SOUL[16]

The Faithful are many, but their Faith is one; their bodies are numerous, but their soul is one.

Besides the understanding and soul which is in the ox and the ass, Man has another intelligence and soul.

Again, in the owner of the Divine breath, there is a soul other than the human soul.

The animal soul does not possess oneness: do not seek oneness from that airy spirit.

If its owner eat bread, his neighbour is not filled; if he bear a load, his neighbour does not become laden;

Nay, but he rejoices at his neighbour's death and dies of envy when he see his neighbour prosperous.

The souls of wolves and dogs are separate; the souls of the Lions of God are united.

I speak nominally of their souls in the plural, for that single Soul is a hundred in relation to the body,

Just as the single light of the sun in heaven is a hundred in relation to the house-courts on which it shines;

But when you remove the walls, all these scattered lights are one and the same.

When the bodily houses have no foundation remaining, the Faithful remain one soul.

## THE MYSTIC WAY[17]

Plug thy low sensual ear, which stuffs like cotton
Thy conscience and makes deaf thine inward ear.
Be without ear, without sense, without thought,
And hearken to the call of God, "*Return!*"
Our speech and action is the outer journey,
Our inner journey is above the sky
The body travels on its dusty way;
The spirit walks, like Jesus, on the sea.

## THE SOUL OF PRAYER[18]

Jalalu'l-din was asked, "Is there any way to God nearer than the ritual prayer?" "No," he replied; "but prayer does

16 *Ibid.*, p. 51.
17 *Ibid.*, p. 74.
18 *Ibid.*, p. 92.

not consist in forms alone. Formal prayer has a beginning and an end, like all forms and bodies and everything that partakes of speech and sound; but the soul is unconditioned and infinite: it has neither beginning nor end. The prophets have shown the true nature of prayer. . . . Prayer is the drowning and unconsciousness of the soul, so that all these forms remain without. At that time there is no room even for Gabriel, who is pure spirit. One may say that the man who prays in this fashion is exempt from all religious obligations, since he is deprived of his reason. Absorption in the Divine Unity is the soul of prayer."

## THE FRIEND WHO SAID "I"[19]

A CERTAIN man knocked at his friend's door: his friend asked, "Who is there?"

He answered, "I." "Begone," said his friend, "'tis too soon: at my table there is no place for the raw."

How shall the raw one be cooked but in the fire of absence? What else will deliver him from hypocrisy?

He turned sadly away, and for a whole year the flames of separation consumed him;

Then he came back and again paced to and fro beside the house of his friend.

He knocked at the door with a hundred fears and reverences, lest any disrespectful word might escape from his lips.

"Who is there?" cried his friend. He answered, "Thou, O charmer of all hearts!"

"Now," said the friend, "since thou art I, come in: there is no room for two I's in this house."

## "RIPENESS IS ALL"[20]

SINCE thou canst not bear the unveiled Light, drink the Word of Wisdom, for its light is veiled,

To the end that thou mayst become able to receive the Light, and behold without veils that which now is hidden,

And traverse the sky like a star; nay, journey unconditioned, without a sky.

'Twas thus thou camest into being from non-existence.

[19] *Ibid.*, p. 93.
[20] *Ibid.*, p. 189.

How didst thou come? Thou camest insensibly.

The ways of thy coming thou rememberest not, but I will give thee an indication.

Let thy mind go, then be mindful! Close thine ear, then listen!

Nay, I will not tell, for thou art still unripe: thou art in thy springtime, thou hast not seen the summer.

This world is as the tree: we are like the half-ripened fruit upon it.

The unripe fruits cling fast to the bough, because they are not fit for the palace;

But when they have ripened and become sweet and delicious—after that, they lose hold of the bough.

Even so does the kingdom of the world lose its savour for him whose mouth has been sweetened by the great felicity.

Something remains untold, but the Holy Spirit will tell thee without me as the medium.

Nay, thou wilt tell it to thine own ear—neither I nor another, O thou who art one with me—

Just as, when thou fallest asleep, thou goest from the presence of thyself into the presence of thyself

And hearest from thyself that which thou thinkest is told thee secretly by some one in the dream.

O good friend, thou art not a single "thou": thou art the sky and the deep sea.

Thy mighty infinite "Thou" is the ocean wherein myriads of "thou's" are sunken.

Do not speak, so that thou mayst hear from the Speakers what cannot be uttered or described.

Do not speak, so that the Spirit may speak for thee: in the ark of Noah leave off swimming!

# -8-

# Jewish Mysticism

What is called Jewish mysticism by the major authorities on the subject does not in a general way conform to the pattern of mysticism as unfolded in this book. In that pattern, which we have found present in Hindu, Buddhist, Christian, and Islamic mysticism, the essence of the experience is the undifferentiated unity. When it is not interfered with by theologians and ecclesiastical hierarchies it is interpreted nondualistically as transcending the distinction between subject and object, between the individual self and the Infinite. In Hinduism, Christianity, and Islam it is interpreted as union with God or with the Absolute. Professor G. G. Scholem, however, tells us that the concept of union is not an essential of mystical experience as understood in the Jewish tradition. He adds, "To take an instance, the earliest Jewish mystics . . . in Talmudic times and later . . . speak of the ascent of the soul to the Celestial Throne where it obtains an ecstatic view of the majesty of God." [1] Professor Scholem also writes, "It is only in extremely rare cases that ecstasy signifies actual union with God. . . . The Jewish mystic almost invariably retains a sense of the distance between the Creator and his creature. The latter is joined to the former, and the point where the two meet is of the greatest interest to the mystic." [2] The word commonly used for this "joining" of the two is "devekuth," which literally means "adhesion." Furthermore, what Professor Scholem calls

[1] Gershom G. Scholem, *Major Trends in Jewish Mysticism*. New York: Schocken Books, Inc., 1954, p. 5.
[2] *Ibid.*, pp. 122-23.

"Throne-Mysticism" consists in "perception of God's appearance on the Throne as described by Ezekiel." In this kind of mysticism we find "descriptions of . . . the heavenly halls or palaces through which the visionary passes and in the seventh and last of which there rises the Throne." [3] The Jewish mystical tradition does include instances of the experience of union with God, for instance in Abulafia and some of the later Hasidim. But this, in Professor Scholem's opinion, is atypical.

Professor Scholem is the leading authority in this field, and if we accept his views as correct, we have to conclude that in the Jewish tradition mysticism does not mean what it means in other religions. It is not, save in atypical cases, what we have understood as mysticism in this book. There are two reasons for this judgment. First, the concept of union, which is essential in Christian, Islamic, and Hindu mysticism, is not a part of typical Jewish mysticism. Secondly, visions of the throne and of celestial mansions are in Judaism called mystical experiences although, as we saw in Chapter I and have illustrated in all the later chapters, visions are excluded from non-Jewish concepts of mysticism because they involve sensuous imagery while the genuine mystical experience is nonsensuous.

As regards the first point, the absence of the experience of union, there might perhaps be some argument. The difference between Christian and Jewish mystical experience seems to be that the former includes union while the latter does not. But it might be suggested that this is only a matter of words. The Christian talks of union but understands it dualistically. It could be the case that both have the same experience and that both interpret it in the same dualist terms but that the Christian calls it union while the Jew does not. We should be in a better position to decide this if we could get some idea of what the Jewish experience is when it is distinguished so far as possible from interpretation. But unfortunately Professor Scholem does not pay any attention to the all-important distinction between experience and interpretation. In these circumstances all the present writer, who does not pretend to be a specialist in Jewish mysticism, can do is to follow Professor Scholem's opinion. This inevitably leads to the view that what is meant by mysticism in Jewry is not what is meant by mysticism elsewhere.

[3] *Ibid.*, pp. 44-45.

In these circumstances I think we ought, in choosing a selection for this chapter, to take one which exemplifies the Jewish concept of mysticism although it differs from that which we have so far sought to illustrate in this book. The selection which follows is taken from the Zohar, or Book of Splendor, which is so highly esteemed in Jewish circles that Professor Scholem refers to it as "a source of doctrine and revelation equal in authority to the Bible and the Talmud." [4] It is also said to be thought of in Judaism as the supreme example of Kabbalistic mysticism. It does not include reference to any experience or concept of union.

A great part of the Zohar consists in commentary on passages in the Old Testament and gives what is alleged to be their inner or esoteric meaning. The words of the Bible, it is supposed, have a literal meaning which is open for all to understand. But they also have a secret meaning which the Zohar purports to disclose. To some extent in Judaism the concept of mysticism seems to mean what is secret, hidden, or esoteric. This is no part of the concept of mysticism elsewhere, although it is true there are occasional hints of esotericism in Dionysius the Areopagite, as when he warns his readers against disclosing his teachings to "the uninitiated."

Much of the Zohar's commentary on the Torah is such that it seems to be intended exclusively for a Jewish audience. Many such passages are too narrowly national to be of interest to non-Jewish readers. I have therefore selected three passages of a sort which—rarely found in the Zohar—are likely to have a wider appeal and can be to some extent linked up with parallel conceptions in world mysticism.

The Zohar teaches a doctrine of emanation of ten *sefirot* —aspects or attributes of the Divine Being. God as He is in Himself prior to the creation of the world is called *eyn sof*, the formless Infinite, which is unknowable and ineffable. He is the "hidden" God, totally incomprehensible to the human mind. Being formless and empty, he yet causes himself to be apprehended in the ten *sefirot* or divine attributes. This may be compared with Eckhart's distinction between the Godhead, which is the dark emptiness and silence, and God who is the creator. Such a comparison seems to endow it with some tincture of world-wide mysticism. But even this is far

<hr>

[4] *Zohar, The Book of Splendor*, selected and edited by Gershom G. Scholem. New York: Schocken Books, Inc., 1949, Introduction, p. 7.

from certain. For although *eyn sof* is in itself an undifferentiated void, which sounds like mysticism, it is also similar to the ordinary philosophical concept of substance and quality which descended from Aristotle through the middle ages to Spinoza and persisted in modern thought until David Hume's criticism destroyed its influence. Substance, too, was an undifferentiated void—although not usually described in that language—and yet substance was a concept of rationalistic and not mystical origin. However that may be, *eyn sof* is at least a possible candidate for the status of a mystical concept in the usual sense and as understood in non-Jewish cultures.

FROM *the Zohar*[5]

### The Beginning

"In the beginning" [Gen. 1:1]—when the will of the King began to take effect, he engraved signs into the heavenly sphere [that surrounded him]. Within the most hidden recess a dark flame issued from the mystery of *eyn sof,* the Infinite, like a fog forming in the unformed—enclosed in the ring of that sphere, neither white nor black, neither red nor green, of no color whatever. Only after this flame began to assume size and dimension, did it produce radiant colors. From the innermost center of the flame sprang forth a well out of which colors issued and spread upon everything beneath, hidden in the mysterious hiddenness of *eyn sof.*

The well broke through and yet did not break through the ether [of the sphere]. It could not be recognized at all until a hidden, supernal point shone forth under the impact of the final breaking through.

Beyond this point nothing can be known. Therefore it is called *reshit,* beginning—the first word [out of the ten] by means of which the universe has been created. . . .

### The Ten Sefirot [6]

If one should ask: Is it not written, "For ye saw no manner of similitude" [Deut. 4:15], the answer would be: Truly, it was granted us to behold him in a given similitude, for concerning Moses it is written, "and the similitude of the

5 *Ibid.,* p. 27.
6 *Ibid.,* pp. 77-81.

Lord doth he behold" [Num. 12:8]. Yet the Lord was
revealed only in that similitude which Moses saw, and in
none other, of any creation formed by His signs. Therefore
it stands written: "To whom then will ye liken God? Or
what likeness will ye compare unto Him?" [Isa. 40:18].
Also, even that similitude was a semblance of the Holy One,
be blessed, not as he is in his very place which we know to
be impenetrable, but as the King manifesting his might of
dominion over his entire creation, and thus appearing to
each one of his creatures as each can grasp him, as it is
written: "And by the ministry of the prophets have I used
similitudes" [Hos. 12:11]. Hence says He: Albeit in your
own likeness do I represent myself, to whom will you compare me and make me comparable?

Because in the beginning, shape and form having not yet
been created, He had neither form nor similitude. Hence is it
forbidden to one apprehending him as he is before Creation
to imagine him under any kind of form or shape, not even by
his letters *hé* and *vav*, not either by his complete holy
Name, nor by letter or sign of any kind. Thus, "For ye saw
no manner of similitude" means, You beheld nothing
which could be imagined in form or shape, nothing which
you could embody into a finite conception.

But when He had created the shape of supernal man, it
was to him for a chariot, and on it he descended, to be
known by the appellation YHVH, so as to be apprehended by
his attributes and in each particular one, to be perceived.
Hence it was he caused himself to be named *El, Elohim,
Shaddai, Zevaot* and YHVH, of which each was a symbol
among men of his several divine attributes, making manifest that the world is upheld by mercy and justice, in ac-
cordance with man's deeds. If the radiance of the glory of the
Holy One, be blessed, had not been shed over his entire creation, how could even the wise have apprehended him? He
would have continued to be unknowable, and the words
could not be verily said, "The whole earth is full of His
glory" [Isa. 6:3].

However, woe to the man who should make bold to identify the Lord with any single attribute, even if it be His own,
and the less so any human form existent, "whose foundation
is in the dust" [Job 4:19], and whose creatures are frail,
soon gone, soon lost to mind. Man dare project one sole
conception of the Holy One, be blessed, that of his sovereignty over some one attribute or over the creation in its
entirety. But if he be not seen under these manifestations,
then there is neither attribute, nor likeness, nor form in him;

as the very sea, whose waters lack form and solidity in themselves, having these only when they are spread over the vessel of the earth.

From this we may reckon it so: One, is the source of the sea. A current comes forth from it making a revolution which is *yod*.* The source is one, and the current makes two. Then is formed the vast basin known as the sea, which is like a channel dug into the earth, and it is *filled* by the waters issuing from the source; and this sea is the third thing. This vast basin is divided up into seven channels, resembling that number of long tubes, and the waters go from the sea into the seven channels. Together, the source, the current, the sea, and the seven channels make the number ten. If the Creator who made these tubes should choose to break them, then would the waters return to their source, and only broken vessels would remain, dry, without water.

In this same wise has the Cause of causes derived the ten aspects of his Being which are known as *sefirot*, and named the crown the Source, which is a never-to-be-exhausted fountain of light, wherefrom he designates himself *eyn sof*, the Infinite. Neither shape nor form has he, and no vessel exists to contain him, nor any means to apprehend him. This is referred to in the words: "Refrain from searching after the things that are too hard for thee, and refrain from seeking for the thing which is hidden from thee."

Then He shaped a vessel diminutive as the letter *yod*, and filled it from him, and called it Wisdom-gushing Fountain, and called himself wise on its account. And after, he fashioned a large vessel named sea, and designated it Understanding [*binah*] and himself understanding, on its account. Both wise and understanding is he, in his own essence; whereas Wisdom in itself cannot claim that title, but only through him who is wise and has made it full from his fountain; and so Understanding in itself cannot claim that title, but only through him who filled it from his own essence, and it would be rendered into an aridity if he were to go from it. In this regard, it is written, "As the waters fail from the sea, and the river is drained dry" [Job 14:11].

Finally, "He smites [the sea] into seven streams" [Isa. 11:15]. that is, he directs it into seven precious vessels, the which he calls Greatness, Strength, Glory, Victory, Majesty, Foundation, Sovereignty;** in each he designates himself thus: great in Greatness, strong in Strength, glorious in Glory,

---

* The first letter in the name of God.
** These designate the seven lower *sefirot*.

victorious in Victory, "the beauty of our Maker" in Majesty, righteous in Foundation [cf. Prov. 10:25]. All things, all vessels, and all worlds does he uphold in Foundation.

In the last, in Sovereignty, he calls himself King, and his is "the greatness, and the strength, and the glory, and the victory, and the majesty; for all that is in heaven and in the earth is Thine; Thine is the kingdom, O Lord, and Thou art exalted as head above all" [1 Chron. 29:11]. In his power lie all things, be it that he chooses to reduce the number of vessels, or to increase the light issuing therefrom, or be' it the contrary. But over him, there exists no deity with power to increase or reduce.

Also, he made beings to serve these vessels: each a throne supported by four columns, with six steps to the throne; in all, ten. Altogether, the throne is like the cup of benediction about which ten statements are made [in the Talmud], harmonious with the Torah which was given in Ten Words [the Decalogue], and with the Ten Words by which the world was created.

## Consuming Fire [7]

Rabbi Simeon said: In one place it is written, "For the Lord thy God is a consuming fire" [Deut. 4:24], and elsewhere, "But ye that cleave unto the Lord your God are alive every one of you this day" [Deut. 4:4]. The Companions have already discussed the seeming inconsistency between these texts, but I offer yet another interpretation.

It has been affirmed by the Companions that there exists a sort of fire which is stronger than other fire, and the one consumes and annihilates the other. If we continue this thought, it can be said that he who cares to pierce into the mystery of the holy unity of God should consider the flame as it rises from a burning coal or candle.

There must always be some material substance from which the flame thus rises. In the flame itself may be seen two lights: the one white and glowing, the other black, or blue. Of the two, the white light is the higher and rises unwavering. Underneath it is the blue or black light upon which the other rests as on a support. The two are conjoined, the white reposing upon the throne of the black. The blue or black base is, likewise, connected to something beneath it, which feeds it and makes it to cling to the white light above.

[7] Zohar, The Book of Splendor, pp. 38-41.

At times this blue or black light turns red, but the light above remains constantly white. This lower light, at times black, at times blue, at times red, serves to link the white light above it with the material substance below to which it is bound and through which it keeps kindled. This lower light is in its nature an instrument for destruction and death, devouring whatever comes near it. But the white light above neither consumes nor demolishes, nor does it ever change.

Therefore Moses said, "For the Lord thy God is a consuming fire" [Deut. 4:24], consuming, actually, all that is beneath him; for this reason he said "thy God" and not "our God," inasmuch as Moses stood in the supernal light which does not consume and does not demolish.

Remark further. It is Israel alone which impels the blue light to kindle and to link itself with the white light, Israel, who cleave to the blue light from below. And though it be in the nature of the blue or black light to destroy whatever it touches beneath, yet Israel, cleaving to it from beneath, are not destroyed; so it is said, "But ye that cleave unto the Lord your God are alive every one of you this day." *Your* God and not *our* God; that is to say, it is the blue or black flame, consuming and annihilating whatever cleaves to it from below, and still you cleave and are alive.

Only just perceptible above the white light and encompassing it, is yet another light, this one symbolizing the supreme essence. So does the aspiring flame symbolize the supernal mysteries of wisdom.

Rabbi Phineas went to him and kissed him, and said, Blessed be God who guided me here. And they went out with Rabbi Phineas, accompanying him for three miles. When they had returned, Rabbi Simeon spoke: The description I have given may be taken as a symbol of the holy unity of God. In the holy name YHVH,* the second letter *hé* is the blue or black light attached to the remaining letters *yod, hé, vav,* which constitute the luminous white light. But there come times when this blue light is not *hé* but *dalet,* which is to say, poverty; this means, when Israel fail to cleave to it from beneath and it in turn fails therefore to burn and cleave to the white light, the blue light is *dalet,* but when Israel make it to cleave to the white light, then it is *hé.* If male and female are not together, then *hé* is erased and there remains only *dalet* [poverty]. But when the chain is perfect, the *hé* cleaves to the white light, and Israel cleave to

* The four letters of the name of God represent four stages of ever increasing divine manifestation.

the *hé* and give substance for its light, and are yet not destroyed.

In this we see the mystery of the sacrifice. The rising smoke kindles the blue light, which then joins itself to the white light, whereupon the entire candle is wholly kindled, alight with a single unified flame. As it is the nature of the blue light to demolish whatever comes into touch with it from beneath, therefore if the sacrifice be acceptable and the candle wholly kindled, then, as with Elijah, "the fire of the Lord descends and consumes the burnt-offering" [1 Kings 18:38], and this reveals that the chain is perfected, for then the blue light cleaves to the white light above, while at the same time consuming the fat and flesh of the burnt-offering beneath, nor can it consume what is below, except it rise and join itself to the white light. At such time, peace reigns in all worlds, and all together form a unity.

The blue light having devoured every thing beneath, the priests, the Levites, and the laity gather at its base with singing and meditation and with prayer, while above them the lamp glows, the lights are merged into a unity, worlds are illumined, and above and below, all are blessed. Therefore it is written, "ye, even while cleaving to the Lord your God, are alive every one of you this day." The word *atem* [you] is here preceded by the letter *vav* [and], which indicates that while the fat and flesh cleaving to the flame are devoured by it, you who cleave to it are yet alive.

# -9-

# A Contemporary
# Mystical Experience:
# Arthur Koestler

The following selection is part of Chapter 33 in Arthur Koestler's book *The Invisible Writing,* which is part of his autobiography. Mr. Koestler relates his early experiences as a Communist, and how in the Spanish Civil War he was accused by Franco's Falangists of being a spy for the popular front. In the prison where he was kept in solitary confinement he knew that prisoners were constantly being taken out at night, placed against the cemetery wall, and shot. He would hear the jailer unlocking cells adjacent to his own and taking the inmates out for execution. He would hear them pass his cell door on the way out. He had every reason to fear the same fate himself. It would appear that in the fearful tension of prison life and under the constant threat of death the mystical experiences which he relates in this selection came to him. The first seven paragraphs contain the actual description of the experiences. The remainder gives some of his later reflections on them.

The experiences were of the introvertive type, and the emphasis is on the dissolution of the individuality. "The I had ceased to exist" because it had been "dissolved in the universal pool." It is this which is sensed "as the draining of all tension, the absolute catharsis, the peace that passeth all understanding." This losing of one's individuality by merging into the Infinite is a universal characteristic of the introvertive experience. At the same time in Koestler's case the experience was apparently incomplete, or not fully developed, because it did not include the total disappearance of all sensations and thoughts, the full experience of the wholly undifferentiated unity. We also note that it came upon him suddenly, unsought and unprepared for, and that he was not able to reproduce it at will as can those more fully developed mystics who have reached the mystical consciousness by prolonged techniques of meditation and concentration.

But Koestler's case throws a great deal of light back on the experiences of the older mystics in the various cultures represented in these selections. We notice that although the experience is the same as theirs—except for its incompleteness—he does not interpret it in terms of any conventional religious creed. His being "dissolved in the universal pool" is undoubtedly the very same experience which Christian mystics interpret as "union with God." It is the same experience as Eckhart describes by saying of the individual self that "it is sunk and lost in this desert where its identity is destroyed" (see page 156). We note Mr. Koestler's view—which is the same as that which I have expressed in the introduction and throughout this book—that a genuine mystical experience, because it is formless, lends itself to transcription in many forms and may "mediate a *bona fide* conversion to practically any creed, Christianity, Buddhism, or Fire-Worship."

It is important to note that these experiences gradually but completely altered the author's life, his philosophy, and his attitude toward the world. They caused him to "see the light" and to abandon communism. As he says in the opening paragraph of the book, "I went to communism (in 1931) as one goes to a fresh spring of water, and I left communism (in 1938) as one climbs out of a poisoned river strewn with the wreckage of flooded cities and the corpses of the drowned. . . . The reeds to which I clung and which saved me from being swallowed up were the outgrowth of a new faith" [1] which resulted from the mystical experiences in prison. He also tells us that, as a result of these experiences, "it struck me as self-evident that . . . we were all responsible for each other—not only in the superficial sense of social responsibility, but because, in some inexplicable manner, we partook of the same substance or identity, like Siamese twins or communicating vessels. . . . If everybody were an island, how could the world be a concern of his?" [2]

This has always been the contention of mystics. They teach that morality ultimately springs out of our subconscious or potential mystical experience. For in the undifferentiated

[1] Arthur Koestler, *The Invisible Writing*. New York: The Macmillan Company, 1954, p. 15.
[2] *Ibid.*, pp. 355-56.

unity in which all distinctions are lost, the distinctions between "I" and "you" and "he" and "she" also disappear, so that, to use Koestler's phrase, we are all "of one substance." Immorality, evil, selfishness, the war of all against all, spring, on the contrary, from the separateness of individuals, their failure to realize in experience the fact that they are not "islands."

If anyone thinks that mysticism consists in useless dreaming, or in the idle and selfish enjoyment of wonderful experiences without any practical and valuable effects in life, they have here their answer. It is the universal testimony of those who know that mystical experience transforms human life, and alters character—often from the squalid and mean to the noble and selfless.

## The Hours by the Window [8]

I was standing at the recessed window of cell No. 40 and with a piece of iron-spring that I had extracted from the wire mattress, was scratching mathematical formulæ on the wall. Mathematics, in particular analytical geometry, had been the favourite hobby of my youth, neglected later on for many years. I was trying to remember how to derive the formula of the hyperbola, and was stumped; then I tried the ellipse and parabola, and to my delight succeeded. Next I went on to recall Euclid's proof that the number of primes is infinite. . . .

Since I had become acquainted with Euclid's proof at school, it had always filled me with a deep satisfaction that was aesthetic rather than intellectual. Now, as I recalled the method and scratched the symbols on the wall, I felt the same enchantment.

And then, for the first time, I suddenly understood the reason for this enchantment: the scribbled symbols on the wall represented one of the rare cases where a meaningful and comprehensive statement about the infinite is arrived at by precise and finite means. The infinite is a mystical mass shrouded in a haze; and yet it was possible to gain some knowledge of it without losing oneself in treacly ambiguities. The significance of this swept over me like a wave. The wave had originated in an articulate verbal insight; but this evaporated at once, leaving in its wake only a wordless essence, a fragrance of eternity, a quiver of the arrow in the

8 Ibid., pp. 350-54.

blue. I must have stood there for some minutes, entranced, with a wordless awareness that "this is perfect—perfect"; until I noticed some slight mental discomfort nagging at the back of my mind—some trivial circumstance that marred the perfection of the moment. Then I remembered the nature of that irrelevant annoyance: I was, of course, in prison and might be shot. But this was immediately answered by a feeling whose verbal translation would be: "So what? is that all? have you got nothing more serious to worry about?"—an answer so spontaneous, fresh and amused as if the intruding annoyance had been the loss of a collar-stud. Then I was floating on my back in a river of peace, under bridges of silence. It came from nowhere and flowed nowhere. Then there was no river and no I. The I had ceased to exist.

It is extremely embarrassing to write down a phrase like that when one has read *The Meaning of Meaning* and nibbled at logical positivism and aims at verbal precision and dislikes nebulous gushings. Yet, "mystical" experiences, as we dubiously call them, are not nebulous, vague or maudlin—they only become so when we debase them by verbalisation. However, to communicate what is incommunicable by its nature, one must somehow put it into words, and so one moves in a vicious circle. When I say "the I had ceased to exist," I refer to a concrete experience that is verbally as incommunicable as the feeling aroused by a piano concerto, yet just as real—only much more real. In fact, its primary mark is the sensation that this state is more real than any other one has experienced before—that for the first time the veil has fallen and one is in touch with "real reality," the hidden order of things, the X-ray texture of the world, normally obscured by layers of irrelevancy.

What distinguishes this type of experience from the emotional entrancements of music, landscapes or love is that the former has a definitely intellectual, or rather noumenal, content. It is meaningful, though not in verbal terms. Verbal transcriptions that come nearest to it are: the unity and interlocking of everything that exists, an interdependence like that of gravitational fields or communicating vessels. The "I" ceases to exist because it has, by a kind of mental osmosis, established communication with, and been dissolved in, the universal pool. It is this process of dissolution and limitless expansion which is sensed as the "oceanic feeling," as the draining of all tension, the absolute catharsis, the peace that passeth all understanding.

The coming-back to the lower order of reality I found to

be gradual, like waking up from anæsthesia. There was the equation of the parabola scratched on the dirty wall, the iron bed and the iron table and the strip of blue Andalusian sky. But there was no unpleasant hangover as from other modes of intoxication. On the contrary: there remained a sustained and invigorating, serene and fear-dispelling after-effect that lasted for hours and days. It was as if a massive dose of vitamins had been injected into the veins. Or, to change the metaphor, I resumed my travels through my cell like an old car with its batteries freshly re-charged.

Whether the experience had lasted for a few minutes or an hour, I never knew. In the beginning it occurred two or even three times a week, then the intervals became longer. It could never be voluntarily induced. After my liberation it recurred at even longer intervals, perhaps once or twice in a year. But by that time the groundwork for a change of personality was completed. I shall henceforth refer to these experiences as "the hours by the window."

Religious conversion on the deathbed or in the death-cell is an almost irresistible temptation. That temptation has two sides.

One plays on crude fear, on the hope for individual salvation through unconditional surrender of the critical faculties to some archaic form of demonology. The other side is more subtle. Faced with the Absolute, the ultimate *nada*, the mind may become receptive to mystic experiences. These one may regard as "real" in the sense of subjective pointers to an objective reality *ipso facto* eluding comprehension. But because the experience is inarticulate, has no sensory shape, colour or words, it lends itself to transcription in many forms, including visions of the Cross or of the goddess Kali; they are like dreams of a person born blind, and may assume the intensity of a revelation. Thus a genuine mystic experience may mediate a *bona fide* conversion to practically any creed, Christianity, Buddhism, or Fire-Worship. . . .

The "hours by the window," which had started with the rational reflection that finite statements about the infinite were possible—and which in fact represented a series of such statements on a non-rational level—had filled me with a direct certainty that a higher order of reality existed, and that it alone invested existence with meaning. I came to call it later on "the reality of the third order." The narrow world of sensory perception constituted the first order; this perceptual world was enveloped by the conceptual world which contained phenomena not directly perceivable, such as gravitation, electromagnetic fields, and curved space. The second order of reality filled in the gaps and gave meaning to the absurd patchiness of the sensory world.

In the same manner, the third order of reality enveloped, interpenetrated, and gave meaning to the second. It contained "occult" phenomena which could not be apprehended or explained either on the sensory or on the conceptual level, and yet occasionally invaded them like spiritual meteors piercing the primitive's vaulted sky. Just as the conceptual order showed up the illusions and distortions of the senses, so the "third order" disclosed that time, space and causality, that the isolation, separateness and spatio-temporal limitations of the self were merely optical illusions on the next higher level. If illusions of the first type were taken at face value, then the sun was drowning every night in the sea and a mote in the eye was larger than the moon; and if the conceptual world was mistaken for ultimate reality, the world became an equally absurd tale, told by an idiot or by idiot-electrons which caused little children to be run over by motor cars, and little Andalusian peasants to be shot through heart, mouth and eyes, without rhyme or reason. Just as one could not feel the pull of a magnet with one's skin, so one could not hope to grasp in cognate terms the nature of ultimate reality. It was a text written in invisible ink; and though one could not read it, the knowledge that it existed was sufficient to alter the texture of one's existence, and make one's actions conform to the text.

I liked to spin out this metaphor. The captain of a ship sets out with a sealed order in his pocket which he is only permitted to open on the high seas. He looks forward to that moment which will end all uncertainty; but when the moment arrives and he tears the envelope open, he only finds an invisible text which defies all attempts at chemical treatment. Now and then a word becomes visible, or a figure denoting a meridian; then it fades again. He will never know the exact wording of the order; nor whether he has complied with it or failed in his mission. But his awareness of the order in his pocket, even though it cannot be deciphered, makes him think and act differently from the captain of a pleasure cruiser or of a pirate ship.

I also liked to think that the founders of religions, prophets, saints and seers had at moments been able to read a fragment of the invisible text; after which they had so much padded, dramatised and ornamented it, that they themselves could no longer tell what parts of it were authentic.

# -10-

# Retrospect and Prospect

I hope it will be understood that in the introduction and commentaries of this book I have given my own views on mysticism, with which other commentators may well disagree. In this sphere of human thought and experience it would be unprofitable merely to set forth a set of facts which would be admitted by all competent persons and to leave the matter there. A writer on the subject can hardly, without being intolerably jejune, avoid giving his own interpretations. Some very good European writers have viewed mysticism from a strictly Christian standpoint, and of course their comments have been strongly colored by this fact. I have attempted something different. I write as one who is sympathetic to mysticism and who believes that mystical experience is in touch with that cosmic Spiritual Presence toward which the great world religions all dimly grope. But I do not write from the special standpoint of any one religion. I have attempted an impartial survey of the phenomenon of mysticism as it has appeared in all the more advanced cultures of the world.

In this chapter I shall do two things. I shall first of all try to bring together in a brief retrospective survey the main points which have emerged in our study. Secondly, I shall inquire what are the prospects of mysticism in the future.

The mystical consciousness seems to be of two kinds. One of these looks outward through the eyes, sees the physical world transfigured so that the One, the supreme Spiritual Presence of the universe, shines through it. The other, looking inward introspectively, sees the One hidden at the bottom (or at the top, if that metaphor is preferred) of the

236

individual self. Of these two kinds the latter is both historically and spiritually vastly the more important.

This introvertive or introspective experience is reached by systematically suppressing the elements of sensation, sensuous imagery, and conceptual thought, as well as the emotional and volitional states which accompany them—getting rid, in fact, of the entire multiplicity of the empirical contents of the mind or self. What then supervenes is not unconsciousness or sleep, as one might expect, but a new kind of nonsensuous, nonconceptual consciousness which is an undifferentiated unity. The entire contents of our sensory-intellectual consciousness is gone, and what is left is "pure" consciousness. It is not a consciousness *of* anything. It has no objects (not even itself as object to itself) for all objects have disappeared with the suppression of sensations, images, and thoughts. This consciousness is therefore pure Emptiness, or nothingness. Nevertheless it is a fullness of effulgent beatitude. The negative side, the Emptiness, is usually expressed by the metaphor of darkness, since in darkness all distinctions disappear. The positive side is commonly expressed by the metaphor of light. This is a complete paradox. The paradox is not that there is an emptiness *and* a fullness, a darkness *and* a light. The paradox is that the emptiness *is* the fullness, the fullness the emptiness; the darkness *is* the light, the light the darkness.

All mysticism is paradoxical and self-contradictory. In Buddhism the paradoxicality is overt, and the Buddhist mystic delights in it. In Christianity the contradictions are often glossed over because logic is a special characteristic of the West. This is not because the paradoxes are any fewer or milder in Christianity than in Buddhism; they are exactly the same paradoxes which appear in all mysticism in all cultures. The reason is that the West is frightened of logicians and tends to conceal contradictions. But it is a simple reflection that you can only have logic where you have distinctions and multiplicity; and that in an experience which is an undivided unity, wherein all distinctions have disappeared, there can be no logic. The very existence of an experience which is pure unity with no internal multiplicity is a standing contradiction.

If this contradictory character of all mysticism should persuade the many logicians and professional philosophers to dismiss mysticism as a delusion, by all means let them do so. I should accept it as a matter of course that conventional professionals will hold conventional professional opinions. But here and there a few rare spirits among the thousands of run-of-the-mill professional philosophers, being less hidebound than their colleagues, may go the length of wondering, or even seriously inquiring, whether the foundations of logic, as now taught with complacent self-assurance in the dogmas of the schools, may not require revision. In another place I shall myself suggest what the revision should be.

The mystical consciousness, then, is undifferentiated unity. This is the core of the experience. In all cultures, with the possible exception of Buddhism, this undifferentiated unity is interpreted as the unity of the self. And this unity of the individual ego is further interpreted as being either identical with, or at least as having reached "union" (in some sense) with, the Universal Spirit. Buddhism denies, on much the same grounds as Hume did, the existence of the individual self (the ego) and interprets the undivided unity as Nirvana.

There is a great cleavage between the East and the West in regard to the nature of mystical "union." According to the Upanishads, the individual self comes to realize in the mystical state that it is identical with Brahman, the Universal Self. The Western religions, Christianity, Judaism, and Islam, consider it heretical or even blasphemous for the creature to claim identity with the Creator. They therefore interpret "union" dualistically. There is union but not identity between God and the soul. In this writer's opinion the Indian view is nearer the truth. The fully developed mystical consciousness involves the disappearance of *all* distinctions, including that between subject and object, between the individual self and the Universal Self. Nevertheless there is something obviously wrong with the bald statement "I am God." What is wrong is that it is only half of the paradox. The other half says, "I am not God." The truth will be not mere identity, nor mere difference, but identity in difference. This phrase may seem to smack of Hegel. But I am not preaching Hegel. Hegel, I hold, was wrong in pretending that identity in difference is a new kind of logic. On the contrary, it is entirely nonlogical. The paradox is not resoluble by a so-called "synthesis" or in any other way.

The undifferentiated unity is not in itself a Christian, or an Islamic, or a Jewish, or a Hindu, or a Buddhist phenomenon. It is world-wide. It is not the property of any religion. It does not favor any one religion above any other. But every religion can appropriate it and interpret it in terms of its own dogmas. Thus Eckhart interprets it in terms of the doctrine of the Trinity, Plotinus as the One, Buddhism as Nirvana. Moreover, mysticism can flourish outside the boundaries of any of the conventionally recognized religious creeds. Plotinus adhered to no religion but wove his mystical experience into the fabric of Platonic metaphysics. Many contemporary persons who are either agnostics or not followers of any specific religion have reached the mystical consciousness and have still remained outside the pale of any religious dogma. This is not because they are less religious than Christians, Mohammedans, and others, but because they are more so. Or at least it means that the spirit of religion is not necessarily united to the body of any recognizable creed. For in the last analysis mysticism is not any theory about the Divine, and does not imply any theory. It is a direct experience of the Divine which can, as such, exist without any theory at all.

It may be asked what the prospects of mysticism are in the future of the world. Is it not a phenomenon whose force has been spent in the past?

Very little can be said on this subject. Sri Aurobindo has suggested that the universe shows a process of emergent evolution of which the terms are matter, life, mind, and supermind. Supermind, which is the mystical consciousness, should then be the next stage beyond which nothing can now be seen. If we could accept this we should expect that the small minority of men who have now reached the mystical stage will gradually—perhaps in the course of a million years or so—become a majority. This long-range expectation, however, can only be justified on the basis of a teleological view of the world—only if evolution is proceeding according to a plan. Certainly no evidence of this is to be found in Darwinism or in any later version of the theory of biological evolution. So far as biology is concerned, it would seem that blind chance, not planning, has presided over evolution in the past. Nor, in my opinion, can evidence of a world purpose be detected within the mystical consciousness itself. We have therefore to regard Aurobindo's idea as a pious hope, founded in religious faith and not in any concrete evidence.

But the reader who suggests that mysticism is a spent force and who asks about its prospects in the future is presumably not greatly concerned about what may happen in a million years. His question is concerned with the near future. As to this I can only say that, unless civilization is destroyed by hydrogen bombs, I see no reason to think that mysticism is a thing of the past. Mysticism is a form of religious spirituality, and spirituality continues to exist through all world crises. Materialistic civilization is against it, but the good and the beautiful and the true manage to survive from generation to generation. In general, spiritual values manage to survive. And this will surely be true of mysticism.